Irish For A Day

Saint Patrick's Day Celebrations in Québec City 1765-1990

Nancy Schmitz

CARRAIG BOOKS

OTHER PUBLICATIONS BY CARRAIG BOOKS

James Mangan, F.S.C.

The Voyage of the Naparima
La Traversée du Naparima (Robichaud/Dompierre)

Jeannette V. Masson

A Grandmother Remembers Grosse Île (Massé)

R. Clive Meredith

In All Weathers In All Seasons

M. O'Gallagher

Saint Patrick's Quebec 1824-1834
Saint Brigid's Quebec 1856-1981
Grosse Ile Gateway to Canada 1832-1937
Grosse Île Porte d'Entrée du Canada (Bourbeau)

Cover: Stained glass window of Saint Patrick, Church of Saint Charles de Limoilou, Québec. Anonymous, between 1919 and 1920.

Back cover: Stained glass window of Saint Patrick, Church of Saint Sauveur, Québec. Gift of Martin Madden, around 1870. Photos Nancy Schmitz

Typesetting, Composition and Printing: Les Éditions Marquis, Montmagny

Carraig Books
P.O. Box 8733
Ste-Foy Québec
G1V 4N6

Dépôt Légal: Bibliothèque nationale du Québec
Legal Deposit: National Library of Canada
First trimester, 1991
ISBN 0-9690805-5-7

Irish For A Day

Saint Patrick's Day Celebrations in Québec City 1765-1990

Nancy Schmitz

Canadian Cataloguing in Publication Data

Schmitz, Nancy, 1938-
Irish for a day: Saint Patrick's Day celebrations in Quebec City, 1765-1990

Includes bibliographical references and index.
ISBN 0-9690805-5-7

1. Saint Patrick's Day—Quebec (Province)—Québec—History. 2. Irish—Quebec (Province)—Québec—Social life and customs. 3. Québec (Quebec)—Social life and customs. I. Title

GT4995.P3S34 1991 394.2′683 C90-090159-7

CONTENTS

ACKNOWLEDGEMENTS

This study first began as a research project in 1978, and received a grant in 1979 from the Department of the Secretary of State for Multiculturalism. A sabbatical leave from Laval University in 1989-1990 allowed me to finish gathering material and complete the written text. Local historian and editor Marianna O'Gallagher was the guiding light behind the original project proposal, as well as the final publication. Rita Brown, Austin Edwards, Patricia Fitzpatrick Kiley, and Leo McCullen were helpful at many stages of the project. Thanks also go to my principal fieldwork assistants: Margaret Low, Monik Simard, and Frances Slaney, and to *Quebec Chronicle-Telegraph* editor, Karen Macdonald, for her ongoing collaboration. And I wish to thank my husband for his unfailing patience and encouragement.

My thanks for their help and cooperation go to all the people who over the years have generously given of their time and expertise, in particular the staff of the Archives de la Ville de Québec, of the City Hall of Sillery, of Saint Patrick's High School, of various city schools, and of Saint Brigid's Home; to Irene Calfat, Cynthia Dooley and Cilma Landriau of the Literary and Historical Society of Québec, to Brother Joseph-Marie Legault of Saint Charles de Limoilou, to Nicole Beaulieu, André Cochrane, Lucien Fréchette, Paul Poirier, and Colette Sills of the Bibliothèque de l'Assemblée nationale du Québec, to Pierre Cayer of the audiovisual service of Laval University, to Vilia Cox of the *Quebec Chronicle-Telegraph*, to Dr Patricia Lysaght of the Department of Irish Folklore at University College Dublin, and to Mrs Doris Rooney and Pádraig Ó Laighin of the Saint Patrick's Society of Montréal. Gerry McNulty and Guthrie Scott furnished helpful reflections on the manuscript. The chapter on the Shannon Show was also read and commented upon by the people most concerned with its production.

Except where they appear within quoted sources, place and street names have been standardized to correspond to the present official map designations, such as Québec, Montréal, Saint Malachie, Saint Patrice, Côte de la Montagne and Saint Jean street, for example, rather than the anglicized forms: Quebec, Montreal, Saint Malachy, Saint Patrick, Mountain Hill and John street. This is done simply to avoid the confusion such double designations often cause the modern reader.

Photo credits have been assigned wherever the photo is reproduced. Cecil Frances Alexander's translation of "The Breastplate of Saint Patrick", available from many non-copyrighted sources, is apparently in the public domain. The arrangement of the "Coulin" is from a non-copyrighted source. The maps were prepared by the author and by Marianna O'Gallagher.

In the end, this publication would not have been possible without the generous collaboration and patience of the people of Québec City and the neighbouring communities, many of them anonymous, who cooperated with us in our search for information about the Saint Patrick's Day celebrations. Wherever possible, their names will be found in their rightful places, throughout the text itself. They are the people who lived Saint Patrick's Day, and whose testimony, whether actually quoted or not, helped us bring it to life on these pages.

Nancy Schmitz
Québec City
1991

PREFACE

We wish to thank the Author and Publisher for granting us the privilege, indeed the honour, of writing this preface for a book about "How We Celebrated Saint Patrick's Day in Years Gone By".

The 17th of March is a special day! and always has been in the hearts of the Irish Community! Pleasant to recall the Solemn High Mass in the Old Church on McMahon Street with Cardinal Bégin as Celebrant. His Eminence had a special affection for the Irish Members of his "flock".

It would be unfair to single out particular Societies or individuals who contributed to keeping alive the observance of the Wearin' of the Green. However, it would be equally unjust to omit Saint Patrick's Literary Institute, the Ancient Order of Hibernians, also that talented and gracious lady, Miss May Derouin, of happy memory!

The Great Occasion was marked by Parades, Concerts, the Soirée and Matinée. Curling Clubs held their annual contest of Ireland vs the World, the Service Clubs remembered the day, Guest Speakers were instructed to bear in mind the reason they were invited!

Hopefully readers will cherish the book, and enjoy this word picture of the past two centuries. Even a newspaper clipping can evoke the lilt of laughter and the Irish love of music. These many pages should encourage the present generation, and, indeed, future generations to celebrate the day with pride equal, at least, to that of our predecessors who worked so hard to make the feast as big as it was. It has been truly said

"A journey back in Time
Refreshes both Mind and Spirit"

The author, Nancy Schmitz, is to be congratulated for taking us back in time to those days of yore, and heartily thanked for giving us such a good picture of Québec in days of long ago. The book will surely refresh both the mind and spirit of its readers.

Leo McCullen
Québec, 1990

Overleaf:

Front page of the special Saturday supplement of *Le Soleil*, 16 mars 1907. Such artist's conceptions of popular saints were a common feature in *Le Soleil* at this period whenever an important feast-day occurred. Another feature was the publishing of portraits of prominent members of the community associated with the feast.

DEUXIEME SECTION 8 PAGES

LE "SOLEIL" QUEBEC

SUPPLEMENT GRATUIT

"FAIS CE QUE DOIS"

LA SAINT PATRICE

Fête Nationale des Irlandais

M. EDWARD NEVILLE,

M. Thos. H. MULLINS

M. J. W. H. WALLACE, C. E.,

Président de l'A. O. H., section de Québec.

M. MARTIN FOLEY

M. P. CAMPBELL.

CHAPTER I

Québec City and the Irish

Saint Patrick's Day, March 17, is recognized as the National Holiday of the descendants of Irish immigrants throughout the world. It is a time for them to express their ethnic appurtenance and to proclaim their Celtic heritage. Everyone is familiar with the Saint Patrick's Day parades in many North American cities, such as Montréal, Toronto, New York, Philadelphia, or Boston, which are regularly covered by the media. The feast is also a commercial success. The greeting card industry showers us with cards, party decorations, and buttons affirming Irishness, even for those who celebrate Saint Patrick's Day without making any claim to Irish ancestry: "Kiss me, I'm Irish", "Think Green", "Honorary Irishman", and similar sentiments. The Saint Patrick's Day celebrations in and around Québec City, capital of the Province of Québec, take on a local colour influenced not only by ethnic affiliation, but also by particular historical and cultural factors. Many of the forces that have shaped the Irish community in the Québec City area, as an Irish enclave within the French enclave in Canada, become apparent when studying the central ethnic event with which they are identified.

The Life and Legend of Saint Patrick

In the context of late 20th century Catholicism, the "cleaning up" of the liturgical calendar resulted in the "disappearance" of many saints whose legends did not correspond to their actual historical existence. This fortunately was not the case for the saint who exemplifies Christian Ireland and whose feast has become so important to people of Irish descent everywhere. Saint Patrick is known to us through his own writings, as well as from hagiographic texts.[1]

Saint Patrick appears at the beginning of the fifth century, at a time when the Roman Empire was beginning to withdraw from its furthest outposts in order to protect Rome from the Gothic invaders. Without Roman protection, Britain was left open to barbarian invasion, especially from the neighbouring Irish who had never come under Roman rule. During the reign of Niall of the Nine Hostages, there were constant raids on Gaul and Britain, and it seems that in the course of one of these, probably about the year 401, the sixteen-year-old Magonus Sucatus Patricius was carried off into captivity.[2] He describes that event in his *Confession*:

> I am Patrick, a sinner, most unlearned, the least of all the faithful, and utterly despised by many. My father was Calpornius, a deacon, son of Potitus, a priest, of the village Bannavem Taburniae; he had a country seat nearby, and there I was taken captive. I was then about sixteen years of age. I did not know the true God. I was taken into captivity to Ireland with many thousands of people.
>
> [ ] after I came to Ireland—every day I had to tend sheep, and many times a day I prayed.
>
> And there one night I heard in my sleep a voice saying to me: "It is well that you fast, soon you will go to your own country." And again, after a short while, I heard a voice saying to me: "See, your ship is ready." And it was not near, but at a distance of perhaps two hundred miles, and I had never been there, nor did I know a living soul there; and then I took to flight, and I left the man with whom I had stayed for six years. And I went in the strength of God, and I feared nothing until I came to that ship.
>
> And the day that I arrived the ship was set afloat, and I said that I was able to pay for my passage with them. But the captain was not pleased, and with indignation he answered harshly: "It is of no use for you to ask us to go along with us." And when I heard this, I left them. — And as I went, I began to pray; and before I had ended my prayer, I heard one of them shouting behind me, "Come, hurry, we shall take you on in good faith". — And thus I had my way with them, and we set sail at once.
>
> And again after a few years I was in Britain with my people, who received me as their son, and sincerely besought me that now at last, having suffered so many hardships, I should not leave them and go elsewhere.
>
> And there I saw in the night the vision of a man — coming as it were from Ireland. And he gave me [a letter] and as I read [it], I thought that at the same moment I heard their voice — "We ask thee, boy, come and walk among us once more."[3]

Some time after Patrick's return, possibly around the beginning of the year 407, he resumed his interrupted education, and eventually found himself in France, where he studied with Saint Germanus at Auxerre. In 429, Germanus was sent to Britain as papal legate, during which time he became aware of the hardships under which the Christians were labouring in Ireland. Patrick had been having visions and dreams which urged him to return to Ireland, but his years of neglected schooling told against him. In 431, Pope Celestine named Palladius as bishop to Ireland, where he founded three Christian communities: *Teach-na-Roman* or House of the Romans, *Kill-fine*, the present Dunlavin, and *Domnach-Ardech* or Donard, near Dunlavin. After Palladius' untimely death, the pope relented and sent Patrick to replace him. Patrick finally returned to Ireland in 432, when he was nearly 50 years old.

Christianity already had a tenuous foothold in Ireland when Saint Patrick arrived there. While tradition mentions several predecessors, apart from Palladius, it is likely that at least two, Declan of Ardmore and Ciaran the Elder were actually of his time and worked under him after his arrival. In spite of the presence of these missionaries and their monastic settlements, most of Ireland remained pagan and Patrick journeyed far and wide in order to convert the population. In his writing he tells of his difficulties.

> They laid hands on me and my companions, and on that day they eagerly wished to kill me; but my time had not yet come. On the fourteenth day the Lord delivered me from their power, and our belongings were returned to us. Daily I expect murder, fraud or captivity. I live among barbarians, a stranger and an exile for the love of God.[4]

He also tells of baptizing many thousands, converting chieftains, establishing monasteries on the pattern he brought from Gaul, and ruling his few bishops from his See of Armagh. Legendary accounts of his deeds feature the encounter on the Hill of Slane, where he dared light the Paschal fire before the druids could light the High King's own fire. The resulting controversy led to his devising his famous homily on the Trinity, using the shamrock as an example, a confrontation which made Patrick famous throughout the country.

On another occasion, during the baptism of Aengus, king of Cashel, he accidentally drove his bishop's crozier through the king's foot. The king, thinking it part of the ceremony, bore it stoically. Upon discovering this heroic behaviour, Patrick immediately healed him. He is credited with driving out all snakes from Ireland, a theme beloved of iconographers. He is also supposed to have encountered Oisín, the blind bard of the hero tales, whose journey to the Land of Youth caused him to outlive his own time by several centuries. Upon his return, he was converted by Saint Patrick, to whom he related the long epic of the heroes of ancient Ireland.

Besides his *Confession*, which tells us much about his life, and his *Letter to Coroticus*, in which he condemns the killing and enslaving of Christian converts, the *Dicta* ("Sayings") and the *Lorica* ("Saint Patrick's Breastplate", also known as "The Deer's Cry") are also attributed to him. According to legend, when Saint Patrick was travelling with his monks to Tara to confront King Laoghaire, the druids set men to ambush him. He led his followers in the recitation of the *Lorica*, and while so doing, he and his monks appeared to the waiting warriors as a herd of deer, thus allowing them to pass unharmed.

He is supposed to have died on March 17th, 461 in Sabhall (Saul), County Down, and was buried in neighbouring Downpatrick. Nearby was the monastery headed by Saint Brigid and it was she who wrapped him in a winding cloth she had made. Saint Patrick left a legacy of Christianity which flourishes in Ireland to this day.

From the Old Country to the New World

Traditionally in Ireland, Saint Patrick's Day has not always been the most important holiday in the cycle of calendar customs. It was generally considered a religious holiday, a day when people were under an obligation to attend Mass. Processions or parades, games and social entertainment did become part of the general feast-day pattern, but the situation of the feast during the Lenten season often affected the tenor of the celebrations.

In previous centuries, young boys and girls wore rosettes which differed according to their sex, the "Saint Patrick's Day Crosses"; this practice died out at the beginning of the 20th century, but we can see these as the ancestors of our present-day badges or buttons. From the 18th century onward, adults would wear a piece of shamrock in their hats in memory of Saint Patrick's use of the shamrock as an analogy to explain the mystery of the Trinity to the Celtic druids. This association of the shamrock explains its presence in decorations around Saint Patrick's Day, as well as its use in such customs as "drowning the shamrock".

> The only two traditions we have for Saint Patrick's Day which seem to go back as far as, perhaps, four or five hundred years, are the wearing of a symbol, Saint Patrick's Cross, and the rather interesting custom of drowning the shamrock. When taking the last drink of the evening, you take the shamrock, which you are wearing, from your hat or your coat, and drop it into the glass as a sort of farewell to the day.[5]

In Québec the saying "to dip the shamrock" has persisted, and is associated more with the drink than with the shamrock itself. When having their Saint Patrick's "pot" or "jar", some would certainly take more than one, while others would wait until the end of the day to "take their shamrock", being content with a single drink.

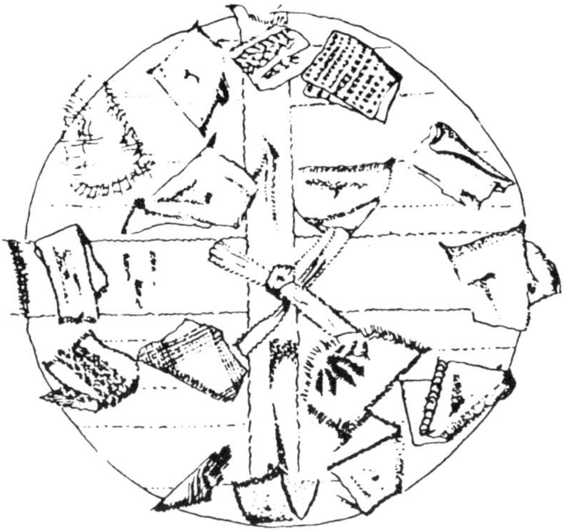

Clare

Kildare

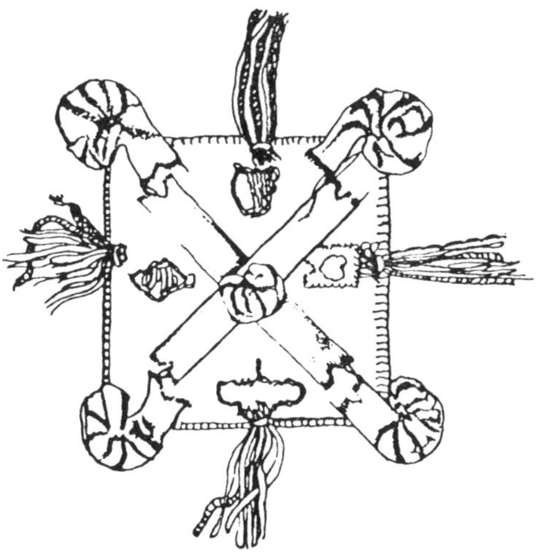

Meath

Saint Patrick's Crosses are one of the few traditions associated with the feast which go back more than one or two hundred years. They were worn by boys and girls in Ireland up until the beginning of the twentieth century, and have since been replaced by various badges or rosettes for young children and the shamrock for older children and adults. The three drawings here illustrated are of Crosses in the National Museum, Dublin, and are reproduced with kind permission from Kevin Danaher's *The Year in Ireland*.

Saint Patrick's Breastplate

I bind unto myself today
The strong Name of the Trinity,
By Invocation of the same,
The Three in One, and One in Three.

I bind this day to me for ever,
By power of faith, Christ's Incarnation;
His Baptism in Jordan river;
His Death on Cross for my salvation;
His bursting from the spiced tomb;
His riding up the Heavenly way;
His coming at the Day of Doom;
I bind unto myself today.

I bind unto myself the power
Of the great love of Cherubim;
The sweet "Well done" in Judgment hour;
The service of the Seraphim,
Confessors' faith, Apostles' word,
The Patriarchs' prayers, the Prophets' scrolls,
All good deeds done unto the Lord,
And purity of virgin souls.

I bind unto myself today
The virtues of the star-lit heaven,
The glorious sun's life-giving ray,
The whiteness of the moon at even,
The flashing of the lightning free,
The whirling wind's tempestuous shocks,
The stable earth, the deep salt sea,
Around the old eternal rocks.

I bind unto myself today
The power of God to hold and lead,
His Eye to watch, His Might to stay,
His ear to hearken to my need.
The Wisdom of my God to teach,
His Hand to guide, His Shield to ward,
The Word of God to give me speech,
His heavenly host to be my guard.

Against the demon snares of sin,
The vice that gives temptation force,
The natural lusts that war within,
The hostile men that mar my course;
Or few or many, far or nigh,
In every place, and in all hours,
Against their fierce hostility,
I bind to me these holy powers.

Against all Satan's spells and wiles
Against false words of heresy,
Against the knowledge that defiles,
Against the heart's idolatry;
Against the wizard's evil craft,
Against the death-wound and the burning,
The choking wave, the poisoned shaft,
Protect me, Christ, till Thy returning!

Christ be with me, Christ within me,
Christ behind me, Christ before me,
Christ beside me, Christ to win me,
Christ to comfort and restore me,
Christ beneath me, Christ above me,
Christ in quiet, Christ in danger,
Christ in hearts of all that love me,
Christ in mouth of friend and stranger.

I bind unto myself the Name,
The strong Name of the Trinity;
By Invocation of the same,
The Three in One and One in Three,
Of whom all nature hath creation;
Eternal Father, Spirit, Word:
Praise to the Lord of my salvation,
Salvation is of Christ the Lord.

[Domini est salus, Domini est salus,
Christi est salus.
Salus tua, Domine,
sit semper nobiscum. Amen.]

ascribed to Saint Patrick
1889 translation by Cecil Frances Alexander [1818-1895]

The feast was also useful as a "Mi-Carême" or Mid-Lent celebration, a continental tradition which did not exist in conservatively Christian Ireland, and served as an occasion for breaking the long Lenten fast.[6] References dating back to the 14th century speak of "Saint Patrick's fish": meat dipped in water before cooking in order to change its "nature", and thus turn it into an approved Lenten food.[7] As is characteristic of festive behaviour everywhere, food and especially drink were consumed in inordinate fashion, thus reinforcing the Irish reputation for celebratory heavy drinking. Today, in the Québec area, certain families serve turkey and ham as festive dishes, but the preparation is not ethnically unique, since Irish cuisine has traditionally been associated with symbolic content rather than a form of presentation. "Corned beef and cabbage", the stereotypical Irish meal in North America, is not as commonly considered as a holiday dish by everyone in Québec, apart from the curling clubs' "beef and greens"[8], while "Irish stews", both beef and lamb, are served by the Veterans Club. In spite of there being no traditional Irish recipes for the food prepared on that day, a popular culinary gesture is to make a cake or a dessert with green icing, gum drops, or colouring. Banquets often included green ice cream and various green desserts, and, of course, there is the green beer served in the pubs and taverns.

In the New World, the Irish fostered the tradition of decorating their houses and the dinner table with shamrocks and green. In the 19th and early 20th centuries, Québec merchants decorated their store windows with green draping, while along the parade routes, in addition to the elaborate arches, the houses and streets were lined with evergreens. These customs have been replaced by mainly indoor decorations, wherever a public celebration of the feast takes place.[9] In rural Ireland, Saint Patrick's day also marks the time when potatoes could be planted: "Saint Patrick promised that after his day every day would 'come hard'."[10] Obvious climatic conditions in Québec preclude the retaining of this tradition.

The founding of the Irish Republic somewhat sobered the Irish celebration of Saint Patrick's Day. An editorial in a Québec newspaper in the 1930s lamented that the parade no longer brought out "the Foresters in their Robert Emmett uniforms, the pipebands with their Irish wolfhound mascots, and the children with the Saint Patrick's Crosses", but that it was reduced to "the annual march-past of the Free State Army after the open air mass at Collins Barracks".[11] In spite of the sports events, such as Irish games in Croke Park, and song-and-dance entertainments of various kinds,[12] modern Irish celebrations in the mother country tend to be less elaborate than those in the New World. Again in the 1950s an AP correspondent commented that

> any Irishman who has whooped it up in south Boston or along New York's Third avenue would get almost homesick for a March 17 among the Irish-Americans, as there's no "drowning the shamrock" here. All bars in the republic are closed on Saint Patrick's Day. — The Emerald Isle celebrates instead with a parade showing off tremendous strides in industrial development. Few politicians even get in the marching.[13]

The 1960s brought a relaxation of this austerity.

> For the first time since the proclamation of the Irish Republic, bars were open—legally that is—on the feast day of Ireland's patron saint.
>
> "Drowning the shamrock this way doesn't quite seem the same," said the man in Mooney's Bar.
>
> One of the Irishman's privileges—and favorite sport—on Saint Patrick's Day was flouting the law to get a drink. He stole into the small snack bar and drowned the shamrock with the extra pleasure that always accompanies a blow for freedom.[14]

A more recent account reveals that Ireland's present economic and political difficulties set a different mood in Dublin: the parade "was a scraggly affair", and though the pubs remain open, their patrons see Saint Patrick's Day as a time for reaffirming nationalist sentiments, singing such songs as "A Nation Once Again" and "The Town I Love So Well". For the Irish in Ireland, Saint Patrick's Day is a reminder that their striving for a united island nation is not yet fulfilled.[15]

On the other hand, in Ireland itself, the traditionally more important feasts were those dating from pre-Christian Europe, common to most European countries, and to French Canada as well. These were: Saint Jean Baptiste (summer solstice), Christmas (winter solstice), and November 1st (the Celtic New Year), now more commonly All Saints or All Hallows, with the accompanying feasts of Halloween and All Souls Day. The Irish themselves often preferred to look forward to the Easter Parade[16], Saint Patrick's Day and its parade having an almost too patriotic and militaristic character.[17]

It is not difficult to see why Saint Patrick's Day took on such importance outside Ireland. The immigrants were faced with the problem of distinguishing themselves from other European ethnic groups whose calendar customs they shared. Saint Jean Baptiste became associated with French Canadian ethnicity; Halloween, though chiefly an Irish borrowing in North America, was too closely attached to general beliefs concerning the dead. Saint Patrick was thus the natural choice, by reason of his being traditionally associated with the Christianisation of the island. As the same 1930s editorialist noted:

> Saint Patrick's Day, which belongs to them alone, is the one day which reunites all the scattered children of the Gael, whether they live in London, New York, Cape Town, Melbourne, Buenos Aires, all are just Irish and proud of it.[18]

Where the Irish settled in large cities: Montréal, Toronto, New York, Boston, Philadelphia, Chicago and Los Angeles, to name the more prominent, they established themselves as an ethnic group in a minority situation. Their celebrations were at first limited to the Irish sector of the city, then as parades became a prominent feature of the holiday, they took place on a larger scale and were recognized by other groups as an integral part of the urban festival cycle.[19] The Montréal parade, for example, is well-known and easily observed, not only because of its importance, but also through its exposure in the media. What is less well-known is how the feast is celebrated in Québec's smaller urban and rural contexts.

The Québec City area is of special interest for several reasons. Firstly, the Irish find themselves in a linguistic context unique in the history of Irish immigration in North America. Elsewhere in Canada, even to some extent in Montréal, the Irish became part of a predominantly English speaking environment, much like the one left behind in post-Famine Ireland. Even though there were Gaelic speakers among the emigrants, their minority position in the Old Country was retained in the New World, where English quickly became the working language.[20] This linguistic choice was also maintained in Québec upon their arrival from the end of the 18th century onward, because of the anglophone domination of Québec after 1760. In spite of the presence of a majority French speaking population, they tended to retain the language of economic and social power at that time. Since the English language naturally set them apart from the French speaking majority, they did not feel the need of the Gaelic language as an additional marker of their ethnicity.[21]

Secondly, the foregoing must be understood as occurring within a peculiar religious context. Their Catholicism placed the Irish immigrants in a position of subordination to the dominant Protestantism of their English and Scottish rulers.[22] This seems at first to be similar to their early status in the United States[23] and other parts of Canada. However, because of the rapid recognition of the civil rights of the Catholic French speaking population following the British Conquest, the Irish were soon in the majority position as far as religion was concerned. As English speaking Catholics, the Québec Irish thus found themselves in an intermediate position. Identified as non-French, because of their language, they were also, particularly during the period of English domination, partially limited in their access to certain positions of power because of their Catholicism. They thus tended to occupy the role of middleman in various occupational sectors. At the same time, their presence in different social strata and their intermarriage with the French population precluded the formation of a ghetto situation in Québec City.

A third factor of importance for a study of the Québec region is the role of ethnic identification as a motivation for the bringing together of rural and urban populations at various Saint Patrick's Day celebrations. Personal involvement in the different activities of the feast frequently depends less on geographical location than on ethnic cohesiveness, as can be seen in the participation in the festive events, in particular the old time parades and the present Shannon Show.

Continuity and Change

It is difficult to establish with certainty the extent of the Irish presence in the Québec City area before the end of the 18th century.[24] Mention is made of "Irishmen" with gallicized names in Montréal during the French régime, and patients at the Hôtel Dieu of Québec during the Battle of Québec. During the 17th and early 18th centuries, we find such Irishmen as pilot and sea-captain Thomas Moore of the Ile d'Orléans, as well as various McCartys and others.[25] But in general, the Irish are well hidden behind possible soldiers of fortune or anonymous settlers who were probably rapidly assimilated into the French Catholic population.[26] At the same time, except for sporadic expulsions and flights into exile of Irish dissidents[27], the bulk of Irish emigration emerged as a result of demographic and economic pressures which built up throughout the 18th century. The decline of the Gaelic language and the spread of English allowed the penetration of English colonial propaganda into the Irish hinterland.[28] This coincided with the British conquest of Québec and the opening of an area to colonisation which also had the advantage of possessing a large Catholic target population, the French Canadians, whose struggle for religious and political autonomy after 1760 was eventually beneficial as well to the Catholic population as a whole and the Irish in particular. This French Catholic presence helped to shape the evolution peculiar to the Irish in Québec, where certain features of the Saint Patrick's Day celebration display interesting variations on such celebrations in other parts of Canada and the United States.

Serious Irish immigration into the Québec area began at the end of the 18th century. In the rural areas outside Québec City, Irish could be found by 1815 in Dorchester and Lotbinière Counties, where they were established in villages such as Frampton, Saint Malachie, Saint Sylvestre and Saint Patrice. By 1821, they had spread into Mégantic County and beyond toward Sherbrooke and other parts of the Eastern Townships, where they joined anglophone immigrants moving north from the United States. On the north shore, between 1820 and 1830, they moved into the areas around Stoneham and Valcartier, founding Sainte Brigitte de Laval, Sainte Catherine and occupying Saint Raymond. Certain of the earlier arrivals were not without some assets, which allowed them to acquire land in such places as Sainte Catherine and Sainte Brigitte. In addition to this rural presence, the immigrants were an important component of the urban population. Since Québec was the first port of arrival, many went no further. Typical later emigrants were from poor rural areas in the old country, and came without funds, singly or in small family groups. In this they differed from the English and the Scots, who usually arrived with some capital and connections. Though a proportion of these families were settled on various land grants by the holders of the concessions, as in Saint Patrice de Beaurivage, the rest found themselves in what was often a totally strange urban environment. Such conditions led the Irish to develop new social ties and a strong sense of community in order to better protect their traditions and culture. Although their competition in the Québec City area with the French Canadians for the same settlement and economic niche was a potential source of conflict, particularly in the waterfront area where the majority settled, the size of their group and their solidarity discouraged too open an opposition.

This continuous influx of Irish during the 19th century greatly influenced the ethnic composition of the city. Québec at this time received the largest anglophone influence of its history; English speakers made up 30% of the total population in 1831 and 40% by 1861. The Irish, however, always outnumbered the English and Scots. In Québec City this Irish presence meant that there were almost a thousand English speaking Catholics in 1819. By 1830 they were 7 000, and by 1861, over 13 000, that is, 23% of the total urban population. Their numbers were drastically affected in the 1830s by the cholera epidemics and in the 1840s by typhus, or ship's fever, brought to the city by the famine emigrants.[29] The Québec Irish nevertheless saw their group increase. The many survivors settled in the city, making their mark on its social, economic and political life. By 1851, however, small groups of Irish had begun to be assimilated by the French, and after 1871, when the decline in the Irish population began, the francophone population gradually improved its numerical superiority.

By 1833 the Irish had their own church building, Saint Patrick's on Sainte Hélène (later McMahon)[30] street. It was given parochial status in 1856, and by special decree was the parish of all English speaking Catholics, no matter what part of the city they inhabited. The majority of its parishioners for more than a century, however, were Irish. The parish served as a focus for the community, and social life revolved around it, particularly under its first pastor, Father Patrick McMahon. The mobility of the community eventually led to the establishing of a further centre of influence, underscored by the construction of an offshoot to Saint Patrick's church on Grande Allée a mere half century later. In spite of this focusing, however, the Irish were never concentrated into a single "quarter" or neighbourhood.[31] This was partly due to the fact that Irish settlement in the city occurred less as a function of national origin than of occupational and economic status. In 1860, the city was divided into three electoral districts, corresponding roughly to Upper Town, Lower Town, and the riverfront localities of today. A brief look at the Irish presence in these various districts shows the degree to which diverse factors shaped the degree of cohabitation or assimilation with the English and Scots on the one hand and the French Canadians on the other.

The first district covered the long, narrow strip in Lower Town between the promontory and the Saint Lawrence river, and included the harbour area, with its wood coves, quays, shipyards, trading houses and warehouses. In the beginning it was the least French sector of the city, with the Irish representing 52% of the total population. In Saint Pierre ward, an industrial and commercial zone, the French were in the majority [59%], with 29% Irish, and 10% English and Scots. In Champlain ward, the Irish were in the majority, making up 72% of the total population. These were the poorest wards of the city, an unstable area, dependent on the lumber industry and harbour traffic, linked to industrial and commercial fluctuations in Canada and the British Empire. The sector suffered a continuous decline until the end of the century, after which there was an adjustment in its administrative limits. The quarter was characterized by small houses that sheltered large, low-income families. Although the Irish, French and other ethnic groups lived separately[32], they shared the same economic and social conditions. The Irish in the area possessed a highly developed community spirit. In 1851, a school for Irish boys was founded on Champlain street. The building would later become the chapel of Our Lady of Perpetual Help when the school was moved to McMahon street[33]. For several decades, Champlain ward remained a political bastion of the English and the Irish.

The majority of the inhabitants worked as ship labourers, carpenters and joiners, coachmen and carters, blacksmiths, shipbuilders, chandlers and seamen, while others were craftsmen or small merchants. Irish merchants found their clients chiefly among the anglophone population. Though the shipbuilding industry was dominated by the Scots and English, the French and Irish also had their share, as can be seen by the enterprises of Valin, Gingras, Brunelle, Carbray, Lane, Powell, Cotnam, and Maguire. The same held true in the lumber industry, where of nineteen coves on the north shore, six were Irish and two French. This was the sector hardest hit by the decline in the shipbuilding and the lumber industry in the last quarter of the 19th century, leading to a drastic decrease in the Irish population. By the end of the First World War, fewer than half the inhabitants of Champlain ward were Irish.

The second district encompassed the area between the north face of the promontory and the Saint Charles river. The main streets, Saint Vallier and Dorchester, were bordered by fine residences, while elsewhere, the inhabitants were mainly members of the working classes, in an industrial and shipbuilding sector. Almost half the total population of the city was found here, with the French vastly in the majority [86%] and only about 8% Irish. Nonetheless, the representative to the Legislative Assembly from the district was an Irishman, Joseph Shehyn. He was so respected by the French, that they continued to vote for him for twenty-five years. In this area were found the tanning, shoemaking and tailoring industries, which were predominantly French, though the lumber coves along the Saint Charles belonged to the Irish.

In contrast, the third district, on the heights overlooking the river, was the administrative and commercial heart of the city, as well as of the province. It was home to the leisured class of all the ethnic groups of the metropolitan area. It included the Old City, whose haphazard development left public buildings crowded together with private dwellings. In its centre was a more open area, shared by the army, the civil administration and various religious congregations. Here were found the City Hall, the Séminaire, Laval University,[34] the Basilica of Notre Dame, the Hôtel Dieu, and the archiepiscopal palace. The Irish made up one-fourth of the population in this district, with Saint Patrick's Church on McMahon street and its presbytery on Saint Stanislas street. In Saint Jean ward, the French predominated, with over 85%, while the Irish were only 7% of the total. Although the Saint Louis ward was about evenly divided between the three groups, with Scots-English, Irish and French each making up a third of the inhabitants, the English were socially dominant. Their spheres of influence included the Anglican Cathedral, Saint Matthew's, Saint Andrew's Presbyterian, Morrin College, and the Governor's residence, Castle Saint Louis.[35]

In the western sector of this district, Saint Brigid's Home, built in 1856 to shelter needy widows and orphans, was the first of a series of institutions which would serve the growing Irish population. Here, in Montcalm ward, the Irish were almost 40% of the population. A fire in 1876 led to a reconstruction of the quarter, and Nouvelle and Saint Jacques streets became Saint Patrice and O'Connell. Another fire in 1881 initiated a movement toward the suburbs of Sillery[36] and Saint Sauveur[37]. As the population shifted, Irish institutions shifted their centre from McMahon street to the Grande Allée area, around Saint Brigid's Home. The first Saint Patrick's school for boys moved from Champlain street to McMahon street, then to de Salaberry, where it became Saint Patrick's High School. In 1935, the Leonard School was opened as an elementary and a high school for girls. In 1956, when a new high school for girls and boys was opened on Maisonneuve, the old school on de Salaberry became the boys' elementary school, until it was reannexed to the high school in later years. The Leonard School on de Salaberry remained an elementary school for girls, until in 1967 it became Saint Patrick's Elementary School for both boys and girls.

During the early part of the century, Saint Brigid's chapel served the growing congregation and became the basis for the construction in 1915 of a new basement church, which would eventually replace the McMahon street Saint Patrick's. The building of the presbytery, the Redemptorist monastery, the parish hall, and finally the construction of an impressive new church, which was consecrated in 1958, completed the establishment of a strong Irish presence in the area.

While most positions of power in the civil and military administration were held by the English, Scots, and Protestant Irish, all persuasions of Irish were often, sometimes overzealously, involved in municipal and provincial politics. Two well-known Irish mayors of Québec during the 19th century were Owen Murphy and Charles

Photos Edwards

Several buildings have housed the Irish congregation of Saint Patrick's parish since the first church on McMahon street. The basement church on Grande Allée, built in 1915, had evolved into an imposing structure by 1958.

Photo Le Soleil

Photos Nancy Schmitz

Old Saint Patrick's Church in the 1960s and 1970s, before and after the fire. In spite of its vicissitudes, the sturdy facade of the McMahon street building remains as a tribute to the character of the Irish of Québec, while the latest church on de Salaberry is a testimony to their persistence and ability to survive.

Alleyn. A large number of the Irish worked in the service sector, as well as in secondary positions in the army and the administration.[38] Those in the liberal professions mingled as equals with the Québec middle class. By the middle of the 20th century, the Irish could be found in every occupational sector: trades, administration, teaching, doctors, lawyers, police, firemen, engineers, professors and so on. The Irish middle class was not a static entity; its membership increased as those of humble origins improved their economic and social position. The greater bilingualism of the Irish, a result of their ties to the English language on the one hand, and the French religion on the other, has always been to their advantage in the labour force. Middle-class anti-Catholic prejudice, which was frequently part of the social reality of Irish settlement in large cities in the United States, was never a factor in Québec City. The positive social interaction of the Irish with the French, English and Scots has always been at least symbolically evident during the Saint Patrick's Day celebrations, particularly during the dinners and the feast-day's High Mass, which is always attended by eminent members of the Protestant and French Catholic clergy.

The Québec Irish Today

As time goes on, it becomes more difficult to pinpoint the numbers of Irish in Québec City who can lay claim an almost unbroken "Irish" descent. Since the 1950s, census figures have grouped them successively with those of "British" origin, or more recently as "anglophones", while intermarriage with French Catholics has led to assimilation in many cases, particularly by the latter half of the 20th century. They continue to follow normal population movements and are dispersed throughout the various newly built-up residential areas of the city, especially the suburbs of Sainte Foy and Charlesbourg, the more semi-rural areas of Beauport, and Val Belair, and the villages, such as Shannon, Valcartier, Stoneham, and Saint Malachie. At the same time, while the anglophone population seems to have stabilized at around 16 000, about 2.7% of the total population,[39] new political adjustments, such as Bill 101, have had an effect on many institutions. In the 1950s, there were Catholic elementary and high schools both in the city and in the suburbs. In the 1980s, it was necessary to reconsolidate these in the face of diminishing enrolments. A compromise allowed the Catholic population to retain a foothold in both city and suburban Québec. The elementary students were assigned to Saint Vincent's in Sainte Foy, while the secondary students remained at Saint Patrick's High in the city. Saint Brigid's Home was rebuilt in Sillery in 1973, when the old buildings on Grande Allée were abandoned as unsafe.

Another significant change in the life of the Québec Irish took place in 1988, when the church and adjoining buildings on Grande Allée had become too great a financial burden on the community. They were sold and torn down to make way for a new business and residential development. The new Saint Patrick's Church, of modest dimensions, situated on de Salaberry avenue, saw its first Saint Patrick's Day celebration in 1989. It continues to share its ministry with Saint Stephen's Church in Sillery. Saint Vincent's, the other English Catholic parish in Sainte Foy, has always been less an Irish than an anglophone institution, since it grew up in response to an English speaking non-Irish Catholic population whose roots were more recent in Québec City.[40] Although all these religiously-oriented institutions are shared by English speaking Catholics of different ethnic origins, they are "felt" to be basically Irish institutions, and as such allow a focusing of Irishness, particularly where Saint Patrick's Day celebrations are concerned.

While the Irish population has seen its numbers grow and diminish, its influence wax and wane, its institutions flourish, decline, and rise again, Saint Patrick's Day continues to function as a high point for Irishness in Québec City, when anyone can be "Irish for a day".

Notes

1. The principal sources for this section are Ludwig Bieler, *The Works of St. Patrick*; Eleanor Duckett, *The Wandering Saints*, p. 30-46; and Paul Guérin, *Les Petits Bolandistes: Vies des Saints*, 17 mars, tome 3 [1872] p. 467-478. All give an idea of the various interpretations of Saint Patrick's life and writings. Recounting the life of Saint Patrick is a regular feature of sermons or newspaper articles on Saint Patrick's Day; for example, on March 17, 1906, an account of the life of "Saint Patrice, apôtre de l'Irlande" occupied the entire front page of *Le Soleil*.
2. Though scholars are not in complete agreement about the location of Patrick's home, most of them place it somewhere on the West Coast of Britain.
3. Saint Patrick, in Bieler, *Confession*, p. 21-28, selected passages.
4. Saint Patrick, in Bieler, *Confession*, p. 37 & 38, and "Letter to the Soldiers of Coroticus", p. 41.
5. Kevin Danaher, "Calendar Customs and Festival Practices in Ireland", p. 115; and *The Year in Ireland*, p. 65. E. Estyn Evans remarks that "Traditionally the cult of Saint Patrick is strongest in Ulster, where hundreds of churches and holy wells are named in his honour, and according to legend he was reluctantly accepted as patron saint in some of the other Irish regions." *Irish Folk Ways*, p. 270.
6. "[On Saint Patrick's Day], we didn't have to fast, and we'd say the French all wanted to be Irish on that day because they wouldn't have to fast." Doris Coveney, interview 1978.
7. Kevin Danaher, *The Year in Ireland*, p. 58-66.
8. The Québec Curling Club served a "Beef and Greens (corned beef and cabbage) Dinner" after their annual "Ireland versus the World" matches on the Saturday nearest Saint Patrick's Day. See *Quebec Chronicle-Telegraph*, March 13, 1957, p. 22.
9. There are a few exceptions, such as the large banner over the entrance to the Shannon Centre during the festivities, and decorations in restaurant and pub windows.
10. "Hard": days of wind and clear weather, which allow the land to dry off. Conrad Arensberg, *The Irish Countryman*, p. 49-50. As Evans puts it: "The countryman likes to have his first ridge of potatoes planted on that day, and he is not greatly moved by the patriotic celebrations which are anyhow more in evidence in New York and Boston than in Ireland." *Irish Folk Ways*, p. 270.
11. *Quebec Chronicle-Telegraph*, March 16, 1935, p. 9.
12. Kevin Danaher, *The Year in Ireland*, p. 58.
13. *Quebec Chronicle-Telegraph*, March 17, 1954, p. 1.
14. *Quebec Chronicle-Telegraph*, March 17, 1961, p. 1.
15. Michelle Sheaff's account of Saint Patrick's Day in Dublin, 1989, in the *Quebec Chronicle-Telegraph*, March 21, 1990, p. 4.
16. Personal communication from a recent Irish emigrant.
17. For example, even though the 1967 parade boasted girl pipers in mini-kilts (signs of the times!) and more than 100 floats, these illustrated new industries growing up in Ireland, maintaining the more "patriotic" and less "festive"

aspect of the "national" feast. Reuters Dispatch, *Quebec Chronicle-Telegraph*, March 17, 1967, p. 1.

18. *Quebec Chronicle-Telegraph*, March 16, 1935, p. 9.
19. Jane Gladden Kelton points out that "the New York City St. Patrick's Day parade is said to be the oldest and largest annual civic parade in the United States. The New York parade generated dozens more after its inception [in 1762], and there are now 175 St. Patrick's Day Parades held each year in the United States." See "New York City St. Patrick's Day Parade: Invention of Contention and Consensus", p. 93. In the province of Québec, the only important annual parade remaining is that of Montréal, which dates from 1824.
20. See John Mannion, *Irish Settlements in Eastern Canada*, p. 15-17.
21. The Irish never felt the need to establish Gaelic language courses in Québec City, either as part of a cultural revival or a search for "roots", the only exception being the Irish language classes which were part of the training of the Hibernian Cadets between 1909 and 1914.
22. This category included the Irish Protestants.
23. In contrast to their experience in Québec, the Irish in the major cities of the Eastern United States, such as New York and Philadelphia, were frequently the victims of nativist anti-Irish and anti-Catholic prejudice. See Kelton, "New York City Saint Patrick's Day parade", p. 104 and Dennis Clark, *The Irish Relations*, p. 11-13, and 199-200.
24. The material in this section is drawn from the following sources: Raoul Blanchard, *Le Canada français*; Thomas Guerin, *The Gael in New France*; John Mannion, *Irish Settlements in Eastern Canada*; Marianna O'Gallagher, "The Irish in Québec"; and Monique Rivet, "Les Irlandais à Québec, 1870-1968". As this last work can still be found only in manuscript form, the statistical material included here summarises Rivet's findings, except where otherwise indicated.
25. O'Gallagher, "The Irish in Québec", p. 253.
26. Certain French surnames may conceal an Irish origin: Aubry for O'Brien, Sylvain for Sullivan, Mainguy for McGee, Jourdain for Jordan, Binet for Bennet, Bourque for Burke, and so on. For the information which substantiates this evidence of Irish settlement, see the reprint of John O'Farrell's 1872 address, "Irish Families in Ancient Québec".
27. The "Flight of the Earls" in 1607, or the "Wild Geese" of 1652, the Irish "soldiers of fortune" of the 17th and 18th centuries.
28. Mannion, *Irish Settlements in Eastern Canada*, p. 15-17.
29. For example, in 1832 the cholera epidemic killed 3 451 people in the city, of whom the majority were Irish; in 1847, typhus brought catastrophe on a national scale: of 100 000 emigrants who left Ireland, 17 000 perished at sea, 5 300 died on Grosse Ile, 14 706 died at Québec, Montréal, Kingston and Toronto; 1 120 in New Brunswick, and 25 000 in Canadian hospitals. Rivet, "Les Irlandais à Québec", p. 7.
30. In honour of the first parish priest, Father Patrick McMahon.
31. To a lesser extent, this absence of the ghetto settlement pattern and mentality is characteristic of all ethnic minorities in Québec City, and is another example of its particular socio-cultural personality.
32. The French enclave was situated in the Cap Blanc sector, and had as its focus the parish church of Notre Dame de la Garde on Champlain street.

33. James Hewitt, *in* Richard Walling et al., *Our Heritage*, p. 3. The building is still referred to by the older inhabitants of Cap Blanc as the "Irish Chapel".
34. Which has since moved to the Cité universitaire in Sainte Foy.
35. Castle Saint Louis was destroyed by fire in 1834, and was replaced by a promenade, Terrasse Durham, today's Terrasse Dufferin. The name Castle Saint Louis was then given to the neighbouring building, Château Haldimand, which was torn down in 1892 to make room for the Château Frontenac.
36. In the middle of the 19th century, Sainte Foy was the sole parish to the east of Notre Dame de Québec. In 1847, the Irish and French of Sillery petitioned for a parish of their own. The present stone church was built in 1854, and Saint Columba, or Columban, was officially erected as a parish in 1855. Since the majority of the Catholics of the municipality were Irish, its first pastor was an Irishman, Father Peter Henry Harkin. The most famous pastor was the son of Judge John Maguire, Father Alexander Eustace Maguire (1854-1934), who was parish priest for forty years. Around the year 1900, his parishioners banded together to construct the avenue which bears his name. In 1969, the parish was renamed Saint Michel, in honour of the patron of the first chapel, erected at the time of the Jesuit mission in Sillery. Saint Michael's Anglican Church on Saint Louis road was also constructed in 1854.
37. A stained glass window depicting "St Patrice" in the parish church of Saint Sauveur, a gift of Martin Madden, recalls the Irish presence in the area.
38. O'Gallagher, "The Irish in Québec", p. 255.
39. *Quebec Chronicle-Telegraph*, March 9, 1988, p. 1.
40. This parish was established mainly in response to the needs of the nearby military housing establishment.

Overleaf:

The Quebec Gazette, a bilingual periodical during the first years of its existence, published an account of the first recorded celebration of Saint Patrick's Day in Québec City in 1765. The *Gazette* first appeared on June 21, 1764.

NOMB. 40.

THE
QUEBEC GAZETTE.
THURSDAY, MARCH 21, 1765.

LA
GAZETTE DE QUEBEC.
JEUDY, le 21 de MARS, 1765.

Sunday laſt, being the Feaſt of ST. PATRICK, the Tutelar of Ireland, the Chief Juſtice of the Province, with other Civil and Military Officers, Gentlemen, and Merchants, of that Ancient and Loyal Kingdom, attended Divine Service at the Recolets Church; a Sermon ſuitable to the Day, on the Duty of Praiſe and Thankſgiving for national Benefits and Bleſſings, was preached by the Revd. Doctor BROOKE, Chaplain of the Garriſon, from Iſaiah xlii. 12. *Let them give Glory unto the Lord, and declare his Praiſe in the Iſlands.* From Church they proceeded to the SUN-TAVERN, where an Entertainment was prepared for them; after which many Loyal and Patriotic Toaſts were drank: And on Monday Evening they gave a Ball, with a cold Collation, to all the Gentlemen and Ladies of the Place, at Concert-Hall; and the whole was carried on and concluded at both Places, with becoming Cheerfulneſs, perfect Harmony, and Decorum.

Dimanche dernier, etant la Fête de St. PATRICE, Tutelaire d'Irlande, le Juge en Chef de la Province, avec d'autres Officiers Civils et Militaires, Gentilhommes, et Négocians, de ce Roiaume ancien et loyal, furent au Service Divin à l'Egliſe des Recollêts, où le Revérend Docteur Brooke, Aumonier de la Garniſon, prêcha un Sermon convenable au jour, ſur le devoir des louanges et remercimens qu'on doit pour les biens et benedictions nationales; le texte tiré d'*Iſaiah* xlii. 12. " Qu'ils rendent la gloire au Seigneur, et qu'ils " publient ſes louanges dans les Iſles." Ils ſe rendirent enſuite à la taverne à l'enſeigne du Soleil, où on leur avoit preparé un repas, après lequel ils ont bû à pluſieures ſantés (ou toaſts) loialles et zélées pour la patrie; et Lundi au ſoir ils donnerent un Bal et une Collation froide à tous les Meſſieurs et Dames du lieu, dans la Salle des concerts: Et le tout a été conduit et a terminé aux deux endroits avec une gaité convenable, une union parfaite, et avec beaucoup de bienſéance.

CHAPTER II

In the Beginning

Because of the ephemeral nature of the records of the Irish presence during the French colonisation of New France[1], it is only after the English Conquest of 1760 that Irish visibility was great enough to warrant a recognition of Saint Patrick's Day activities in Québec City.

Earliest Saint Patrick's Day Celebrations

The first clear mention of a celebration of the feast-day appeared in *The Quebec Gazette* in 1765.

> Sunday last, being the Feast of Saint PATRICK, the Tutelar of Ireland, the Chief Justice of the Province, with other Civil and Military Officers, Gentlemen, and Merchants, of that Ancient and Loyal Kingdom, attended Divine Service at the Recolets Church; a Sermon suitable to the Day, on the Duty of Praise and Thanksgiving for national Benefits and Blessings, was preached by the Revd. Doctor BROOKE, Chaplain of the Garrison, from Isaiah xlii. 12. *Let them give Glory unto the Lord, and declare his Praise in the Islands.* From Church they proceeded to the SUN-TAVERN, where an Entertainment was prepared for them; after which many Loyal and Patriotic Toasts were drank: And on Monday Evening they gave a Ball, with a cold Collation, to all the Gentlemen and Ladies of the Place, at Concert-Hall; and the whole was carried on and concluded at both Places, with becoming Cheerfulness, perfect Harmony, and Decorum.[2]

The Church of the Recollet Fathers had been heavily damaged during the Battle of Québec, and soon made way for the Anglican Cathedral which was completed at the beginning of the 19th century.[3] This first celebration was a Protestant one, as can be seen by the presence of Dr John Brooke, one of the first Anglican clergymen in Québec City. The "Sun" Tavern, owned by Miles Prentice, was located on Saint Jean street.[4]

The next record comes out of the siege of Québec by Benedict Arnold, during the American Revolutionary War. The journal of

William Lindsay, a Scottish businessman who had settled in Québec around 1770, was first published in 1826. On March 17, 1776, in the middle of the siege, Lindsay wrote in his diary:

> This being Saint Patrick's Day, the Governor (who is a true Hibernian) has requested the garrison to put off keeping it until the 17th May, when he promises they shall be enabled to do it properly, and with the usual solemnities.[5]

The journal of an "Artillery Officer" has this entry for the same day:

> As this was Saint Patrick's day, it was expected the Rebels would attack the town in hopes that a great number of the Garrison would be drunk; & what confirmed us in our opinion was the junction of a great number of the Enemy at their ordinary rendezvous about a Mile from town—Greatly to the Credit of the Irish, not a man was seen the least in liquor in the garrison.[6]

It would seem that the Irish reputation for festive drinking, whether deserved or not, had an indirect influence on military strategy. At the same time as these entries were made from inside the city, Caleb Haskell, a devout member of Arnold's army outside the city, noted in his journal:

> March 17th, Sunday. It being Saint Patrick's Day we had the curiosity to go to Mass in Bonpoir.[7]

Although the feast has always been celebrated by both Protestants and Catholics, by the beginning of the 19th century the festivities in Québec City had begun to take on a predominantly Catholic character, due to the increasing number of Irish Catholic immigrants. The first recorded Catholic celebration of Saint Patrick's Day dates from March 17, 1819. The Reverend Michel Dufresne of Notre Dame de Québec had taken an interest in the growing number of Irish in the city, and on that day he celebrated a High Mass with a special sermon in honour of the occasion in the Church of the Congregation, or Jesuits' church, built two years earlier on Esplanade Hill.[8]

During the next decade, there are sporadic reports of the observance of the feast. These reports treat it as an item of ordinary news, which would indicate that it was a customary occurrence. At this time, the two major components of the day seem to have been a morning church service coupled with an evening banquet. In 1824 a High Mass was celebrated "in the French Cathedral".[9] The band of the 37th Regiment was present. Quite likely they played the Irish airs before Mass which would quickly become a time-honoured custom of Saint Patrick's parish. A recently ordained curate, Irish-born

Father Patrick McMahon, preached the sermon before a congregation composed not only of Irish and French Catholics, but of many English Protestants as well. Lieutenant Governor Burton was present and "contributed largely to the collection".[10] In 1829, the scenario was much the same. The public dinner in the evening was held at Robert Lafontaine's Ottawa Hotel.[11]

From 1829 on, the newspaper reports become more regular. The *Quebec Gazette*, the *Quebec Mercury*, *Le Canadien*, the *Quebec Telegraph*, and later the *Quebec Chronicle*, and *Le Soleil*, either mention the events directly, or comment on connected issues. Around this period the feast also expanded from its mainly liturgical and feasting observance to an annual spring festival. The Irish formed the greater part of the immigrants arriving in Québec during the 1820s. In consequence, the naming of Father McMahon as a curate of Notre Dame de Québec in 1828, was a recognition by the Catholic hierarchy of the existence and of the needs of the expanding Irish population, which numbered around 7 000 at that time.[12]

The Liturgical Observance

From 1830 to 1834, the Saint Patrick's Day Mass was celebrated either at the Basilica or at Notre Dame des Victoires, which had been put at the disposal of the Irish before they had a church and parish of their own. The founding of Saint Patrick's parish and the building of the church (on Sainte Hélène street, later McMahon street in Old Québec)[13] stabilized the Irish population and the parish became a focal point for the Saint Patrick's Day's activities. The Church was dedicated on the 7th of July 1833. The first Saint Patrick's Day High Mass was held there on March 17th, 1834.

> This morning the usual High Mass was chaunted in the new church of Saint Patrick, in honor of the Patron Saint of that church and of Ireland. The Rev. Mr Holmes delivered an excellent discourse to a crowded congregation, and about £80 were afterwards collected in aid of finishing the interior of the church. His Excellency the Governor in Chief attended the service.[14]

A certain amount of feeling was generated by the presence of Governor Aylmer at the Mass. It was said he did so "in an effort to get the Irish to refuse to sign the 92 Resolutions". That same year, Father McMahon was invited to dine at the Castle Saint Louis.

The celebration of a High Mass at the beginning of the day's festivities is one custom linking the Old World with the New. The notion of a holy day, an obligatory one in Ireland as the feast of the national patron saint, carries with it traditionally the necessity of attending Mass in honour of the religious holiday, whatever other celebrations may be involved. It is natural then to suppose that many of the elements of the Mass would be similar to other high holy days of the liturgical year, with the addition of special touches for the feast being celebrated. The Solemn High Mass was magnificent, the sanctuary crowded with important ministers and notables, robed in the parish's most precious vestments, as when in 1836 and frequently thereafter the Co-Adjutor Bishop of Québec, C.F. Baillargeon came regularly, either to celebrate the Mass or at least to assist.

The music was furnished by a military band, and eventually, in 1837, by a pipe organ, with a programme of sacred music and singing, the organist (first Miss Hill in the 1840s and later Adolphe Hamel) adding Irish medleys before and after Mass. The service became more and more elaborate toward the end of the century. In 1880, the choir, under the direction of organist Calixa Lavallée, performed Cherubini's Coronation Mass in D, accompanied by an orchestra made up of the Union Musicale, the Septuor Haydn and various amateur instrumentalists. Adolphe Hamel was at the organ, while Gustave Gagnon played the harmonium in the orchestra.[15]

There was generally standing room only (several thousand persons would attend), even after the upper balconies were added to the church. The *Mercury* noted in 1837 that the church "was crowded to excess; several females fainted". Various national flags and the banners of the various societies, as well as the ribbons and badges proudly worn by the members of the congregation, added a colourful note to the occasion. A partial description in the *Gazette* and the *Mercury* of the 1835 observance gives an idea of the atmosphere which reigned at that time.

> The religious services yesterday in the Church of the Patron Saint of Ireland, were attended by a great concourse of persons, probably exceeding 4000. The Rev. Mr McMahon delivered a very eloquent sermon, in which he introduced with candour, but proper reserve, some notice of the public institutions of the Province, and of the respect and protection they afforded to all religions. The collection taken for finishing the Church was £84.[16]
>
> The building, which as yet shows but a set of bare walls, will in course of time be a fine sample of elegance and utility, if the fostering hands of kindliness continue stretched in its favour: the Church was crowded to excess notwithstanding the severity of the weather, which blew a ragged snow storm. In the vast assemblage were here and there to be seen persons of different creeds, and opinions, every one of them anxious to hear the panegyric of Saint Patrick preached. — The excellent band of the 32nd Regiment — struck up the national tune of Saint Patrick's day in the morning, slow and gay. — Next followed that fine old Irish melody "The Harp that once thro' Tara's hall."[17]

Father McMahon "was labouring under severe illness",[18] but nevertheless felt it his duty to give the sermon, even though he was obliged to rest from time to time (allowing several musical selections to be played).[19] The next day, *Le Canadien* reacted promptly and severely to the English papers' partisan reportage of McMahon's sermon.

> If the persons who did not attend yesterday's Saint Patrick's Day Mass were in any doubt about the rumours concerning the sermon, the use of "candor" and "proper restraint" by the correspondents of the *Quebec Gazette* and the *Mercury* simply confirms what was openly whispered even in the Church and elsewhere. Instead of trying to justify the unjustifiable, these writers would have better spent their time, with all due reverence for the brilliant talent of the preacher, regretting that during a religious feast, at which were gathered persons of every party, nationality and persuasion, he found it necessary to foment discord among his hearers and consequently among the whole population of this city.[20]

On more than one occasion Father McMahon's sermon on Saint Patrick's Day stirred up emotions both for and against him. The large and varied attendance on the feast day encouraged him to point out the similarities that drew people together in order to emphasize the decent conditions allowed the Irish people in Québec. But when he chose to give "some notice of the public institutions of the Province, and of the respect and protection they afforded to all religions", his listeners from the reform camp chose to interpret his words not only as support of the administration, but as condemnation of themselves.[21]

The ecumenical nature of the Saint Patrick's Day Mass has always allowed the members of the Irish community of Québec, their friends and sympathizers to come together without enmity, but it was impossible to banish politics altogether. Nevertheless, Father McMahon's successors were generally more successful in avoiding the kind of controversy represented by the events of 1835-1838.

The collection taken up on Saint Patrick's Day was usually intended for the relief of the poor, particularly during the outbreaks of cholera in the 1830s and typhus in 1847-48. In 1837 Father McMahon abandoned politics for a "charity sermon"[22], and it was even decided to "forego the usual festivities of public dinners, and devote the sums which would have been expended on such entertainments to the relief of the necessitous poor."[23] The same thing occurred during the upheaval surrounding the Irish potato famine in 1847[24] and again in 1850[25]. On certain occasions the collection was otherwise designated, as for example from 1833 to 1836, when the new Saint Patrick's church was nearly completed and the money was earmarked for the building fund. In another year it was used to purchase the first bell for the new church. In the beginning, the Saint Patrick's Society took charge of the money, but this function was later taken over by the Saint Vincent de Paul Society.

While other elements of the festival might wax or wane according to political climate or economic need, the Mass has always remained a constant and vital part of the Saint Patrick's Day celebration. There were, however, religious services of other denominations, though these were not as extensive as those of the Irish Catholics. For many years, the Irish Protestant Benevolent Society held a divine service in honour of Saint Patrick's Day, with a collection in aid of their funds for the relief of the destitute and aged. It was held at different churches in different years: in 1865, a service was held in Saint Andrew's Church, while in 1866 and 1885, the anniversary was commemorated at the Anglican Cathedral, the "Recolets Church" of the 1765 service; in 1875, 1876, and 1880, it was held at Chalmers Church on Sainte Ursule street and in 1900 at Trinity Church on Saint Stanislas street. These anniversary services were generally held on Sunday evening, and thus not always on the day itself. For example, the 1875 service was held on the 16th of March and was attended by Mayor Owen Murphy, John Hearn, M.P.P., and other Irish Catholics. The Protestant services did not conflict with the Catholic Mass, thus allowing the members of the Catholic and Protestant congregations to participate fully with their Irish fellow citizens.

From Procession to Parade

The Saint Patrick's parish authorities, represented by the Committee of Management, were not the only ones responsible for the celebrations. The various national, political and benevolent associations which had grown up around the anglophone population contributed very largely in these early years. Already in 1831 the Hibernian Benevolent Society had come to the Mass in procession "from their rooms".

One of these associations, the Saint Patrick's Society, was founded in February 1836, mainly by men from a group called the Québec Constitutional Association. Its basic purpose was "to make arrangements for the due celebration of Saint Patrick's Day, by Public Dinners."[26] The society attracted both Catholics and Protestants into its ranks, since one of the articles of its constitution strictly prohibited all religious or political subjects or discussions. In 1848, however, during the struggle for responsible government, political differences led to the temporary existence of a splinter group, the Friendly Sons of Saint Patrick, but by 1851 the breach was healed and Irishmen again reintegrated the Saint Patrick's Society regardless of creed or political persuasion.

Once the Saint Patrick's Society was founded, its members began to proceed to the celebration of the Mass at Saint Patrick's Church in a more formal way. From the very beginning, the Society invited its sister societies of Saint George, Saint Andrew and the Caledonian to accompany them. In 1836 the members of the Society met the members of two of the other societies, Saint George's and Saint Andrew's at the Albion Hotel and proceeded from there to the Church. In return, the Saint Patrick's Society joined in the celebrations of the national days of the sister societies, as on April 23rd, 1836, when they went to the English Cathedral for Saint George's Day.[27] It took some time for them to get organized, however. In 1837, the Society gave notice that it had not as yet "provided itself with badges or banners", and rather than march in procession without them, requested the members of the other societies to come directly to the Church where they could enter either in procession or individually. The Saint George and Caledonian Societies went in procession to the Church, while the members of the Saint Andrew's entered individually. The Saint Patrick's Society was waiting for the others at the entrance, and conducted them to their reserved seats. By the following year, however, all was in readiness, and the Saint Patrick's Society made up for its previously modest showing by a grand procession from the Albion to the Church. The order of procession was as follows:

SAINT PATRICK'S SOCIETY

Two Marshals, with white wands.

Band.

The Union Jack, (supported on each side.)

Six of Committee, } Two abreast
Six Members, }

First Banner, (supported on each side.)

Six of Committee, } Two abreast
Six Members, }

Second Banner, (supported on each side.)
Six of Committee, } Two abreast
Six Members, }
IRISH FLAG, (supported on each side.)
Two Marshals, with wands
Members of Society, two abreast
Remainder of Committee of Management
Two Physicians
Treasurer
Two Secretaries
Two Vice-Presidents
President

SAINT GEORGE'S SOCIETY
(According to their arrangements)

SAINT ANDREW'S SOCIETY
(According to their arrangements)

CALEDONIAN SOCIETY
(According to their arrangements)[28]

Further instructions were given as to how to proceed upon reaching the Church, and the whole was conducted with pomp and solemnity.[29] Once the Saint Jean Baptiste Society had come into being in 1842, its officers and members also participated, and on several occasions furnished elements for the parade, in particular its marching band.

The period of immigration of the 1840s had swelled the Irish population of Québec City, and the processions correspondingly expanded into full scale parades, their routes becoming longer and longer, according to the dwelling places of the presidents of the marching societies and of the various civil and ecclesiastical dignitaries. At its most complete, the Parade might include any or all of several elements. Marshals on horseback led the parade, leading to much lending and borrowing of horses and boots and saddles between civilians and military cavalry. The national societies, Saint Patrick's, Hibernian Benevolent (and later the Ancient Order of Hibernians), the Saint George's, Saint Andrew's and Caledonian, marched with flags, banners and guards of honour. Military bands occasionally provided the music. In 1851 and 1852, the Saint Jean Baptiste Society band did the honours. The *Quebec Mercury* gives

Saint Patrick's Day.

The following will be the order of Procession of the different National Societies in Quebec, to-morrow morning, in honour of the Patron Saint of Ireland:—

SAINT PATRICK'S SOCIETY.

Two Marshals, with white wands.
Band.
THE UNION JACK, (supported on each side.)
Six of Committee, } Two abreast.
Six Members, }
FIRST BANNER, (supported on each side.)
Six of Committee, } Two abreast.
Six Members, }
SECOND BANNER, (supported on each side.)
Six of Committee, } Two abreast.
Six Members, }
IRISH FLAG, (supported on each side.)
Two Marshals, with wands.
Members of Society, two abreast.
Remainder of Committee of Management.
Two Physicians.
Treasurer.
Two Secretaries.
Two Vice-Presidents.
President.

SAINT GEORGE'S SOCIETY.
(According to their arrangements.)

SAINT ANDREW'S SOCIETY.
(According to their arrangements.)

CALEDONIAN SOCIETY.
(According to their arrangements.)

The Quebec Gazette
16th March 1838

REFERENCES:

1 Catholic Cathedral
2 English Cathedral
3 Old Chateau
4 Parliament Buildings (start of the parade in 1848)
5 Court House
6 Seminary
7 Ursuline Convent
8 Jesuits' Barracks (City Hall 1990)
9 Hotel Dieu
10 St. Patrick's Church (ruins 1990)
11 Theatre
Betwen 11 & 12 McMahon's residence
12 Trinity Church
13 Congregational Church (1819 Mass, see p. 24)

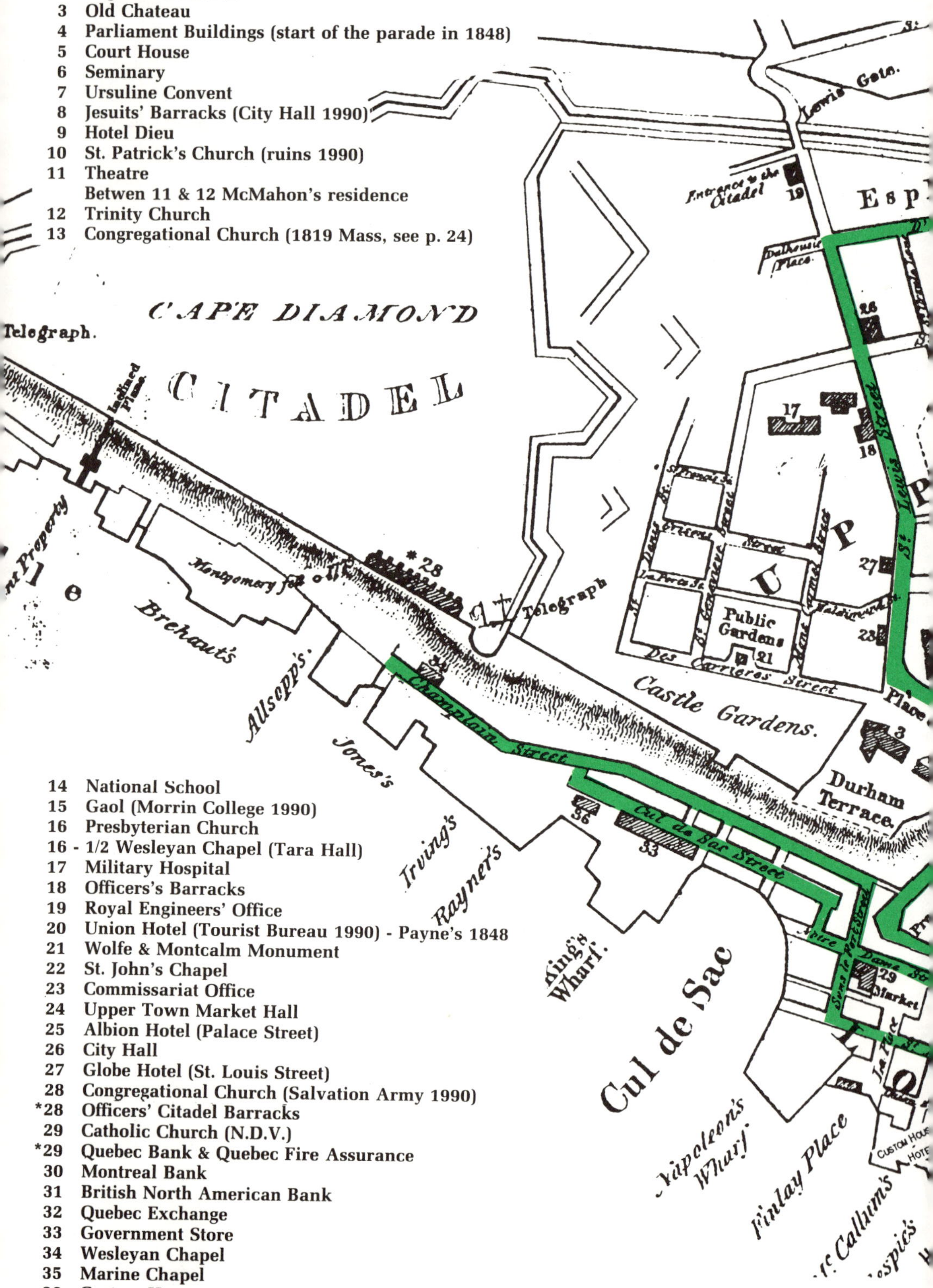

14 National School
15 Gaol (Morrin College 1990)
16 Presbyterian Church
16 - 1/2 Wesleyan Chapel (Tara Hall)
17 Military Hospital
18 Officers's Barracks
19 Royal Engineers' Office
20 Union Hotel (Tourist Bureau 1990) - Payne's 1848
21 Wolfe & Montcalm Monument
22 St. John's Chapel
23 Commissariat Office
24 Upper Town Market Hall
25 Albion Hotel (Palace Street)
26 City Hall
27 Globe Hotel (St. Louis Street)
28 Congregational Church (Salvation Army 1990)
*28 Officers' Citadel Barracks
29 Catholic Church (N.D.V.)
*29 Quebec Bank & Quebec Fire Assurance
30 Montreal Bank
31 British North American Bank
32 Quebec Exchange
33 Government Store
34 Wesleyan Chapel
35 Marine Chapel
36 Custom House
37 St. Paul Market Hall

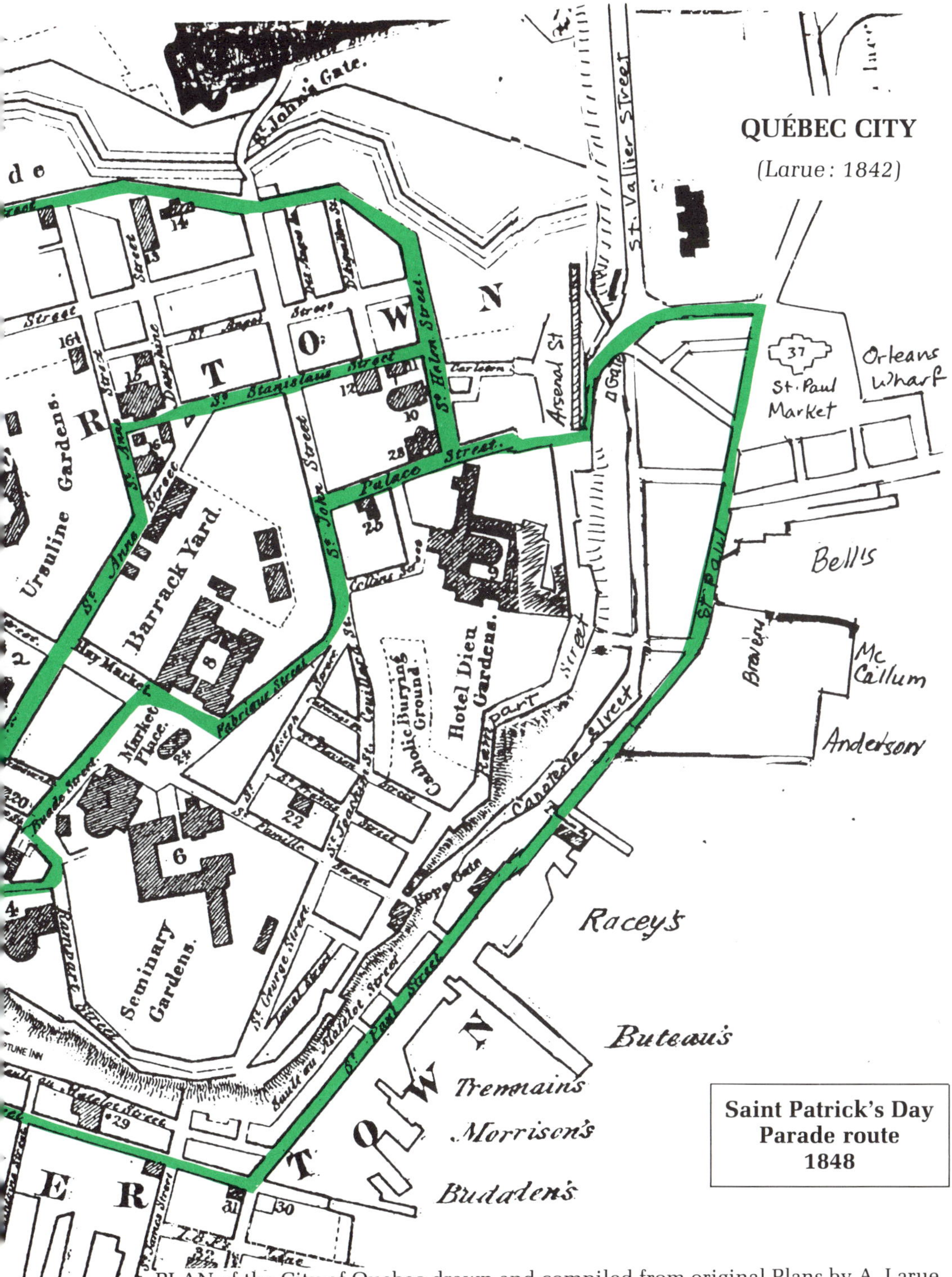

PLAN of the City of Quebec drawn and compiled from original Plans by A. Larue, published by A. Cowan and Son, Quebec 1842. Adapted by M. O'Gallagher.

THO' THE LAST GLIMPSE OF ERIN.

AIR—COULIN.

3

And I'll gaze on thy gold hair, as graceful it wreathes,
And hang o'er thy soft harp, as wildly it breathes;
Nor dread that the cold-hearted Saxon will tear
One chord from that harp, or one lock from that hair.*

* "In the twenty-eighth year of the reign of Henry VIII. an Act was made respecting the habits and dress in general of the Irish, whereby all persons were restrained from being shorn or shaven above the ears, or from wearing Glibbes, or *Coulins* (long locks), on their heads, or hair on the upper lip, called *Crommeal*. On this occasion a Song was written by one of our bards, in which an Irish virgin is made to give the preference to her dear *Coulin* (or the youth with the flowing locks), to all strangers (by which the English were meant), or those who wore their habits. Of this song the Air alone has reached us, and is universally admired." — WALKER'S HISTORICAL MEMOIRS OF IRISH BARDS, page 134. — Mr. WALKER informs us also, that about the same period there were some harsh measures taken against the Irish Minstrels.

Moore's Irish Melodies Arrangement from Stevenson, 1852.

a glowing account of the 1848 parade. It is worth quoting as fully as possible, in order to have an idea of the extent of Irish occupation of the city at that time. The account mentions that "at least 2,500 persons were assembled and marched". The composition of the parade was as follows:

PROGRAMME OF THE PROCESSION

Two Marshals on Horseback, with wands of office, will head the Procession and lead off, followed by the sons of members, and boys of Irish descent, four deep, with flags and banners prepared for them. Then will come the "Saint Patrick's Band", headed by their Drum Major. Immediately after them will be the Banner of Erin, with the arms of Ireland, preceded by two spearmen, supported by two axemen, with Battle-axes, followed by members of the Society, and other Irishmen, and the Descendants of Irishmen, four deep; then the Banner of Saint Patrick, with the Harp, supported by two axemen, with Battle-axes, followed by the Committee of Management, the Physicians, the Treasurer and Secretary, the two Vice-Presidents and the President, on either side of whom will be a spearman and a Marshal on Horseback, behind him will be the Red Cross Banner, supported by two axemen, with Battle-axes. Then will follow the "Erin go Bragh" and "Faugh-a-ballagh" Fire Companies, headed by the Band of the 93rd Highlanders, with the other Fire Companies, in the order which they have arranged among themselves. Two Marshals on Horseback will bring up the rear.

ROUTE

At nine o'clock, the Procession will pass up from the Parliament Buildings,[30] through Buade Street, Fabrique Street, Saint John Street, and Palace Street to Saint Patrick's Church, where the Society will hear Divine Service. On leaving the Church the Procession will form in the same order, and pass along Helen Street[31] to Saint John's Gate, turn up the Esplanade to Saint Lewis Street, pass down Saint Lewis Street, stopping at the residence of the Hon. R.E. Caron, President of the Saint Jean Baptiste Society, towards which the Band will face and play "A la Claire Fontaine," after which the Band will face round to the residence of the President, and play the "Sprig of Shillelagh"; the procession will then move on towards Payne's Hotel, where it will halt and salute the Saint George's Society, the band facing round and playing "the Roast Beef of Old England". It will then proceed along Saint Ann Street to Saint Andrew's-school-house, when it will again halt and salute the Saint Andrew's Society, the band facing round and playing "Auld Lang Syne"—It will then descend Saint Stanislas Street to the residence of the Rev. Mr McMahon, when it will again halt, the band facing round and playing "the Coolin". The line of march will then be resumed, the procession passing by Saint Patrick's church (which it will salute without stopping,) down through Palace Gate to Saint Paul's Market, where it will turn and pass along Saint Paul Street, Saint Peter Street, turn up Sous-le-Fort Street to Champlain Street, pass along the whole length of Champlain Street to the Toll-Gate, Cap-Blanc, when the Procession will halt and open out; the line of March will be resumed through the centre, returning through Champlain Street to the New Custom House, then along Cul-de-Sac Street, Notre Dame Street and up Mountain

Street to the Parliament Buildings, in front of which the Procession will form round the band, who will play in concert, "God save the Queen", and the meeting will then disperse, with three cheers for Old Ireland.

After giving the programme, the *Mercury* went on to describe the actual happenings:

On arriving at the residence of the Hon. R.E. Caron, the President of the Saint Jean Baptiste Society, facing which is the dwelling of John Patrick Bradley, Esq., the President of the Saint Patrick's Society, the procession halted, and loud cheers were given. On behalf of the former institution the Hon. L. Panet, Vice-President, responded. He was surrounded by his officers, and flanked by the handsome banners of the Society. Suspended from Mr Bradley's house was a huge drawing of the renowned Brian Borohme, and a string of Irish flags was suspended across Parloir Street, from the same dwelling.

The next halting place was at Payne's Hotel, where the officers of the Saint George's Society had assembled in line, with their beautiful banners and rich insignia, and where an exchange of gratulation passed between the Presidents of the two Societies. Each Fire Company in passing halted and gave three cheers for Saint George, which was heartily responded to, and the ladies who crowded the balcony of the hotel were also loud in their cheering, and waved their snow white scarfs (or handkerchiefs) in graceful accompaniment. With uncovered heads, and drooping banners, all did homage to the National Anthem, played, respectively, by the Saint Patrick's Band, the band of the 93rd Highlanders, (who preceded the Fire Brigade) and that pertaining to the No 5 Fire Company.

From thence the vast multitude passed onward, until its leaders reached the point of turning, a long—though not wearisome—travel enlivened and invigorated as all were by the general enthusiasm which pervaded the line of march. From the foot of Palace Street to the Turnpike beyond Cap Blanc, when the retrograde movement was made, the many marching treaded beneath graceful arches of evergreen; and between rows of fir saplings, flags waving above and around them, and sentiments of welcome and of patriotism studding both arches and houses, while salvos of mimic artillery resounded from side to side along their path. The windows, thresholds, and street-corners were crowded;

You would have thought the very windows spoke—
So many greedy looks, of young and old,
Darted through casements their dreaming eyes
Upon the pageant, and that all the walls
Painted with imagery, had said aloud
"Jesu preserve ye! Welcome Erin's Sons!"

In concluding this portion of our notice we must not omit to mention, that in passing through Sous-le-Fort Street, at O'Doud's [sic] auction rooms, on a platform projecting from a window, stood a harper[32], with his harp, attired in the ancient Irish costume, and decked with the crown of Ireland's Old Kings, who, by his strains, aptly reminded of the "Harp which once thro' Tara's Hall."[33]

Having just come into existence, the Friendly Sons of Saint Patrick were conspicuously absent from this gathering, but they made up for it the following year.

Saint Patrick's Day was celebrated here on Saturday with unusual *éclat*, the two Irish Societies vying with each other in honoring the memory of the Apostle of Ireland. The streets in the Lower and several parts of the Upper Town, through which they walked in procession, with their banners and bands of music, were overhung with flags and lined with evergreens, and here and there discharges of fire arms were heard on their passage.[34]

In 1850, the problem such rivalry posed was avoided by a technicality. Saint Patrick's Day fell on Passion Sunday, and since at least two weeks had to elapse before the feast could be decently celebrated, it was decided to forego the procession and other festivities altogether in favour of a charitable donation. In March of 1851, however, thanks to the personal efforts of Paul Lepper, retiring president of the Saint Patrick's Society, and John Maguire, president of the Friendly Sons, the two parties were reconciled. The Friendly Sons disbanded upon approving the following resolution: "Deeming the existence of two National Societies harmonizing in their objects as unnecessary and inexpedient, we shall join the Saint Patrick's Society"[35]. The celebration that year reflected this successful restoration of harmony.

The procession was the most numerous we have witnessed for several years, and this, perhaps, may be accounted for from the welcome fact that the division in the ranks of Irishmen has been healed by the amalgamation of the Friendly Sons with the elder Society. Irishmen, in Québec, are now what they should be—united; at all events *one* in the glorious cause of charity.[36]

John Maguire himself would be elected president of the Saint Patrick's Society and march in the 1852 parade. That parade was at least as, if not more elaborate than the one in 1848. The route also varied slightly from the previous one. After forming up in Place d'Armes, the participants marched to the church. When the Mass was ended, the parade reformed behind the Marshals, Ed Hartigan and Luke Brothers. John Maguire and his fellow officers of the Saint Patrick's Society brought up the rear. The marchers, accompanied by the band of the Saint Jean Baptiste Society, went first to the priest's residence, where, to the tune of "Coulin" they saluted their new pastor[37], Father James Nelligan who had just given the sermon in the church. From there they went up Saint Stanislas to Saint Jean Street and then down to Côte du Palais to play the National Anthem before the residence of the Governor General, Lord Elgin. Going back to Saint Jean Street by way of Collins street, they halted at Russell's Concert Hall to salute the Saint George's Society to the tune of "The Old English Gentlemen". From there the parade proceeded up Saint Jean Street and Saint Stanislas to Saint Andrew's School to salute the Saint Andrew's Society with "Auld Lang Syne".

At the corner of Saint Louis and Sainte Ursule, the band saluted the Mayor by playing "Vive la Canadienne". In the same neighbourhood, at John Maguire's, they played "Let Erin Remember the Days of Old." They marched back through Place d'Armes down Du Fort street to the Archiepiscopal Palace, there to greet the Archbishop with "Le Chant des Évêques". At Parliament House at the top of Côte de la Montagne, the band played "À la Claire Fontaine" as a salute to the Saint Jean Baptiste Society. The Grand Battery[38] was next, where they halted before the house of Thomas Kelly, the retiring president of the Saint Patrick's Society, to play "Saint Patrick's Day". From there the parade continued on through the Hope Gate[39], down Côte de la Canoterie, into and through Saint Paul street to Saint Pierre street to salute the house of Mr William Quinn, vice-president, with the band playing "The Exile of Erin". They continued playing as they progressed down Saint Pierre, Sous le Fort, Cul de Sac and Champlain streets. Stopping at John Doran's, another vice-president, they played "The Boys of Kilkenny." Their last call in Lower Town was the Mariner's Chapel[40], before turning and marching back by way of Petit Champlain, Notre Dame, Côte de la Montagne, Place d'Armes and Saint Louis street, to the president's house for one last rendition of "Saint Patrick's Day".

The account of the 1848 procession contains the description of a very typical feature of the Québec parades. Around this time people living along the route began to erect "arches of evergreen" over a framework spanning the narrow streets from house to house, with "rows of fir saplings" in front of the houses.[41] Flags would be strung across the street, and the houses and arches draped with bunting and banners carrying appropriate "sentiments of welcome and of patriotism", such as "God Save Ireland", or "Faith and Fatherland". A "huge drawing" of Brian Boru was suspended from the Bradley dwelling in 1848. Often there would be images of Saint Patrick[42] and shamrocks. This practice was possibly inspired by the custom of similarly decorating the route followed by the summertime Corpus Christi procession, when as well as the usual decorated procession altars, arches of evergreen boughs, flags or ribbons were erected.[43] It was but a short step from a sprig of green on the door to a row of little green trees in front of the houses on the parade route. This custom continued well into the 20th century. It began on Saint Pierre street and soon spread to Champlain street in Lower Town and Saint Patrice street, among others, in Upper Town.[44]

The parade could be affected by several factors. During the 19th century, it was never held if the feast fell on a Sunday, as in 1839, or during Passion or Holy Week, as in 1845 and 1850, a natural hazard, since Saint Patrick's Day always occurs during Lent. However, weather seemed to be the least of its problems. As with most activities in Québec, only the very worst weather could prevent its occurring or daunt the participants. The *Gazette* remarked in 1858 that

> Notwithstanding the moist drizzly disagreeable weather which prevailed here this forenoon, there was a most decidedly great turn out of the natives of Erin ... to do honour to the anniversary of their patron saint. ... There were the usual accompaniments of pistol firings, squibs, crackers, music and banners; and there was underfoot a perfect flood of water, or a sheet of frozen snow, slippery as glass, to make up the sum total of the demonstration, and bedraggle those who formed the procession, and those who followed in its train.[45]

Not even the famous "Saint Patrick's Day Storm" (which could as easily fall on Saint Joseph's Day, the 19th) ever seems to have done more than delay the festivities a day or so. Political differences, though, could and often did affect it more than any physical factor ever would.

The Fenians

In the 1860s, as Canada was moving toward Confederation and the United States was engaged in Civil War, the Fenian uprising in Ireland had its own repercussions on Saint Patrick's Day in Canada and in Québec. The American "Fenian Brotherhood", a secret revolutionary society, had been formed in the 1850s to come to the aid of their brethren in Ireland.[46] Among its other activities, it planned an invasion of Canada in the spring of 1866, in order to incite Irish and other Canadians to revolt against English rule. They badly miscalculated Irish Canadian sentiments and their efforts came to nothing. In the meantime, however, all across the country during the weeks preceding Saint Patrick's Day, rumours of an imminent invasion caused a great deal of excitement. The government's counter-measures led to people seeing Fenians everywhere.[47] As *Le Canadien* put it:

> The wildest rumours abound in the city. Some say the city gates will be closed all day and business suspended. Others say that an insurrection will erupt in the city, while an invading army, commanded by Sweeney himself, will arrive at the Pointe-Lévis at one o'clock. We assure those who give in to foolish fears that the city has never been safer, and we will go so far as to say that today and tonight will be the quietest of the year in Québec.[48]
>
> The fatal day, earmarked for the Fenian invasion, has come and gone, without a single hostile demonstration troubling the peace from one end of the country to the other. Perhaps now such useless alarms will cease.[49]

The "prevailing excitement in the city" caused the Irish Protestant Benevolent Society "to forego its celebration of the national festival".[50] A subscription for the charitable fund was opened to cover the deficit caused by the loss of the collection on Saint Patrick's Day. The Irish Catholics, at the request of their pastor, cancelled their parade, and put off the Soirée until after Easter. Notwithstanding, the Solemn High Mass took place as scheduled, in a church crowded with the faithful and a "large number of strangers". At the same time, although Ottawa cancelled its parade, Montréal and Toronto did not, and their parades came off peaceably. *Le Canadien* noted that the same trouble free atmosphere prevailed in the principal cities of the United States as well.[51]

The American Fenians' abortive attempt finally took place in June and rumours of further activity continued to circulate into the following year. The papers noted the Fenian news from Ireland, but Saint Patrick's Day passed without the feared uprising occurring there or elsewhere. Since the 17th fell on a Sunday in 1867, the Mass and most of the other festivities in Québec took place on the Monday. It was as if the Québec Irish wished to make up for the restrictions which the Fenian scare had imposed upon them the previous year, and the resulting Mass, parade and evening concert were evidences of their "redoubled ardour".[52]

By 1868, things were back to normal. The 1873 procession went off without a hitch.

> We are glad that the weather has been so favourable for the outdoor demonstrations connected with this national celebration. The usual procession, with bands of music and mounted marshals passed through principal streets, the line of route being decorated with trees and bunting.[53]

The 1876 parade was somewhat less fortunate. The notorious Saint Patrick's Day storm caused the parade to be postponed from Friday the 17th to Monday the 20th, when it did go off with the usual éclat. Its composition had been modified by the founding of new groups and associations, and it was made up of

ST. PATRICK'S DAY.

1876  1876

GRAND CELEBRATION

—OF THE—

NATIONAL ANNIVERSARY.

ORDER OF PROCESSION:

PUPILS OF CHRISTIAN BROTHERS' School (Sons of St. Patrick), St. Joseph Society of Diamond Harbour, Irishmen members of the Quebec Ship Laborers' Benevolent Society, St. Patrick's Total Abstinence Cadets, St. Patrick's Total Abstinence Society. St. Patrick's Catholic and Literary Institute, Members of St. Patrick's Congregation and Irishmen and descendants of Irishmen generally.

LINE OF MARCH:

Assemble and form in Procession at Champlain Market, starting from there at 8.30 A. M., sharp. Proceed by Notre Dame Street, Mountain Hill.

ADDRESS

to His Grace the Archbishop of Quebec, by the President of the Quebec Ship Laborers' Benevolent Society, in the name of all the Societies in line of march—Buade Street, Fabrique Street, Palace Street, McMahon Street to St Patrick's Church.

REFORM PROCESSION.

STANISLAS STREET,

Address to the Pastor and Clergy of St. Patrick's Church, by the President of the St. Patrick's Total Abstinence Society, in name of all the Societies in line of march—continue St. Stanislas Street,

SALUTING

D. A. Ross, Esq., President St. Andrew's Society, by all Societies as they pass, along St. Ann Street to the Place d'Armes, St. Louis Street,

SALUTING

Hon. D. E. Price, President St. George's Society, by all Societies as they pass; also

SALUTING

Denis Murray, Esq., President of St. Patrick Society, at St. Louis Hotel, by all Societies in line of march—continue St. Louis Street,

ADDRESS

to Mayor and Corporation at City Hall, by President St. Patrick's Catholic and Literary Institute, in name of all Societies in line of march—continue St. Louis Street,

SALUTING

Master J. Hawley, President St. Patrick's Total Abstinence Cadets, by all Societies as they pass, Amable Street, Lachevrotiere Street,

SALUTING

The Ladies of the Good Shepherd, by Societies as they pass, Artillery Street, St. Eustache Street, out St. John Street,

SALUTING

C. J. L. Lafrance, Esq., President St. Jean Baptiste Society, by all Societies as they pass, down St. Augustin Street to D'Aiguillon Street,

SALUTING

Jas Creighton, Esq., President St. Patrick's Catholic and Literary Institute, by all Societies in line of march, along D'Aiguillon Street

SALUTING

Thos. J. Molony, Esq., President of the St. Patrick's Total Abstinence Society and Master McClutchy, President of Sons of St Patrick Society, by all the Societies in line of march—up St. François Street, along St. John Street, down Palace Street, St. Nicholas Street, St. Paul Street, Sault-au-Matelot Street, St. Antoine Street, St. Peter Street, Sous-le-Fort Street, Little Champlain Street, Champlain Street,

SALUTING

J. Cassidy, Esq., President Ship Laborers' Benevolent Society, and Master Thos. Scanlan, President of the St. Joseph Society, by all Societies as they pass—continue to Toll Gate, where the Societies will halt, and by countermarching return to the Champlain Market and disperse, after giving three cheers

FOR OLD IRELAND AND HOME RULE.

God Save Ireland!

By order,

JOHN HOWARD,
Secretary Q. S. L. B. S.
P. MORGAN,
Secretary St. P. T. A. S.
J. M. KENNEDY,
Secretary St. P. C. & L. I.

March 15, 1876.

The Morning Chronicle

Atlas of the City and County of Québec from Actual surveys based upon the Cadastral Plans deposited in the office of the Department of Crown Lands by and under the supervision of H.W. Hopkins, 1879. Adapted by M. O'Gallagher.

Upper Town
(Hopkins: 1879)

St. Patrick's Day.

1885. 1885.

ORDER OF PROCESSION !

PATRICK LEWIS—Grand Marshal on Horseback.

BAND.

FIRE BRIGADE.

SONS OF ST. PATRICK.

BAND.

St, Joseph's Society of Diamond Harbor.

BOYS OF HOLY FAMILY.

Total Abstinence Society.

BAND.

IRISH NATIONAL LEAGUE.

IRISH PIPER.

YOUNG GIRLS OF HOLY FAMILY.

BAND.

IRISH NATIONAL ASSOCIATION,

BAND.

CLERGY.

All to assemble at CHAMPLAIN MARKET HALL, at 8.30 o'clock A. M., *sharp.*

At the sound of the Bugle, all are requested to take their respective places.

The Signal to Advance will be gi en also by the sound of the Bugle.

The Procession will Start at 9.15 o'clock *sharp.*

As the wants of the Procession will be attended to by the Grand Marshals and Buglers, mounted men, to avoid confusion or accident, are requested to keep their respective places in the Procession.

By order,

PATRICK LEWIS,
Grand Marshal on Horseback.
JEFFERY ROWE,
Grand Marshal on Foot.

March 16, 1885. Bp

The Morning Chronicle
March 17, 1885

La fête de St-Patrice

C'est demain que les Irlandais célèbrent la fête de leur patron, St Patrice. Cette année, à Québec, il y aura démonstration religieuse et nationale.

La procession promet d'être grandiose. Elle partira du Tara Hall à 9 heures et se rendra à l'église St Patrice en passant par les principales rues de la Haute Ville.

La messe aura lieu à 10 h. 30.

Voici l'ordre de la procession :

1o Fanfare.

2o Enfants d'écoles de la Congrégation de St Patrice.

3o Young Men's Sodality.

4o Fanfare.

5o Association irlandaise nationale.

6o Société de tempérance totale.

7o Fanfare.

8o La C. M. B. A. ; la C. B. L. ; la C. O. F., et la A. O. H.

Le soir, il y aura représentation théâtrale à l'Académie de Musique.

Le Soleil
16 mars 1896

> A platoon of Provincial Police, marshals on horseback, a car containing the bard of Erin drawn by four white horses in green trappings, the Sons of Saint Patrick, the Saint Joseph Society, the Temperance Cadets, the Saint Patrick's Total Abstinence Society, the Irish section of the Ship Labourers' Benevolent Society, the Saint Patrick's Catholic Institute, and the members of Saint Patrick's congregation not belonging to any of the Societies together with three brass bands.[54]

That same year, the parade and soirée in Sillery which were to be held on the 17th were both postponed to the following Monday, although the Mass took place as scheduled. The suburban community also had its arches, the one on what is now Saint Louis road between William street and Maguire avenue being

> as pretty and tasteful a triumphal arch as could well have been designed. Several young ladies were, in spite of the gale that howled around them, putting the finishing touches, in the shape of flowers, golden hearts, crosses, anchors, and other religious symbols upon the evergreens. In the several alcoves there were places arranged so that they might be occupied by appropriately dressed little children. Over the centre of the arch was a compartment in which was a harp, also made of evergreens and flowers.[55]

There was another arch on Sillery Hill[56], "gay with flowers, floating pennons and radiant bunting".

In 1880 and 1881, the effects of the recession of the 1870s were being felt, and for those two years the procession was dispensed with, as it would have seemed like "dancing at a wake", in view of the "national distress in the mother land" and the "suffering which several succeeding years of commercial depression have left behind them here".[57] By 1885, however, the parades were back in full swing and would continue until well into the 20th century.

The Saint Patrick's Day Dinner

In the 1765 account of Saint Patrick's Day, besides the divine service, there is mention of an entertainment and toasts at the tavern, followed on the Monday night by a ball, "with a cold Collation". Almost every year after the beginning of the 19th century, a much heralded dinner, particularly the one sponsored by the Saint Patrick's Society, was held on or about the 17th. It appears from the first that the events themselves were all-male affairs. No one Saint Patrick's Day Dinner was exactly the same as any other. John Cannon, M.P., chaired the 1829 banquet, while in 1831, a group of 40 to 50 members and friends of the Hibernian Benevolent Society dined at Hugh Maguire's Shamrock Inn in the Haymarket. The decorations included orange and green ribbons, as well as a large picture of Daniel O'Connell. Another delightfully extravagant dinner occurred in 1835 under the auspices of the men who the next year founded the Saint Patrick's Society.

The 1835 dinner was a public one, well advertised ahead of time in the Gazette and Mercury. The tickets at 15 shillings each could be purchased at Mr T. Cary & Company Book Store, from Mr Brent of Côte du Palais, and at Hugh Maguire's Inn. The dinner itself, catered by Hugh Maguire, was served in the Old Theatre in the Haymarket, property of Ben Cole.[58] Dominick Daly presided over the five tables of gentlemen, Irish Protestants and Catholics, Scots and English, military and civic dignitaries present.

> In the evening, in honor of the day, the most brilliant public dinner ever got up in Québec, was given in the old Theatre, Haymarket. The room was decorated with mottoes, flags, and painted scenes and evergreens, in excellent taste, having a capital effect in its *ensemble*; while outside, beautiful transparencies of the Patron Saints of England, Ireland and Scotland, faced the Haymarket. The four ranges of tables, headed by the cross-table occupied by the Chairman, were laid out with the most substantial elegance.
>
> Dominick Daly, Esq. was in the Chair, and on his right and left were, among the several guests, Col. Nicholls, commandant, Colonels Gore, McDougall, and Godby, Major Wingfield, Captain Doyle, and Messrs. A. Stuart and J. Neilson, and others.—The four tables were each closely filled by from fifty to sixty gentlemen, the four croupiers terminating them, and stewards being disposed at equal distances at each. The whole offered a brilliant *coup d'œil* of upwards of 225 persons at table; and we believe some were precluded from getting seats, and others were absent from indisposition.[59]
>
> The toasts were drunk with enthusiasm and great unanimity, and a number of speeches, with scarcely a word in allusion to the politics of the day, were made. Among those who addressed the company were, Cols. Nicholls and Gore, Capt. Doyle, Messrs. A. Stuart, J. Neilson, J. Duval, G. Pemberton, Lt. Waller, R.N., Dr. Fisher, Mr E. Bowen, Dr. Parnell, Mr Ford, Mr Power, Mr Collard. A couple of groups of amateurs and professional vocalists were placed near the centre of the tables, and gave some original and other songs in excellent style, and one or two with great spirit.
>
> No meeting was ever distinguished by a more entire unanimity of sentiments, and more cordial, free and easy enjoyment.[60]

The guests were of "every profession and class", including "Merchants from the Lower Town, Advocates, and gentlemen moving in the first circles. There were present also several Canadian[61] gentlemen, who seemed to enter fully into the spirit of the entertainment." Their reputation was such, that one lady qualified the men's celebration as "a stupid gormandising dinner."[62] And well she might, for there were twenty-one toasts drunk at that 1835 dinner. Each toast was greeted by the rendition of an appropriate melody played on that occasion either by the Band of the 79th Regiment, or by Mr Macnally on the Irish union pipes[63], or by the Scottish piper. Toasts were offered to a wide spectrum of personalities, ranging from the King and the Royal family, through the Governor, the military and naval authorities, and after those, patron Saint of the day, and the "heroes, orators and poets of our own Green Isle"; the Shamrock; the Rose and Thistle, "our fellow Canadian subjects; the land we left and the land we live in"; and others to the ladies, to the reverend preacher[64], and other guests.[65]

While the Québec *Gazette* and *Mercury* reported the Haymarket feast in full detail, *Le Canadien* carried an account of the 1835 Saint Patrick's Day dinner given by the "Irish Reformers of Québec" (who had also earlier taken exception to the sermon). Their dinner had been held at Mr Murphy's Custom House Hotel in Lower Town. The hall was too small to accommodate all who had wished to attend, but it was hoped to do better the following year, so that all "friends of the Reform who so desired could meet with their Irish fellow citizens on that occasion." The account also mentioned that

> Several Liberal Members of the House of Assembly assisted, and the Canadian gentlemen who attended, returned enchanted with the vivacity of spirit, the brilliant eloquence and the distinguished manners of their Irish friends. It was the first time that they shared the pleasures of an Irish gathering, and promised never to miss such an occasion in the future.[66]

It was at the evening dinners that people separated into rival political camps. This was especially noticeable during the time of the Reformers.[67] In 1836, for example, the 17th was begun with the High Mass well attended by French and English speaking, of different religions and political persuasions. However, there were three significant Saint Patrick's Day dinners that night. The Irish Reformers sat down to a dinner chaired by the visiting Edmund Bailey O'Callaghan, with E. Toomey, Al. Taschereau, and C. Drolet at Mr Murphy's Custom House Hotel[68]. Michael Connolly, President of the Hibernian Benevolent Society was there with many of his fellow Hibernians. The president was Michael Quigley, with vice-presidents T. Cotteral and John Maguire. The group probably did not toast the administration with the verve of the Saint Patrick's Society if they did so at all.

> In the evening there were several dinners in honor of the day, at different taverns in the city. At Mr Maguire's, in the Haymarket, Mr Power presided over a party of upwards of eighty persons. [At the Albion,] the President of the Saint Patrick's Society presided, [and] the Presidents, Vice-Presidents and

> the Officers of the Saint George and Saint Andrew's societies were invited as guests.[69]

The Saint Patrick's Society dinner at the Albion Hotel[70] was chaired by Dominick Daly, then provincial secretary, surrounded by, among others, William King McCord, G.H. Parke, H. Caldwell, W. Burke, J.M. Muckle, E.G. Cannon, J.P. O'Meara, Thomas Ryan, Patrick Lawler, and John Patrick Bradley. It is possible that the Irish who wanted to celebrate were too numerous to be accommodated even in the larger halls, perhaps there existed even further political divisions, but in any case Judge Power's friends also held a Saint Patrick's Day dinner at Hugh Maguire's Shamrock Inn on the Haymarket.[71]

Outside the period of the troubles, when differences were accentuated and interest groups wooed new adherents, the March 17 dinners were otherwise occasions when the basic spirit of understanding and accommodation with which Québec City had come to operate was underlined by the active participation of French Canadians, along with English and Scottish personalities. For example, at the banquet of 1829, the vice-president for the occasion was Amable Berthelot, who sang a song he had composed for the circumstance.[72] Again in 1841, the Mayor of Québec, pleading that he could not speak English well enough to reply to the toast in his honour, sang "À la Claire Fontaine" instead. With the passage of time, more entertainment was added to the dinners. In 1840, the Glee Singers of the Coldstream Guards performed. In 1841, Governor General Lord Sydenham granted the use of Castle Saint Louis for the dinner, which was catered by Hugh Maguire.[73]

The famine years, at the end of the 1840s, marked a shifting of priorities in the work of the different societies. They devoted their energies to raising money for relief in the home country and for caring for the destitute immigrants who arrived in large numbers at the immigration station on Grosse Ile, near Québec, during that time. The Saint Patrick's Day dinner took a back seat to these more pressing concerns, and either did not take place or did so in a more subdued atmosphere. Once the urgency of this period had diminished, however, the dinners continued. In 1848, the Saint Patrick's Society Dinner took place at Baimbrice's Hotel (the former Old Hay Market Theatre). The account of 1851 mentions that the dinner at the Saint George's Hotel was "not of the Saint Patrick's Society, but of Irishmen disposed to do honor to the occasion." This would seem to indicate that partisan feelings had become more subdued in reference to Saint Patrick's Day.

In the 1870s the Saint Louis Hotel became the Saint Patrick's Society's headquarters, and it was in its "large dining hall" that the "great convivial and gastronomic gathering of the year" took place, still catered by the Messrs Russell, still attended by the notables of the city and the other National Societies.[74] In 1880, the same year that the parade was cancelled, the dinner was also "dispensed with out of sympathy for the suffering poor of Ireland, though the flag of the Society floated all day from the window of their rooms at the Saint Louis Hotel".[75] In 1881, it was held again and attended by about 60 members of the Society and their friends.

There is little mention, however, of the dinners during the last two decades of the century. In 1885, the only one considered worthy of mention, was that of the Hon. Mr Lynch who apparently held a dinner following the Soirée that year "at the restaurant of the Parliament Buildings". There were the usual toasts, speeches and songs and the party broke up at one o'clock in the morning. The menu combined several national and political connotations in its presentation:

Potage
Printanière à la Royale
Hors d'Oeuvre
Vol au Vent Financière
Releve
Filets de Caribou braizés [sic] à la Canadienne
Entrée
Cotelettes d'agneaux aux petits pois verts, sauce Irlandaise
Croquettes de Volaille à la Princesse
Rôtis
Dindes farcies à la Québécquoise
Rosbeefs
Légumes
Pommes de terre à la Parisienne, Carottes, etc.
Patisserie
Pudding à la crème, Sauce au Vin Rouge, Tartes à la Saint Patrick
Dessert
Pommes, Oranges, Biscuits, Bonbons cristallisés, Fromage,
Thé, Café, etc. Vins assortis[76]

It was not until well into the 20th century that the dinners began to resume the importance that had been accorded them during most of the 19th century and which has been maintained up to the present day.

The Saint Patrick's Day Ball

In its account of the 1851 celebration, the *Quebec Mercury* referred to the fact that a ball "had been contemplated, but circumstances occurred to stop it." The question of a ball was brought up again in a letter to the editor of the *Mercury* on April 5, 1851.

> Mr Editor.—I perceive that the gentlemen of the Saint George's Society have determined to have a Ball on Saint George's Day, and I understand that active preparations are now making for it—this is as it should be, and does credit to the Sons of Saint George. But, may I ask you, Mr Editor, what are the Sons of Saint Patrick about? They certainly determined to substitute a Ball on Saint Patrick's Day for the stupid, gormandising dinner. I, as well as many other ladies of my acquaintance, (though the notice given was short) set immediately about making preparations, and I went to no little trouble and expense in so doing, when circumstances occurred to prevent the Ball taking place on Saint Patrick's Day. Here was a disappointment—but we ladies did not blame the gentlemen of the Saint Patrick's Society; we knew that it was not their fault, and consoled ourselves fully when we learned that the Committee had decided to have the Ball on Easter Monday. As it is now but a couple of weeks from that day, my friends Eliza and Wilhelmina, have with me decided, that it would be well, Mr Editor, to request that you will, with your usual attention to the wishes of our sex, give a hint to the gentlemen at the head of the Saint Patrick's Society, through your paper, that it is time they were up and doing, if they intend to fulfil their promise. I assure you, Mr Editor, the ladies of Quebec anxiously expect to be treated by the gentlemen of the Saint George and Saint Patrick's Society, to a couple of delicious Balls, on a magnificent scale, in Easter week. By complying with our request, Mr Editor, you will add one more link to the long chain of obligations which the ladies of Quebec owe you.
>
> I am, Sir, your's [sic] very sincerely,
> A Friendly Daughter of Saint Patrick.[77]

The "Friendly Daughter" was granted her wish. Both Societies celebrated, after Lent to be sure, with a Saint Patrick's Ball on April 28th and Saint George's on May 1st. However, for spectacle and grandeur, little could match the Saint Patrick's Day Ball given the following year, 1852, which was hosted by the ever-present Saint Patrick's Society, its ranks bolstered by its union with the "Friendly Sons of Saint Patrick".

The ball and supper at the Russell Hotel was attended by 600 guests, with two military bands accompanying the dancing. The presence of Lord Elgin and his suite gave a vice-regal tone to an already crowded day. The president of the Saint Patrick's Society, John Maguire, welcomed the guests, among whom were Mr Caron, the president of the Saint Jean Baptiste Society, the heads of departments of Government, the Commandant of the Garrison, the colonels of the

The Music Hall or Academy of Music was the scene of the earliest dramatic and musical presentations. It stood on Saint Louis Street, next to the Saint Louis Hotel on the corner of Haldimand.

The Music Hall (Academy of Music) on Saint Louis Street, after the destructive fire of the night of March 17, 1900.

Place d'Armes Square showing the Anglican Cathedral on the left, the Catholic Basilica in the background, and largest of all: the Union Building, also known as Payne's Hotel, Saint George's Hotel, the Morgan Block, and in 1990, the Tourist Bureau.

regiment and other military men. The parish was represented by the O'Mearas, Alleyns and Hearns. Lord Elgin was the first to be toasted and in his graceful reply spoke warmly about Irish-Scottish connections: he said he always found the Irish and Scots in his government wherever he went. Mr Caron, in reply to the toast offered to him and to the Saint Jean Baptiste Society, said that:

> The older race of this land had tendered freely and with delight a welcome hand to the strangers whom it rejoiced to see rising up and thriving around them, in institutions like those under whose auspices and as whose guests they were now enjoying themselves.[78]

Toasts were also offered to Mr Poston of the Saint George's Society and Mr Gillespie of the Saint Andrew's Society.

The ecclesiastical attitude, both Catholic and Protestant, toward dancing, particularly repressive during the 19th century, can be found in an episcopal letter in 1853 from Bishop Turgeon, addressed to Saint Patrick's Congregation. Though his reprimand was couched in formal terms, the bishop enjoined the parishioners not to engage in "certain lascivious dances recently introduced into this country and which are repugnant to the rules of Christian modesty."[79] The response of the organizers of the festivities can be seen in a motion introduced by Patrick Neville, seconded by John Hearne, and adopted under the chairmanship of Charles Alleyn, president of the Saint Patrick's Society, that "should the Society think fit to celebrate Saint Patrick's Day with a Ball, Polkas, Waltzes and similar dances should not be permitted"[80]. Unfortunately the newspapers of 1854 mention the parade only, as well as the firing of guns during the day as elements of the celebrations. While two dinners were held, there is no mention of a ball or dance. As time went on, the dinners continued without an accompanying ball. The organizers probably thought it best to conform to the admonitions of the ecclesiastical authorities. With the passage of time, however, the dance, with the dinner, would again become an integral part of the feast.

The Matinée and Soirée

Under the auspices of the Saint Patrick's [Catholic] Literary Institute, founded in 1852, concerts and other dramatic presentations were offered on various occasions to an ever widening audience. The Institute's first feast-day soirée was held in 1856 in the Saint Patrick's church hall. For almost a hundred years the Literary Institute would sponsor the Matinée and the Soirée of the 17th of March. A look at programmes of these events reveals a mixture of melodrama with solo performances interspersed between acts. Often the Intermission was used by the president of the Literary Institute for a speech and it could be a long one. Songs, poetry and instrumental performances were also offered at the intermission by men and women, boys and girls. Occasionally a visiting artist performed, but in general it was local talent.

Québec was on the circuit for performing artists' North American tours, since the port of Québec was the debarkation point for European shipping lines. The artists were happy to have a place for a first concert or first full scale rehearsal after an Atlantic voyage, so Québecers were accustomed to the best of up-to-date entertainment. Being aware of that, the players in the Matinées and Soirées no doubt adopted the costumes and manners of the international artists, but the contents of the concerts were Irish—the pathos, the patriotism, the pride—all are there in the plays, the poetry, the songs. Such performances have been at the heart of the Saint Patrick's Day festivities for over a hundred years. Before examining them more closely in a later chapter, we shall follow the development of the celebrations up to the present day.

The end of the 19th century and the beginning of the 20th saw the Québec Saint Patrick's Day celebrations at their height. The imposing parades were a prelude to a Solemn High Mass at which a choir gave an extremely elaborate programme of sacred and patriotic music with choir, orchestra and organ. The Matinées and Soirées involved talented "amateurs of the Irish Society". Boer War fervour and the presence of Irish soldiers in South Africa would lead to a temporary glorification of anything Irish. The hopes for a form of self government in Ireland were high, and the century ended with typically Victorian patriotic optimism and fervour.

Notes

1. In *The Gael in New France*, Thomas Guerin discusses the difficulties involved in correctly assessing the extent of the Irish presence in Québec City before 1760, in comparison with Montréal, where the evidence is more easily available.
2. *The Quebec Gazette*, Thursday, 21st March, 1765. For purposes of comparison, note that the first recorded New York celebration was in 1737: Kelton, "New York City Saint Patrick's Day Parade", p. 93, and in Philadelphia, in 1771: Clark, *The Irish Relations*, p. 193. In Montréal, the first recorded banquet in honour of Saint Patrick's Day was held in 1824.
3. The Recollet Church burned down in 1796, and was rebuilt in 1804 by a gift from King George III to the people of Québec. On September 16, 1990, the Franciscan Fathers held a vespers service in the Cathedral to commemorate the 300th anniversary of the arrival of the Recollet Fathers in Québec.
4. On the present site of McKenna Florist's in Old Québec. George Gale, *Historic Tales of Old Québec*, p. 130.
5. Literary and Historical Society of Québec, Eighth Series of Historical Documents, p. 87; *Bulletin des Recherches Historiques*, Vol. XLV, No. 8, passim. The Governor was Sir Guy Carleton.
6. Literary and Historical Society of Québec, Eighth Series of Historical Documents, p. 33.
7. Kenneth Roberts, *March to Quebec: Journals of the Members of Arnold's Expedition*, p. 492. The place is probably Beauport. Another diarist, James Melvin, simply remarked: "March 17, Sunday. Pleasant weather.... March 19. Snowed."
8. Esplanade Hill: rue d'Auteuil (see map, p. 32). This is the present Jesuit Chapel on the corner of Dauphine and d'Auteuil in Old Québec: see George Gale, *Quebec 'Twixt Old and New*, p. 48 & 141 and James M. O'Leary's *History of the Irish Catholics of Quebec*, p. 7-8: "The first meeting of the Irish Catholics of Quebec, for religious purposes, was held in March, 1819, when it was resolved that efforts be made to celebrate St Patrick's day, by a High Mass. A subscription was taken up to defray the necessary expenses, and the festival was celebrated in the chapel of the Congregationists, on the Esplanade Hill. A sermon was preached by the Reverend Michael Dufresne, vicar at Quebec. This gentleman took a deep interest in the temporal and spiritual affairs of the Irish Catholic immigrants, then arriving in Quebec, where there were very few of their nationality in a position to render them any assistance. From this time, the celebration of Saint Patrick's Day has been continued, but there was no other distinct service for the Irish Catholics until 1822, when they were formed into a separate congregation under the temporary charge of the Reverend Simon Lawlor."
9. The Basilica, Notre Dame de Québec.
10. *The Quebec Gazette*, 18th March 1824.
11. Gale, *Historic Tales of Old Quebec*, p. 215-216.
12. O'Leary, *History of the Irish Catholics of Québec*, p. 9.

13. A complete account of the founding of the parish and the construction of the church is found in Marianna O'Gallagher, *Saint Patrick's Québec: The Building of a Church and a Parish.*
14. *The Quebec Gazette*, 17th March 1834. The Governor in Chief was Lord Aylmer.
15. *The Morning Chronicle*, March 18, 1880, p. 3.
16. *The Quebec Gazette*, 18th March 1835.
17. *The Quebec Mercury*, March 19, 1835.
18. His illness prevented him from attending the banquet that evening.
19. *The Quebec Mercury*, March 19, 1835.
20. *Le Canadien*, 18 mars 1835. Author's free translation.
21. The newspapers took advantage of the occasion to carry the ensuing controversy far into the following summer. The split in the parish caused Reformer adherents Michael Connolly, Michael Quigley, John Teed, and Peter Donoghue to be dismissed from the Committee of Management of the parish. See O'Gallagher, *St Patrick's Québec*, p. 54 and passim.
22. *The Quebec Gazette*, 15th March 1837.
23. *The Quebec Mercury*, March 18, 1837.
24. "Throughout the early part of 1847, a collection was made among the parishes of Québec and the surroundings to aid the starving of the British Isles. The Irish under the direction of Father Patrick McMahon, pastor of Saint Patrick's, had taken the lead in this collection, but were soon joined by all the citizens, English and French, Catholic and Protestant, who contributed more than £1000 in the spring to send to the poor in Scotland and Ireland. Little did they realize that soon the city itself would be actively involved with these people." Marianna O'Gallagher, *Grosse Ile*, p. 49 ff.
25. *The Quebec Mercury*, March 16, 1850.
26. *The Quebec Gazette*, 26th February 1836.
27. Invitation in *The Quebec Gazette*, 11th April 1836.
28. *The Quebec Gazette*, 16th March 1838.
29. *The Quebec Gazette*, 16th March 1838.
30. Opposite the Upper Town Post Office, where Montmorency Park is today.
31. McMahon street today.
32. This personage would be found again heading the 1870 parade.
33. *The Quebec Mercury*, March 21, 1848.
34. *The Quebec Gazette*, 19th March 1849. The account in the March 17th edition of *The Quebec Mercury* alludes only to the Saint Patrick's Society and reports no dissension.
35. *The Quebec Gazette*, 17th March, 1851.
36. *The Quebec Mercury*, March 20, 1851.
37. Father McMahon had passed away on October 3rd, 1851.
38. Des Remparts today.
39. At that time there was a gate at the juncture of des Remparts and Sainte Famille.
40. Formerly the Sarsfield Club, at the foot of the stairs leading from the Cove Fields to Champlain Street.
41. On Champlain street at the beginning of the century, "the men would stay up until midnight to work on the arches". Mrs Vera Kenny, interview 1978.
42. "Father borrowed a picture of Saint Patrick and that was put up in the centre of that arch. They used to cover it all in green cotton. The picture of Saint Patrick was in the middle." Cecilia Ryan, interview 1978.

43. "[For the Corpus Christi procession in June,] arches of evergreens are built and ornamented with pictures, mottoes and flags." W.P. Greenough, *Canadian Folk-Life and Folk-Lore*, p. 75. The same may hold true for the Saint Jean Baptiste parades, particularly those around the turn of the century. As one spectator observed: "It almost seemed as if it were Saint Jean Baptiste's Day, but the snow and the absence of the maple leaf were a reminder that it wasn't yet the feast-day of the French Canadians." *Le Soleil*, 17 mars 1899, p. 1. Author's free translation.
44. "Every family would buy trees. There were wooden sidewalks. They were nailed to the sidewalks, unless there was snow. The whole street was all trees, both sides of the street the parade went down." Cecilia Ryan, interview 1978.
45. *The Quebec Gazette*, Monday evening, 17th March 1858.
46. See Clark, *The Irish Relations*, Chapter 7, "The Philadelphia Fenians", for a study of a local branch of the brotherhood.
47. On March 16, 1866 the *Quebec Gazette* published a letter received from Richard Alleyn, president of the Hibernian Benevolent Society, in which he objected to a reference in the paper on the 15th, where the Society was described as "a sort of quasi-Fenian organisation" and wished that "The citizens in general may feel assured that their Irish brethren feel nothing but good will to them, and are as ready as any class to preserve peace, kindly feeling and the law."
48. *Le Canadien*, 16 mars 1866. Author's free translation.
49. *Le Canadien*, 19 mars 1866. Author's free translation.
50. This must have meant a dinner or some other celebration, since Gale, in *Quebec 'Twixt Old and New*, p. 245, mentions that in 1866 a St Patrick's Day anniversary service was held in the English Cathedral on the 17th at three o'clock in the afternoon. The Society had been founded as a charitable society in 1859.
51. *The Quebec Gazette*, 16th and 19th March 1866; *Le Canadien*, 19 mars 1866.
52. *Le Canadien*, 18 mars 1867; *The Quebec Mercury*, March 19, 1867.
53. *The Quebec Gazette*, 17th March 1873.
54. *The Morning Chronicle*, March 21, 1876.
55. *The Morning Chronicle*, March 18, 1876.
56. Now côte de l'Eglise.
57. *The Morning Chronicle*, March 18, 1880.
58. On the site of the present-day Clarendon Hotel. Maguire's accommodations were not "sufficiently extensive", hence the choice of Cole's premises instead.
59. Father McMahon's absence was due to illness.
60. *The Quebec Gazette*, 18th March 1835.
61. "Canadian" in this context means "French-Canadian".
62. *The Quebec Mercury*, April 5, 1851.
63. Irish union pipes: the Irish bagpipe, inflated by bellows operated by the arm (Encyclopedia Britannica, 1962, vol. 2, p. 923-924, "Bagpipe"); in Gaelic, *uilleann* (elbow) pipes, of which "union" is probably a corruption.
64. Father McMahon's absence did not prevent those present from proposing a toast to him. His place was taken by a Father Macaulay, who responded to the toast with a long speech on the spirit of Christian harmony.
65. On Friday, 20th March 1835, the Gazette devoted six columns to an extensive coverage of the dinner, the speeches and toasts and the complete text of an "original song", on the virtues of Phrenology and Dr Parnell, its practitioner, composed and sung by A. Campbell to the tune of "The Hunting of the Hare".

The text of the song had also been reproduced in the Mercury article of March 19, 1835.

66. *Le Canadien*, 18 mars 1835. Author's free translation.
67. "The time of the *Patriotes* (Papineau's reformers, around 1837-38) caused divisions within the community: John Maguire sided with the reformers and this got him into difficulty with his former teacher and patron, Judge William Power. Charles Alleyn, a fellow Irish Catholic and later Mayor of Québec, was an officer in the government troops, while Maguire and others such as Michael Connolly and John Teed worked for the *Patriote* side. Dominic Daly, another Irish Catholic and member of St Patrick's parish, was provincial secretary, and was later responsible for issuing warrants for the arrest of *les Patriotes*." Marianna O'Gallagher in the *Quebec Chronicle-Telegraph*, March 14, 1990, p. 14.
68. On Dalhousie Street. At that same dinner, someone proffered a toast to Father McMahon. O'Callaghan demanded that the toastmaker be thrown out. McMahon had roused O'Callaghan's wrath and became the object of accusations in O'Callaghan's newspaper for attempting to exercise pressure on the Irish of Québec to win them to the Government side in the reform fight.
69. *The Quebec Gazette*, Friday 18th March 1836.
70. On Côte du Palais.
71. On the corner of Sainte Anne and des Jardins.
72. The newspapers published it in full. The reportage of these events usually included all the verses of such patriotic songs, composed for the occasion and sung to a well-known air of the moment. The 1835 and 1851 accounts are two other good examples.
73. This was actually the Château Haldimand, which replaced the former Castle Saint Louis, until the Governor's residence was moved to Spencer Wood (Bois de Coulonge) in 1849.
74. *The Quebec Gazette*, 17th March, 1873; *The Morning Chronicle*, March 19, 1875.
75. *The Morning Chronicle*, March 18, 1880.
76. *The Morning Chronicle*, March 18, 1885.
77. *The Quebec Mercury*, April 5, 1851.
78. *The Quebec Gazette*, 21st April, 1852.
79. *Archives de l'archevêché de Québec*, St Patrick's I, 55, 1853. See also Barbara LeBlanc (1986: 21-87) for a discussion on the role of the Church in the prohibition of dance.
80. *The Quebec Gazette*, 11th January, 1854.

Overleaf:

The enthusiasm for Saint Patrick's Day that prevailed in 1900 was reflected in the tone of the headlines in both English and French papers of the day. *Le Soleil* even went so far as to publish an article in English on its front page.

7 to 12

DAILY TELEGRAPH.

7 to 12

QUEBEC, SATURDAY, MARCH 17, 1900.

The FEAST OF ST. PATRICK !

Quebec's Patriotic Sons and Daughters of Erin Celebrate the Day !

Other Classes of the Community Pay Tribute to Irish Gallantry by Wearing the Shamrock

Green Flags of Erin Everywhere in Evidence, Together With Evergreen and Bunting

Irish National Association.
BAND.
Banner.
St. Patrick's T. A. and B. Society.
BAND.
Sarsfield A.A.A.
Flag.
St. Patrick's Branch, C.M.B.A.
BAND.
Banner.

the great year 1900—and brings us again to the honored festival of Ireland's patron, the great St. Patrick, a festival ever more and more dear to the children of Erin. No matter in what part of the world their lot may be cast, every recurring return of the day makes our hearts turn more and more fondly to the beloved land of our forefathers, and pray God and St. Patrick to bless her and shorten the days of her bondage.

Imposing Procession and Addresses to Archbishop Begin and Father Henning

Solemn Service at St. Patrick's Church and Full Text of the Eloquent Sermon—Other Notes

Edition quotidienne

Québec, Samedi, 17 Mars 1900

Vol. 4—No 6[illegible]

Probabilités
Pour les prochaines 24 heures

Le Soleil

ORGANE DU PARTI LIBERAL

LA COMPAGNIE D'IMPRIMERIE DE QUEBEC

BUREAUX

Thy sun is but rising when others are set
And the broad light of liberty will shine round thee yet
ERIN GO BRAGH !

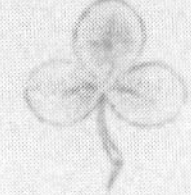

the shamrock is a badge of honor. It has become in the British Empire what the "Etoile des Braves" was in the empire of Napoleon, one of the great distinctions in the land.

And what has occurred to bring about this change? The whole world is aware of what has occurred. The sons of Irish birth have parted with the white haired Mother, the loving wife and children, or the sweetheart and have gone forth to war, as their fathers did before them, and as their fathers they were found in the front rank. As the men of their race have done upon a hundred battlefields, they have fought and died—victorious or vanquished—but as Irishmen alone know how to die.

They have fought beneath the folds of the meteor flag of England in which they found the Cross of Saint Patrick. Their courage has startled the empire. Their leaders, sons of their race, Roberts, Kitchener, French and

Le bulletin du "Soleil" ce matin

Dieu sauve l'Irlande !

ERIN GO BRAGH

Puissant plaidoyer d'unité national[illegible]

CHAPTER III

The Early Twentieth Century

At the beginning of the 20th century, the annual Saint Patrick's Day celebrations continued to be of interest to the general population of Québec City, both French and English. The procession, or parade, before the Mass, as well as the other festivities, were announced beforehand, or were reported on afterwards, in both the English and French papers. The hopes for a form of self-government in Ireland were high, and the century began with a burst of patriotic fervour, prompted by the heroism of Irish troops in the South African war. This state of affairs was too good to last. The progression of events which embraced the First World War, the Easter Uprising and finally the Second World War, on the one hand, and the decreasing numbers of the Québec Irish population on the other, could not help but affect the celebration of Saint Patrick's Day. Nevertheless, the Irish welcomed the new century in an atmosphere of optimism, which was nominally shared by all their fellow citizens in Québec.

Boer War Fervour

The year 1900 itself was the occasion for a unique celebration of Saint Patrick's Day. The sympathy of the French Canadians for the troubles in Ireland, their acceptance of the Irish into Québec society, the high hopes cherished by the Irish both in Ireland and in Canada for the eventual proclamation of Irish independence, none of these managed to draw as much attention to the feast as did the relief of Ladysmith in South Africa during the Boer War, by Marshal F.S. Roberts and his Irish soldiers[1]. The subsequent euphoria motivated Queen Victoria's request that Saint Patrick's Day be celebrated throughout the British Empire in recognition of the victory. In Ottawa the Irish flag was raised over the central tower of the Parliament Buildings on the 17th, and all the regiments were ordered to join in the various Saint Patrick's Day parades wherever possible.

Shamrocks were also distributed widely to members of Parliament[2]. The Mayor of Québec, the Hon. Simon N. Parent, issued the following proclamation:

> In order to comply with the desire generally expressed by the citizens of Québec, and in order also to acknowledge publicly and in a befitting manner the glowing tribute paid by our Most Gracious Sovereign Lady the Queen to the bravery and heroic deeds of valor accomplished by her Irish soldiers in the present South African War, I proclaim [Saint Patrick's Day] as a civic holiday.[3]

Portraits of Felix Carbray and Marshal Roberts were prominently displayed on the front page of *The Quebec Chronicle*, next to an article attempting to discover an Irish ancestry for the Queen. *The Daily Telegraph* waxed lyrical.

> Quebec has never been backward in her observance of the day, but on this occasion she outdid all her previous efforts. — There was, indeed, but one nationality in the whole of Quebec—the Irish—and but one sentiment—"Erin go Bragh".[4]

The 17th was a Saturday, and the *Telegraph* took advantage of its weekend edition to publish a six-page section on the Québec Irish: pictures of the Irish representatives in Parliament, Fitzpatrick, Carbray, Turner; the Québec Irishmen on the City Council and the officers of the Irish Protestant Benevolent Society, the officers of the Ancient Order of Hibernians; pictures of "Our representative Irishmen", and members of the other societies, including the Saint Alphonsus Ligouri Council of the Catholic Benevolent Legion, completely filled another page; there were descriptions of the arches, of the parade, in short, a comprehensive overview of the Québec Irish community and its celebration of Saint Patrick's Day.

Le Soleil not only devoted its entire front page on March 17th to Saint Patrick's Day, it even went so far as to publish half the articles on that page in English. Its banner headline read "Thy sun is but rising when others are set/And the broad light of liberty will shine round thee yet/ERIN GO BRAGH!", and a large space was devoted to pictures of Charles Stuart Parnell, Daniel O'Connell, John Redmond, and Thomas Moore. The entire text of "The Wearing of the Green" appeared on the second page, with music and piano accompaniment.[5] One text remarked that "Irish and English were more united than ever today in order to celebrate this feast, which is popular with and beloved of the French Canadians."[6]

The 17th dawned fine and by seven o'clock in the morning, the streets were crowded with people. "The masses of snow contrasted vividly with the bright green ribbon, or shamrock, that was universal in the crowded streets."[7] The parade formed up at eight o'clock at the Sarsfield Club in Champlain street and was headed by a detachment of eighteen policemen under Captain Pernee. Its composition was typical of the era:

Bugle Band
Flag
Pupils of Saint Patrick's School
Banner
Young Men's Sodality
Band
Flag
Irish National Association
Band
Banner
Saint Patrick's Total Abstinence and Beneficial Society
Band
Sarsfield Amateur Athletic Association
Flag
Catholic Mutual Benefit Association, Saint Patrick's Branch
Band
Banner
Catholic Order of Foresters, Saint Patrick's Court
Band
Flag
Ancient Order of Hibernians
Invited Guests[8]

The streets through which the parade passed were "splendidly" decorated with evergreens and flags. There were three arches on Champlain street, of which the most striking was that of the Sarsfield A.A.A.: it displayed the flags of Ireland, France, the United States, England, and the Dominion of Canada, as well as the flags of the four provinces of Ireland: Connacht, Munster, Leinster and Ulster. The route was a familiar one, Champlain street, Champlain Market Square, Saint Pierre, Côte de la Montagne, with a stop at the Archbishop's Palace to address Monseigneur Bégin, then on up Du Fort, Sainte Anne, d'Auteuil, Saint Patrice, Saint Eustache, Artillerie, Saint Michel, Saint Amable, Saint Augustin, back down Grande Allée, Saint Louis, du Parloir, des Jardins, to stop at the Hôtel de Ville for a salute to the mayor, then down Saint Jean and Saint Stanislas to Saint Patrick's presbytery, to address the pastor, Father Joseph Henning, and finally to McMahon street for the Solemn High Mass.

The Irish community, with their friends and sympathizers filled the church to overflowing. Among the decorations were the grouped flags of Ireland, England and Québec. The choir performed Mozart's 12th Mass, accompanied by an orchestra, presided over by two organists, J. Vézina and N. Levasseur. The recessional was Wiegand's "Hymn to Saint Patrick". The Mass was celebrated by Archbishop Bégin himself, while Father Delargy's sermon recalled the part Saint Patrick played in the conversion of Ireland. The members of the Irish Protestant Benevolent Society were treated to an eloquent sermon at their service in Trinity Church, while the next day, at the Anglican cathedral, Bishop Andrew H. Dunn devoted his Sunday sermon to a eulogy of Saint Patrick.

The evening of the 17th, over 1,500 people attended the 44th Annual Soirée at the Academy of Music on Saint Louis street. James C. Collier, President of Saint Patrick's Literary Institute, opened the programme with a speech about the bravery of the Irish regiments in South Africa. Then the Saint Patrick's Literary and Dramatic Club, under the direction of Edward W. Varney, presented Falconer's Irish Drama "Savourneen Deelish". The evening closed with "God Save Ireland" and the National Anthem. Unfortunately, it was also the last Soirée in the Academy, since a fire broke out near the end of the performance and by morning the building had completely burned to the ground. Thanks to the courage and sangfroid of manager Ed Varney and others, no one was injured.[9] The day which had begun so gloriously narrowly escaped ending in tragedy.

During the first decade of the 20th century, the importance of the Irish presence in the minds of the general public continued to ensure coverage of Saint Patrick's Day celebrations in the papers, though the amount of space devoted to it fluctuated, probably according to the editorial needs of the papers and the concerns of the day. For example, the printing of a text in English on the front page of *Le Soleil* would not be repeated, though on three more occasions the feast itself would make a visual splash. In 1901, there was only a column on the last page of the evening edition, while in 1902, the Saturday edition preceding the Monday feast had another full first page on which were reproduced the picture of the Irish flag (a harp on a green field) and the portraits of Daniel O'Connell and Charles Fitzpatrick.[10] The feast itself was reported on the late dispatch page of the Monday edition. In 1905 and 1906, the front page was devoted to the "Life of Saint Patrick". Again in 1907, the entire first page of the second section was devoted to a fanciful drawing of Saint Patrick chasing the snakes from Ireland, surrounded by nearly a dozen photographs of prominent Québec Irishmen.

The same was true of the English papers. Though the coverage was more extensive, it often varied according to the day of the week on which the feast occurred and the importance accorded the events for a particular year. The Matinée and Soirée were always announced ahead of time and reported on afterwards; the various dinners were announced and complete coverage assured; the parade, or its absence, was noted and commented upon. The religious services were always mentioned, particularly the High Mass at Saint Patrick's Church, variously referred to as a "Solemn High Mass" or a "Grand Mass".[11] As time went on, the entertainment section of the Chronicle began to contain more and more articles of general interest on Ireland, editorial comments on past and present Irish events, poetry, songs and even stories and games with an Irish theme on the children's pages.

In both the English and French papers, the mention of the feast was often accompanied by an appropriate editorial, wishing the Irish well, mentioning their hopes for a swift settlement of the troubles in the home country, and referring to their place in Québec and Canadian society. The 1902 editorial in *Le Soleil* compared the "special status" of the Irish in the British Isles with the "special status" enjoyed by Québec in the Canadian Confederation.

> We should like to express the sentiments which the French Canadians harbour on this occasion towards their Irish compatriots, free and happy in Canada, yet constrained by a constant bitterness because of the perpetual disappointment of their brothers in Ireland. — In Great Britain, Ireland occupies a place analogous to that of Québec in the Canadian Confederation. The Province of Québec enjoys the most complete autonomy; the same favour is requested for Ireland. No one is better placed to understand this than the French Canadians. Never forget, Catholic Irish and French Canadians, that we have a common interest in this immense country which will, in the near future, have a population of several million inhabitants. This common interest necessitates not only the most perfect harmony, but also a kind of confraternity from which we will mutually benefit. ERIN GO BRAGH![12]

A similar sentiment was expressed by the 1908 editorial in the *Chronicle*: "... the French join us in congratulating our Irish countrymen this day...God bless Ireland, God bless the Empire, God bless the Dominion."[13]

The Fate of the Parade

Of all the elements of the feast, the parade was still the aspect of the celebration most sensitive to current social conditions and changes. It was easily cancelled for civil or religious reasons,[14] as when, for example, the 17th fell on a Sunday or during Passion or Holy Week in Lent, or because of the unfavourable political climate in Ireland or Québec. In 1901 the parade was as splendid as ever, unfolding under a brilliantly sunny sky. The decorations for the feast of 1902 were up three days beforehand, with two "magnificent" arches on Champlain street; the parade featured five bands, with Mayor Parent figuring prominently among the dignitaries in the procession. The Irish members of the police were given a holiday in order to participate in the festivities. The arches varied in location and decoration. In 1903, there were three, one on Champlain street, flying the Irish flag flanked by two harps on pillars; one on Sainte Julie, flying the Irish, American and Dominion flags; and one on Saint Eustache, with the flags of Ireland, France, and the Dominion, this last the most elaborate of the three.[15] The 1904 parade featured a large "Star Spangled Banner", while the Mayor and all the Irish members of the City Council were again noticeably present. There were the usual arches and evergreens, and merchants decorated their windows with harps and green ribbons.[16] There were marshals on foot or on horseback, often with plumed hats or bowler hats covered with shamrocks, and sleighs filled with city and provincial dignitaries.

From 1905 to 1907, the parade continued to feature largely in the festivities, with pauses for long addresses and responses before the residences of the Archbishop, the Lieutenant-Governor, the Mayor, and the Rector of Saint Patrick's Parish. During these years the weather was rarely an obstacle to the procession. In 1906, a light snow was falling, while a heavy rainstorm delayed the 1907 parade until two o'clock in the afternoon. A hundred members of the Ancient Order of Hibernians, with Montréal companies 1 and 2 of the Hibernian Knights had come especially from Montréal for the 1907 occasion. The Knights made an impressive picture in their white gloves, navy uniforms, and white plumed hats. During the procession, as they passed in front of the Basilica, they paused to execute a drill with military precision, drawn sabres at the ready. The American, Irish, British, and Papal flags were grouped with the flags of the different societies, and the bands of the Royal Artillery, the Union Lambillotte and the 8th Regiment furnished the music. As it was a Sunday, the "customary addresses" were omitted. That evening, the Hibernian Knights were the guests of honour at the banquet of the Ancient Order of Hibernians, attended by some 200 guests, held in the two main rooms of the Auditorium café. The toasts went

EMMET HOCKEY CLUB
CHAMPIONS QUEBEC CITY JUNIOR LEAGUE
WINNERS OF VICTORIA CUP
1911~12
M·DELANEY
M·REDMOND
W·QUART
J.DOYLE
J·DINAN
F·McLAUGHLIN
M·POWER
J·DREW
P·REDMOND
W·O'CONNEL

The arch of the Emmet [sic] Club near the Sarsfield Athletic Club building on Champlain Street is bordered by evergreens thrust in the snow. The Emmet Club was founded in 1912 and won the Victoria Cup in hockey that year. Its members also practised baseball, lacrosse, and rowing. The founding officers in 1912 were Martin Delaney Jr, president, Frank McLaughlin, vice-president, Michael Power Jr, secretary, and John Doyle, treasurer.

Photos kindness of Jean Egan Gagnon

Photo Chronicle-Telegraph

The parade arch on Saint Patrick street circa 1922 decorated with mottos, portraits and tricolours; during the parade, marshals on horseback are eagerly awaited by the crowd.

Photo Chronicle-Telegraph

Prints Pierre Caver

Decorated Arch on Sainte Julie Street in early 1900s.

Le Soleil artist Joseph Brouilly's rendition of the arches on Saint Eustache and Sainte Julie streets in 1903.

Four horsemen on Champlain Street in front of N° 6 Fire Station (named Faugh-a-Ballagh). Jack Kenny at lower right.

Postcards kindness of Leo McCullen

A Saint Patrick's Day Parade in the 1920s. The photo seems to have been taken facing west from atop the Saint Jean Gate, or from the walls. The Montcalm Hotel with its café is on the left.

Saint Patrick's Day Parade in the same era as the above with the photographer at the same vantage point. Two signs on the telegraph poles point to the YMCA.

on until the visitors had to leave to catch the late evening train back to Montréal.[17]

The 1908 celebration was a quiet one. The usual parade was not held, though no particular reason was given, while the celebrations elsewhere, such as the parade in Montréal, seem to have gone on much as usual. Nevertheless, flags floated from public buildings and private houses, and there were a few banners proclaiming "Erin go Bragh" and "Ireland for ever". The 1909 parade made up for it however. In spite of bad weather, which led to doubts that it would be held at all, the different groups were out in force, led by the marshals in green on horseback and omitting not a single speech at the statutory halts. The 1910 procession featured the Hibernian Cadets, which had been formed the previous year.[18] "The cadets looked smart in their dark 'rifle green' (almost black) uniforms, with light green facings, including the stripe on each leg of their trousers."[19] There were again three arches that year, one in front of the Diamond Harbor Chapel, where the parade began, another on Saint Michel street and the third at the corner of Saint Eustache and Artillerie. Both the 1910 and the 1911 parades enjoyed fine weather, with the usual evergreens lining the streets and appreciative crowds along the way. The route varied slightly, since it was held separately from the Mass, and instead of ending at the church, it finished up at the Tara Hall on Sainte Anne street. Because the 17th fell on a Sunday in 1912, the parade was cancelled again that year, though all the other usual events took place, including a dinner by the Saint Patrick's Young Men's Sodality that evening, and the annual Soirée at the Auditorium.

In 1913, the first slight changes began to appear in the programme of the celebrations. The Soirée was held on Saturday the 15th, while the other festivities took place as usual on Monday the 17th itself. However, for the next two years, in spite of the outbreak of war in Europe, things were back to normal. The parade took its traditional route to the church, stopping as always at the Episcopal Palace to salute the Cardinal, while the mayor and city councillors marched in the procession itself. Captain Emile Trudel, chief of police, who was at the head, would eventually take part in every parade from 1905 to 1926, in an official or unofficial capacity. As the Great War dragged on, many of the civilian and the military members of the community, who would ordinarily have taken part in the parade, were called up, and from 1916 to 1920,[20] no parade was held, though the other events went on as usual and

> In honor of the day, numerous flags are flying from public buildings and private residences throughout the city, besides which a large number of the most prominent store windows are prettily trimmed with green in all shapes and forms, some of them being artfully gotten up.[21]

The troubles in Ireland which would lead to the Easter Uprising of 1916 were an additional reason for considering the parade an inappropriate manifestation under the circumstances, though the uprising itself did not take place until April.[22]

In 1921, the parade was back, and the *Chronicle* hailed it as "the most successful held for nearly a score of years".[23] Both French and Irish were among the crowds lining the parade route. The event was blessed by fine weather and the colour green was very much in evidence; even the marshals' batons were green, and youngsters waved green balloons in front of the horses.[24] At the same time, all the papers carried editorials or comments on the bloody fighting[25] which had followed the partition of Ireland the preceding autumn, and expressed hopes that someday soon the Irish there would enjoy the same freedoms as did their countrymen in Canada. This theme was underlined by the presence in the parade of members of three branches of the Self Determination for Ireland League: the MacSwiny Branch, the Sarsfield Branch and the Kevin Barry Branch. Their hopes began to be realised with the recognition of the Irish Free State in December 1921, though true peace was still to come. The 1922 parade saw the construction of two arches, as in previous years, one on Saint Michel street and the other on Saint Patrice. Mayor Samson and several French city council members rode among the dignitaries in the processional cars, and the parade ended up as before at the Church on McMahon street.

In 1923, the parade was moved to Sunday afternoon, even though the Mass, Matinée and Soirée were held on Saturday the 17th.[26] In 1924, the feast fell on a Monday and the parade was held on that day, but in 1925 the parade was held on Sunday the 15th, and in 1926 on Sunday the 14th. The 1926 parade was "a banner affair"[27], the weather was "ideal", and the Police, the Fire Brigade, and the Societies were out in force. The green, white, and orange of the Free State flag predominated, and a sleigh carried the British, Irish, French and American flags. The parade left at two-thirty in the afternoon from the Diamond Harbor Chapel, accompanied by the band of the Royal 22nd Regiment, and ended with Benediction in the church on McMahon street. This was to be the last of the traditional parades. The absence of the parade in 1927 was treated by the media as temporary, since it had previously been cancelled on

Photo Edwards

The Saint Patrick's Day parade in *Le Soleil*, 1924.

1919

Musical Programme

To be

Rendered at the Solemn Pontifical Mass

KYRIE.......................................T. de la Hache
CHRISTE...................Solo...................T. de la Hache
Mrs. H. S. Quart

GLORIA.......................................T. de la Hache
CREDO.......................................A. Durand
ET IN SPIRITUM...........Solo.......................A. Durand
Miss V. Henchey

GENITUM.................(Quartette).................A. Durand
Mrs. H. S. Quart, Miss V. Henchey, Mr. J. Shields, Mr. R. Timmons
SANCTUS.......................................T. de la Hache
AGNUS DEI.................(Trio).................T. de la Hache
Miss V. Henchey, Mr. J. Shields, Mr. R. Timmons

OFFERTORY SELECTION

O SALUTARIS.......................................Weigand
Mrs. H. S. Quart and Mr. Jos. Shields

Mr. A. JACQUES.......................................Organist

Musical Programme

to be rendered at the

Solemn Pontifical Mass

St. Patrick's Day

1924

Processional—Irish Airs.
Kyrie in B flat.......................................Mercandante
Gloria in C.......................................Hayden
Credo in B. flat.......................................Farmer
Offertory—Selected.
Sanctus in G.......................................Marzo
Benedictus in G.......................................Marzo
Agnus Dei in G.......................................Marzo
Recessional—Hymn to St. Patrick.

Organist...........................Prof. André Jacques

A recital of Irish airs was a typical feature of the Saint Patrick's Day Mass, as was the hymn to Saint Patrick used as a recessional. The choir was made up of talented amateurs, and a military or local orchestra or chamber group might accompany the organ. There was often a visiting organist, who would act as choirmaster or orchestra director, leaving the musical selections to the titular organist. Andre Jacques was parish organist of Saint Patrick's during the 1920s, and also took part in the Matinées and Soirées, as did his successor Léonce Crépault.

various pretexts, but by 1928, the papers noted that the festivities would take place "with the exception of the annual Saint Patrick's Day parade, which has been dispensed with"[28]. The following year, an editorial lamented:

> While fully recognizing that local climatic conditions do not often lend themselves to such a demonstration, we can find it in our heart to regret that the annual parade is apparently a thing of the past.[29]

The "climatic conditions" had never before posed a real problem, as former parades, especially those of 1907 and 1909, had shown.[30] As well, the parades continued as strongly as ever in cities such as Toronto and Montréal, where the weather often posed similar problems to that of Québec. The weather was a convenient way of articulating the effects of the changing social, economic and demographic "climate" surrounding the Irish in Québec.[31]

A form of revival of the procession took place after the Second World War, when the Saint Patrick's High School Cadets[32] began to parade again in 1950 after a ten year absence. This parade was usually composed of the band and one or two platoons; they would march from Saint Patrick's School on de Salaberry avenue, to attend Mass at the old church, and back to the school again. When the Mass was said in the new church, they attended in formation. By the early seventies, however, even this final effort had came to an end. Perhaps one of the last manifestations was seen in the afternoon of the 17th in 1962, when several older students of the boy's section of the High School did parade through the streets of the Old City in decorated convertibles, after which they adjourned to Noonan's Chien d'Or to continue the celebration with their elders.[33]

Religious Services

Protestant observances of the anniversary continued as they had in the 19th century. The Irish Protestant Benevolent Society's annual service was usually held on the Sunday evening nearest Saint Patrick's Day, and was attended by the members of the Saint George's and Saint Andrew's Societies. There was often a musical programme offered by a choir composed of members of the various Protestant churches, which always included the traditional hymn "Saint Patrick's Breastplate".[34] The participation of the Protestant clergy and the sister societies at the Catholic mass seems not to have had as its counterpart an official Catholic presence at the Protestant service, possibly because of the rigorist attitude which prevailed in Catholic thinking from the early 1920s until after the Second Vatican Council in the 1960s.[35] It is worth noting however, that in 1940 a member of Saint Patrick's parish, May Anne Burridge did participate in the entertainment given at the lecture evening held by the Irish Protestant Benevolent Society.[36]

Without a doubt, the most durable feature of Saint Patrick's Day has been the Catholic Mass. Throughout the years, no matter what variations there may be in the other elements of the feast, the Mass quite naturally remains the focal point of the celebrations, in view of the importance of the Catholic element in the Irish population. The two world wars, while affecting certain aspects of the festivities, such as the parade, did not affect its most important component, the Mass. When religious observances by other denominations took place, they did not conflict with the Mass, since representatives of other national or religious bodies have always manifested a certain solidarity by attending the Mass at Saint Patrick's Church, either collectively or individually.

After the turn of the century, the westward movement of the Irish population away from the Old City and the new focusing of parochial activities around the Grande Allée complex led gradually to the construction of another Saint Patrick's church. Nevertheless, the Saint Patrick's Day Mass itself was held in the old church on McMahon street until just before its closing at the beginning of the 1960s. The last Saint Patrick's Day Mass was held there in 1958. From then until 1988, the Mass was held in the Grande Allée church. When the newest Saint Patrick's church was erected on de Salaberry avenue, its official consecration took place on Saint Patrick's Day in 1989.

The Mass was the occasion for an important musical display, which furnished a counterpart to the musical offerings of the Soirée, since both drew upon the talents of many of the same organists, musical ensembles and singers. A great deal of work went into the preparation for the feast-day's music, with amateurs and professionals offering impressive choral and solo performances. The names of the soloists at the 1909 Mass, Bradie, Fitzhenry, Foley, Goyer, Leclerc, Lefebvre, Lesperance, Mahoney, McManamy, Shields, and Timmons (the Richard of Soirée fame), show that the soloists were not only Irish, but were drawn from the French community as well. Only two of these, Shields and Timmons, were still going strong in 1921, but the other names on the programme, Conway, Delaney, Dugal, Faguy, Fecteau, Gosselin, and Quart, illustrate the continued cooperation between Irish and French. Masses by Haydn, Wiegand, Durand, and Gounod were among the selections successfully attempted by the choirs. A typical feature of the service was the recital of Irish airs played by the organist, before and after the service, a tradition begun by Miss Hill in the 1840s and which continues down to the present day.

Two noted organists of the 1800s were Miss Hill[37] and choirmaster Adolphe Hamel. At the beginning of the 20th century, another organist, Joseph Vézina, was choirmaster of Saint Patrick's and responsible for the feast-day programme. In 1904, J. Arthur Bernier, the organist of Saint Sauveur, was the visiting accompanist. Father Peter Costello assisted Vézina in 1914, when J. André Jacques began taking over from him as regular organist of Saint Patrick's. Father Costello continued to be responsible for the musical programme at Mass even after becoming rector in 1918. At the Pontifical High Mass in 1921, organist Léon Dessane conducted a large orchestra, with André Jacques at the organ itself. The latter held the post of parish organist until replaced by Léonce Crépault in the early 1930s.

Visiting Redemptorist preachers from Montréal, Saint John, New Brunswick, and various Ontario parishes continued to give the feast-day sermons, alternating with the rectors of Saint Patrick's, and other Québec clergy, such as Father Eustace Maguire, pastor of Saint Columba's, Sillery. The visitors bore such Irish names as Doyle, Gillen, Maloney, McBrearty, McCormick, McLaughlin, Mulhern, Mullins, Murray, O'Reilly, and O'Sullivan. The fiery sermons of Father McMahon were no more. The 20th century sermons revolved around the themes of the life of Saint Patrick and his contributions to the Christianisation of Ireland, the hopes of the Irish in Ireland, and Irish contributions to Canadian nationhood. Though the clergy took strong positions in the struggle for Irish independence, usually by condemning certain radical factions, the Saint Patrick's Day sermons in Québec tried to hold up Saint Patrick as a model for peace, reconciliation of differences, and patriotism, both in Canada and in the Old Country. In his 1916 sermon, visitor Father Miles Howland referred to the Irish among the Fathers of Confederation[38] and stressed the contributions of all persuasions of Irishmen.

> I wish to correct the erroneous impression that Irish Catholics alone have done so much for their country to secure her rights and freedom. Protestant Irishmen have done their full share in devoting their lives in the welfare of their country, and shedding their blood in her defence.[39]

The feast-day liturgy was usually that of the Pontifical High Mass, celebrated or attended by important members of the Québec hierarchy, such as Paul Eugène Roy, archbishop of Québec, Cardinal Bégin or his representative Bishop Langlois, and Monsignor E. Laflamme and Chanoine Garneau of the Basilica. Cardinal Rouleau attended for the first time in 1927, and regularly thereafter, either as celebrant or participant, formally occupying the episcopal throne. Civil dignitaries included the mayor, the council members, members of federal and provincial parliaments, the officers of the different national Societies, as well as Sir Charles Fitzpatrick, lieutenant governor in the years after the First World War.[40] The Old Church was always filled to capacity; at the 1921 Mass, there was standing room only, and hundreds were unable to gain entrance[41]. Accounts during the 1920s began to mention the dinner given for the officiating and visiting clergy after the Mass in the presbytery dining room, generally also attended by the dignitaries of the Saint Patrick's Society. In 1928, after attending the dinner, Cardinal Rouleau visited Saint Brigid's Home in the afternoon.[42]

The Dinners

The official Saint Patrick's Day dinner, or banquet, which had been played down during the late 1800s, soon began making a comeback. It remained a place for expressing strong patriotic sentiments. Part of the 1907 celebration included a dinner given by the Ancient Order of Hibernians in honour of the Hibernian Knights from Montréal, who had been their guests in the parade; it took place in the two large dining rooms of the Auditorium Café on Saint Jean street. The decorations included the flags which had been carried in the parade, as well as banners carrying the inscriptions: "Cead mille Failte", "Sinn Fein" and "Ireland a Nation". Jeremiah Gallagher, the president of Division no 1, was in the chair, while the guests of honor included Fathers Mulhern, Gannon, and Maguire, J. J. O'Flaherty and P. Scullion, provincial president and vice-president, P. Keane, president of the Montréal division, Captain P. Doyle of the Hibernian Knights, the Hon. John C. Kaine, J.M. Wallace, M. Coleman, P. French, M. Monaghan, J. M. Ahern, president of the Literary Institute, pro-mayor Foley, and aldermen Madden, Hogan, Mulrooney, Dinan and Campbell.[43]

The 1907 dinner was catered by W. Dugal. Toasts were proposed to "The day we celebrate", "Ireland a nation", "Our hosts", "Canada our Home", "The clergy", "The press", "The ladies", "The president of the banquet". The dinner ended early for once, because of the need for the Montréal Hibernians to catch the last train. The following year, 1908, was a quiet one and it is likely the dinner was cancelled along with the parade, although the Mass and the 52nd annual Soirée took place as usual.

During the 1920s, the "Québec Celtic Association", under the presidency of Richard O'Connor, held a well attended banquet on the eve of Saint Patrick's Day at the Château Frontenac. The guests often included the mayor and city councillors. The speeches took on more dramatic tones when treating the themes of civism and patriotism. In 1925, the speech by the Hon. John Hall Kelly compared the Irish revolutionists to the Patriotes of 1837, showing how both were ready to give their lives for the defense and safeguard of their rights.[44] The banquets were another occasion where musical selections formed part of the entertainment; in 1926, the singer was Keith Allen who gave a selection of traditional Irish songs. The Québec Irish community was not necessarily parochial in its choice of honoured guests, however. The speaker for the 1928 Celtic Banquet was Mr Lindsay Crawford, Irish Free State representative of Trade and Commerce in New York. The Ancient Order of Hibernians took over from the Celtic in the early Thirties. Their 1930 banquet was presided over by John Slavin, with guests Mayor Henri Edgar Lavigueur, Father Maguire of Sillery, Father Coughlin of Saint Patrick's, Joseph Cannon, Martin Egan, Bernard Devlin, Richard Timmons, and Father Byrne, A.O.H. chaplain. The after-dinner speeches were broadcast by the French language radio station, CHRC, live from the Victoria Hotel.[45]

The 1920s also ushered in a period of increasing severity in Catholic religious practices, especially regarding the Lenten observance. While the Irish had previously taken for granted that they could consider the 17th of March a holy day and a holiday by virtue of their ethnicity, it was now deemed necessary to formalize this dispensation. A newspaper article noted in 1925 that there were "a number of private functions held in different parts of the city" and that

> These have been made possible through the kindness of His Eminence Cardinal Bégin who, although the festival falls in Lent, has granted a dispensation to the Irish members of his diocese to enable them to regard it as a feast day.[46]

The Optimist and Kiwanis Clubs of Québec went "Irish" at their weekly or monthly luncheon in the month of March. For example, the Kiwanians' invited speaker in 1927 was a visiting artist from Ireland. The Québec Athletic Club would hold a feast-day dinner. The Québec and Victoria Curling Clubs had both instituted an annual curling match on or near Saint Patrick's Day with the theme "Ireland versus the World". These usually pitted the Irish and anglophone members against the French contingent, and the match was followed in the afternoon or evening by a banquet, complete with invited speakers and a programme of musical entertainment. The menu at the Québec Club's dinner was usually "Beef and Greens", the corned beef and cabbage associated with Irish tradition.

The 1935 Celebrations

The Saint Patrick's Day festivities of 1935 were typical of the 1930s and the period between the two wars. The activities were many and varied, and there were enough participants of all ages, all ethnic groups, and all walks of life to more than satisfy the organizers of the different events. Above all, 1935 was the "Diamond Jubilee" year of the incorporation of the Saint Patrick's Literary Institute.[47] One of the first events was the Kiwanians' annual "Irish" Luncheon on March 14th, where the speaker was Robert Brown, a professor at Saint Patrick's High School, who spoke on the "Life History of T. D'Arcy McGee". Then, on Friday the 15th, the annual Irish concert of the Ladies Auxiliary of the YMCA drew a large audience.

The usual "Ireland versus the World" matches of the Québec and Victoria Curling Clubs took place on Saturday the 16th. The Victoria Club's luncheon was at one o'clock in the afternoon, and the speaker was Father Lambert of Saint Patrick's, while the Québec Club's dinner was at six, and their speaker was Father B.J. O'Doherty, also of Saint Patrick's.

Saint Patrick's Literary Institute's 79th Annual Matinée and Soirée, both under the direction of May Derouin[48], were held on Saturday the 16th, at the Capitol Theatre. "Unfavorable weather had an effect on the attendance and there were a few vacant seats, although the afternoon and evening attendance ran well into the thousands."[49]

On Sunday the 17th, the Choir of Saint Patrick's parish gave a special musical programme under the direction of V. Rees Hansen, followed by an informal supper in Saint Patrick's parish hall, presided over by Theodore J. Carbray. There were addresses by Dermot O'Gallagher, Father James McCandlish, and Father John Gallagher,

Photo kindness of Leo McCullen

Photo Le Soleil.

Saint Patrick's Athletic Club Banquet at the Victoria Hotel in 1924.
Québec Curling Club celebration of Saint Patrick's Day under president C.H. Handley in 1944.

Photos Edwards

War years, old friends together: Bertha Rooney, Dermot O'Gallagher, Evarista O'Donnell, Wallie Rooney, Norma O'Neil O'Gallagher and John O'Donnell at the Saint Patrick's Day banquet at the Château Frontenac c. 1941.
A dance at the YWCA on Sainte Anne Street, March 17, 1945.

followed by specialty numbers by Alice Walsh, Kathleen McKeaney and Dermot O'Gallagher. Mary O'Gallagher Conway, Sophie Tessier, Henry Weber, Theodore J. Carbray and Léonce Crépault furnished the music.[50] The Irish Protestant Benevolent Society also held their annual service at Saint Andrew's Church on Sunday evening, attended by "a number of Irish Protestants wearing the green." The invited speaker was the Rev. J.P. Graham of Saint Andrew's Church, Sherbrooke, and the usual sister societies were present.[51]

The annual banquet of the Ancient Order of Hibernians on Sunday evening the 17th at the Victoria Hotel, was presided over by Thomas Prendergast. The principal speaker was Major Charles G. [Chubby] Power, then M.P. for Québec South, and other speakers were Lt Col John S. [Jack] O'Meara, president of the Québec Harbor Commission, Richard Timmons, Father John Gallagher and James A. McManamy.

The events concluded with the Pontifical Mass, held on Monday morning the 18th, at ten o'clock in Old Saint Patrick's Church on McMahon street. The celebrant was Cardinal Villeneuve, assisted by the rector of Saint Patrick's, Father Charles Kelz, and English speaking priests from the Séminaire de Québec. Father Aidan Murphy, also of Saint Patrick's, gave the feast-day sermon.

The War Years

As the threat of war was drawing nearer in Europe, the Saint Patrick's Day celebrations of the late 1930s continued to express the vitality of Québec's Irish community.[52] An important step was taken by the Ancient Order of Hibernians in 1936, when the members of its Ladies Auxiliary attended the dinner "for the first time in recent years" and "enhanced the gathering with their charming presence". The banquet, held in the Chateau Frontenac, was followed by a social evening, with songs and entertainment, and dancing in the ballroom. It was a model for all the banquets to come, the all-male dinners, particularly those of the 19th century, passing into history. In addition to the usual speakers and toasts, there was an address by Mrs Mary Connolly from Montréal, national vice president of the A.O.H.'s Ladies Auxiliaries, who congratulated the members of the Québec division on their initiative. She was thanked by the local president, Mrs Winifred Wallace.[53]

The 1937 observance was marked by a special Mass on Sunday the 14th, to commemorate the 105th anniversary of Old Saint

Patrick's Church, as well the ten o'clock Mass on the 17th, which was attended by Cardinal Villeneuve, Premier Maurice Duplessis, and Sir Charles Fitzpatrick. The music was furnished by the Saint Patrick's men and boy's choir, under the direction of Fathers William Murphy and William Cassidy. There was also a Mass on the 17th at Saint Columba's in Sillery[54] at 7:30 in the morning, for the families of the suburban community, with a programme of selected chants by the Children of Mary. Greetings from the Saint Jean Baptiste Society to the Hibernians were read at the banquet, which was held on the evening of the 16th at the Chateau Frontenac, in spite of the day's bad weather.

The Saint Patrick's Day storm[55] came into its own in 1937. A "severe blizzard of driving snow", accompanied by a fifty mile an hour gale, roared through the streets on the 16th, leaving "flooded cellars, derailed street cars, delayed trains and ferries, broken wires, numerous chimney fires, masses of ice in the river and many minor accidents on the windswept streets."[56] It was equalled, if not bested, by the storm on March 15, 1940, the "worst storm in years and the worst of the season", which destroyed telephone communication between Québec and Montréal, leaving the city cut off from the outside world for over twenty-four hours.[57]

In different years, various other groups held activities related to Saint Patrick's Day. The Renaissance Club invited T.J. Coonan, M.P.P. to lecture on the Irish at their weekly luncheon on March 16th, 1938. On the evening of the 17th, there was also an "Irish versus the World" Bowling Match at the Canadian Legion Club, as well as the usual matches and supper at the Victoria Curling Club. The Irish tricolour was flown atop the City Hall and other public buildings.[58] The Rotary Club's weekly luncheon paid tribute to "the Irish" on March 15th, 1939, with invited speaker J.J. Marnell, and guests J.S. O'Meara, Harry S. Quart, and Irish Protestant Benevolent Society president, T. Allen Begley. That same year, Father Gerald M. Crowley's sermon at the Mass on the 17th carried strong political overtones, when he "voiced strong opposition to undue nationalism", and upheld Christian patriotism: "when we value and respect the gifts of our racial neighbors and live in harmony with all classes."[59]

The 17th of March fell on Palm Sunday in 1940, a phenomenon which, according to the Saturday paper, had not occurred since 1799 and would not occur again until 2199.[60] Nevertheless, several activities took place as usual,[61] although the Matinée, Soirée and A.O.H. banquet were put off until the beginning of April. On the 16th, both

Hibernian Knights lined up before the Saint Patrick's School building on McMahon Street. The FOR SALE sign would indicate that the de Salaberry Street School, dating from 1917, was already in use. The Carleton Street sign is legible. Both these buildings are standing in 1990. The second rider from the right is Robert Crotty.

The 1940 banquet of the Ancient Order of Hibernians was held on April 2nd, because Saint Patrick's Day fell on Palm Sunday. The guest speaker that year was John Hearn, Irish High Commissioner to Canada.

the Québec and Victoria Curling Clubs held their matches and evening dinners. Brother Fidelis was the speaker at the Québec Club, and May Anne Burridge and Vincent Munro gave a programme of Irish airs. Green was much in evidence the next day at the various Palm Sunday services around the city. On the evening of April 1st, the Irish Protestant Benevolent Society held a lecture evening in Saint Matthew's Parish Hall, at which May Anne Burridge again sang Irish airs.

The A.O.H. banquet took place on Tuesday evening, April 2nd, at the Chateau Frontenac. The guest speaker, Irish High Commissioner to Canada John Hearn, addressed his audience in Gaelic and in French, before continuing in English. There were more than twenty-five dignitaries seated at the head table. Among them were Cabinet Minister Frank Connors, Mayor Lucien Borne, Aldermen Frank Dinan and Emile Poulin; Fathers Patrick Gallery, Charles McCormick, and James McCandlish; Brothers Raymond, Gregory, Fidelis, and Thomas; Captain Emile Trudel, former chief of police, who was attending his 35th banquet, Chief of Police A.S. Bigaouette, Assistant Provincial Police Commissioner Lt-Col. Léon Lambert, and Fire Chief Rosaire Beaulieu. The national societies were all represented: Edouard Coulombe, Saint Jean Baptiste, T. Allan Begley, Irish Protestant Benevolent, Arthur Rawland, Saint George's, and Captain E.E.B. Rattray, Saint Andrew's. Also present were John O'Connor, provincial vice-president of the A.O.H.; Mrs Mary Slaney, provincial president, and Geraldine Egan, provincial vice-president of the Ladies Auxiliary of the A.O.H.; Mrs M.J. Hatchett, diocesan president of the Catholic Women's League, Leo McCullen, president of Saint Patrick's high school Old Boys Association, John K. Leonard, parish trustee, and Andrew Walsh, of Saint Patrick's Amateur Athletic Association.

The 1940 celebrations closed with the Solemn High Mass at Old Saint Patrick's on the morning of April 3rd, attended by Rodrigue Cardinal Villeneuve.[62]

Throughout the war years, the celebrations continued, even if some activities had to be partially or completely curtailed. With the young adults caught up in the war effort, the Matinée and Soirée were the most affected. The two performances consisted of variations on a single show, composed mainly of school children and adolescents. The Mass and the banquet continued to unite various elements of the community, French and English, Catholic and Protestant. In 1941, a Saint Patrick's Dance was held at the Alouette Club on the evening of the 17th, for members of the armed forces. Mae Derouin prepared several numbers from the matinée as entertainment, accompanied by Mrs H.P. Bouffard on the piano. The banquet and the Curling Club dinners were held on the evening of the 16th as usual. As the war dragged on, however, some inevitable adjustments were made. In 1943, the banquet was suppressed, and at the Mass, the church was filled with members from all branches of the armed services. The usual dinner after the Mass was held for the clergy in the presbytery of Saint Patrick's. The Curling Club matches and dinners were still being held in 1944.

In 1945, the Kiwanians held their Saint Patrick's Day luncheon at the Château Frontenac at noon on the 15th, attended by a hundred members and guests. The feast-day Mass at the McMahon street church brought together the usual dignitaries, among them Auxiliary Bishop Georges Pelletier, representing the Cardinal, Premier Duplessis, Mayor and Mrs Lucien Borne, Chief Justice Albert Sévigny, Alderman and Mrs Frank Dinan, and representatives of various religious communities, as well as parochial, patriotic and civic organisations. As the war years ended, the Saint Patrick's Day celebrations had managed to survive. The community again faced the future with the usual Irish optimism.

Notes

1. The news was confirmed on March 1st, 1900.
2. *Le Soleil*, 16 mars 1900, p. 1.
3. *The Quebec Chronicle*, March 16, 1900, p. 2. Although Saint Patrick's Day never became a legal holiday, city employees of recognized Irish descent would continue to be given the 17th as a "personal" holiday for several decades to come. The Catholic High School has a free day on the holiday. Saint Jean Baptiste, June 24th, was only declared a legal holiday in 1925.
4. *The Daily Telegraph*, March 17, 1900, p. 7.
5. It was published again on page 3 in *Le Soleil*, 16 mars 1903. In the first decade of the century, it was a common practice for the newspapers to publish the complete text and musical accompaniment of popular songs on various occasions, particularly in the Saturday editions.
6. "...cette fête toujours populaire et aimée des Canadiens-français." *Le Soleil*, 17 mars 1900, p. 12.
7. *The Daily Telegraph*, March 17, 1900, p. 7.
8. *The Daily Telegraph*, March 17, 1900, p. 7. *Le Soleil* of March 15th noted that the guests included the Mayor of Québec, Simon Parent, Mayor William Lee of Notre Dame de Québec (Banlieue) [Montcalm district today], Mayor Michael Brophy of Sainte Foy and Mayor James Timmony of Sillery.
9. Had the fire begun much earlier, the Irish population of Québec City could have been for all intents and purposes wiped out.
10. The caption under his picture reads: "Charles Fitzpatrick, minister of justice; chief of the Catholic Irish in Canada".
11. Possibly due to the influence of the French term "grand-messe".
12. *Le Soleil*, samedi 15 mars 1902, p. 2. Author's free translation. The editorial the following year, also on page 1, took up substantially the same points and ended with a word for word repetition of the final paragraph.
13. *The Quebec Chronicle*, March 17, 1908, p. 2.
14. This was in contrast to other Canadian cities whose English population was more important, such as Montréal, Toronto or Ottawa, where it was rarely cancelled.
15. Drawings in *Le Soleil*, 17 mars 1903, p. 3.
16. The windows of the "marchands de nouveautés" in Upper Town, in the Faubourg Saint Jean and elsewhere, were decorated with harps, green silk, and ribbons: all displayed with taste and intelligence. *Le Soleil*, 16 mars 1904, p. 8.
17. *The Daily Telegraph*, March 16, 1907, p. 8; *The Quebec Chronicle*, March 18, 1907, p. 1; *Le Soleil*, 18 mars 1907, p. 5.
18. In 1909, a cadet corps was established under the auspices of the A.O.H. It was named the "Hibernian Cadets" and for years it formed a basic part of the parade. The boys were drilled by militiamen, but the corps lived up to its Hibernian title by having classes in Irish history and in the Gaelic language offered by two of its founders, Denis Coveney and Jeremiah Gallagher. The cadet corps later came under the jurisdiction of St Patrick's High School, when it was integrated into the Canadian Army Cadet system. From the 1950s to the 1970s the cadets *were* the parade.

19. Information from Guthrie Scott, 1990, who attended the parades as a young child. They wore civil war type caps: information from Dermot Conway, 1990. Maguerite Scott O'Donnell remembers the horses coming out of Campbell's Livery Stable wearing green plumes on their heads.
20. "The absence was conspicuous of an outdoor demonstration such as occurred in the Ancient Capital in the good old days of the past." *The Quebec Chronicle*, March 18, 1920, p. 3.
21. *The Quebec Telegraph*, March 17, 1916, p. 1.
22. The Sinn Feiners seized the General Post Office at noon on Easter Monday, April 24th. The general reaction of the Québec papers was to treat it as an unfortunate happening; it was eclipsed by the news from the European War.
23. *The Quebec Chronicle*, March 18, 1921, p. 3.
24. *The Quebec Telegraph*, March 17, 1921, p. 1.
25. This was the time of the infamous "Black and Tans".
26. That same day, the Irish of Montréal sent a message of encouragement to the president of the Free State, W.T. Cosgrave. In Ireland itself the holiday was marked by bloody civil war encounters between the Free State Government and De Valera's Republicans.
27. *The Quebec Chronicle*, March 15, 1926,p. 3.
28. *Quebec Chronicle-Telegraph*, March 17, 1928.
29. *Quebec Chronicle-Telegraph*, March 16, 1929.
30. In fact, looking at the period from 1899 to 1918, ten of those years boasted fine, sunshiny, "ideal" weather on the day, while in four years the celebrations took place in spite of the "most inclement" weather. For the other six years, the weather was not considered worth mentioning, generally because no parade was held.
31. In a interview with the *Quebec Chronicle-Telegraph*, March 17, 1961, Dermot O'Gallagher maintained that "the parade was discontinued because of traffic congestion and seasonal conditions and the general lack of interest from the local Irish element."
32. *Quebec Chronicle-Telegraph*, March 17, 1954, p. 1: picture of Cadets and caption: "Perennial parade of the Saint Patrick's Hibernian cadet corps".
33. *Quebec Chronicle-Telegraph*, March 17, 1962, and author's personal observations. The Cadets did march around the corner from the school to the Church on Grande Allée on other occasions after that, as late as 1972, but not as more than part of the procession into church.
34. This sung version of Cecil Frances Alexander's translation of the "Lorica" or "Deer's Cry", the prayer attributed to Saint Patrick, while a regular feature of the Protestant observances, is rarely sung in Catholic services. See above, page 6.
35. Cf. Desmond Bowen, "Ultramontanism in Quebec and the Irish Connection," passim.
36. *Quebec Chronicle-Telegraph*, April 2, 1940, p. 3.
37. "The Musical arrangements of the Mass were under the management of Miss Hill, the Organist of Saint Patrick's Church, and reflected much credit on all those who took a part in them." *The Quebec Mercury*, March 17, 1849.
38. Thomas D'Arcy McGee, Hon. Edward Whalen, Sir Edward Denny, Archbishop Connolly of Halifax.
39. *The Quebec Telegraph*, March 17, 1916, p. 10. References were made to Emmett, Swift, Grattan, Tone, Parnell and Davis.

40. Fitzpatrick was lieutenant-governor from 1918-1923.
41. *The Quebec Telegraph*, March 17, 1921, p. 1.
42. *Annales de l'Asile Sainte Brigitte*, 1928.
43. *Le Soleil*, 18 mars 1907, p. 5; *The Quebec Chronicle*, March 18, 1907, p. 1.
44. *Le Soleil*, 17 mars 1925, p. 16.
45. CHRC also broadcast the festivities live from La Meunerie in Sillery in 1983 and 1984. The local English-language CBC-affiliated radio and television stations play Irish music, conduct topical interviews, and report on local festivities during the feast-day period. CKMI-TV first began broadcasting on March 18, 1957.
46. *The Quebec Chronicle and Quebec Gazette*, March 17, 1925, p. 1.
47. Although the Institute was founded in 1852, it was only incorporated under that name in 1875. See below p. 132.
48. Over the years, Miss Derouin's name appears variously as May or Mae.
49. *The Quebec Chronicle-Telegraph*, March 18, 1935, p. 3. The details of the concerts, Matinées, and Soirées may be found in chapter V.
50. *Quebec Chronicle-Telegraph*, March 18, 1935, p. 1.
51. *Quebec Chronicle-Telegraph*, March 18, 1935, p. 3.
52. For example, the March 14th, 1936 edition of the *Quebec Chronicle-Telegraph* ran stories about the upcoming Olympics in Germany, and pictures of German troops crossing the Rhine, as well as a history of Irish schools in Québec as part of a series on "English Schools of the Ancient Capital", and a verse for children on the Life of Saint Patrick.
53. *Quebec Chronicle-Telegraph*, March 17, 1936, p. 3. The "Friendly Daughter of Saint Patrick" would have approved. See above p. 50.
54. Saint Columba's [Columban's] or "Columbus"', as the centenary plaque in the church proclaims, now the parish of Saint Michel de Sillery, celebrated its centenary in 1954.
55. For some interesting speculations on the traditions connected with the Saint Patrick's Day storm, see Herbert Halpert, "Ireland, Sheila and Newfoundland", particularly p. 155-166.
56. *Quebec Chronicle-Telegraph*, March 17, 1937, p. 1.
57. *Quebec Chronicle-Telegraph*, March 15, 1940, p. 1.
58. On March 14th, 1938, Hitler made his entry into Vienna.
59. The British, Irish and Canadian flags were flown atop the City Hall. *Quebec Chronicle-Telegraph*, March 17, 1939, p. 1.
60. "An ancient legend says that the 'crossing of the shamrock and the palm' portends great events from which the 'isle of Destiny' shall emerge a free nation after blood has flowed in her streets." *Quebec Chronicle-Telegraph*, March 16, 1940, p. 3.
61. For example, the parade in Montréal took place as usual.
62. *Quebec Chronicle-Telegraph*, April 3, 1940, p. 3.

Overleaf:

The Centenary Mass in Old Saint Patrick's Church, McMahon Street, 1956.

CHAPTER IV

The Late Twentieth Century

The Post-War era marked the beginning of another period of transition in the Québec Irish community, as it began its expansion and dispersion throughout new areas of the city. The Irish continued to enjoy a good relationship with the French, many of whom readily participated in the celebrations.[1] The 1950s brought the centenary of Saint Patrick's Church and Parish, the completion of the building of the new Parish Church on Grande Allée, and a new centering of Irish activities around the de Salaberry-Grande Allée area. The Matinée and Soirée were back in force, although by 1956 the Matinée would be replaced by well-prepared performances given by the individual schools. As in the past, the celebration encompassed a variety of festive activities.

Centenary and Beyond

The focus of the feast remained the morning Mass, attended by the usual civil and religious dignitaries, and followed by a noon dinner for the clergy at the presbytery. Other activities varied according to the years. In 1953 the Young Marrieds Club of the parish held a social evening on the 16th, with music by Roger Anger's Orchestra. In 1954, the Optimists Club held their Saint Patrick's Day luncheon at the Château Frontenac at noon on the 17th. Members wore green ties, shamrocks, and ate green ice cream. The entertainment was furnished by the little girls from Saint Brigid's Home and several acts from the Soirée, followed by a sing-along. Different restaurants and bars advertised Saint Patrick's Day entertainment, with accessories, such as hats, ribbons, shamrocks, to mark the celebration of the feast. The little girls performed again on the 16th for the Optimists in 1955. Ironically, the only "true" Irishman present that year was Jack Gorman, who was made honorary president of the club for the day.[2] The Kiwanians' luncheon on the 17th at the Château Frontenac featured Lawrence Corriveau, who spoke on the love of the Irish for their patron saint.[3]

In 1959, Pat Timmons was president of the Rotary Club of Québec, and their March 17th Saint Patrick's Day luncheon at the Château Frontenac featured Irish songs by France Dion and Claude Bédard, accompanied by Jeannine Bégin on the piano. The Kiwanians' 1959 luncheon at the Château on March 12th was attended by 150 members and their wives. Green hats, ties, shamrocks, and dresses were much in evidence, while green beer and green ice cream were again on the menu. Performers from the Soirée furnished several numbers for the musical programme, which included dances and a choral competition between the Québec and Montréal clubs. The prize was the coveted "Shillelagh", which the Montréal club won for the second year in a row. The day ended at the Jean Talon Vaults, with dancing, singing, and recitations by Bill O'Reilly.[4]

The tradition of giving city employees a holiday on Saint Patrick's Day was still alive in 1955. Although some forty Irish employees took advantage of the holiday on the 17th, they were already fewer than they had been five or ten years previously. Alderman David Burns did attend the city council meeting, where, as the only Irishman, he "received the best wishes of his French colleagues during the meeting."[5] About this time, reminiscences of older members of the community began to appear in the newspapers, evoking descriptions of past holidays. In a 1950 interview, eighty-three year old William George Berrigan, Québec-born former Canadian Pacific Station Head, described the parades as he had known them.[6] Paddy Ryan, an immigrant from Ireland at the age of 18 and a former president of the Québec Ship Laborers, was still celebrating in 1955, at the age of ninety-two. After attending the Mass, "he renewed acquaintances with old friends. — Later in the afternoon, he took in the sing song at the Chien d'Or and set about getting 'into shape' for the soirée at the Palais Montcalm" that evening.[7] He too regretted the absence of the old-time parades.

The first high point of the decade was 1956, the centenary year of the founding of Saint Patrick's Parish and Saint Brigid's Home. The 17th of March fell on a Saturday and there was a large turnout for all the festivities, in spite of the "usual storm". The Centenary celebrations began in the morning with the singing of a Pontifical High Mass by the Rector, Father Robert MacDonald, assisted by Monsignor Omer Garant. Every seat was filled in the Old Saint Patrick's Church on McMahon street. The day ended with the 100th

Photo Oesterwinter Print Pierre Cayer

Photo Edwards Print Pierre Cayer

Rotary Club Saint Patrick's Day luncheon at the Château Frontenac on March 18, 1959. The 1962 Ladies Shamrock Bonspiel was held at the Cambrai Curling Club. The main trophy winners that year were Rita Proulx, Mrs Ray Stevens, Mrs Evelyn Heale and Mrs Gisèle Bouvrette of the Winter Club rink.

Photos Oesterwinter Prints Pierre Cayer

The Kiwanis club annual Saint Patrick's Day luncheon at the Château Frontenac in 1957. Green-decked Kiwanians had earlier visited the Mayor in honour of the day. Mayor Wilfrid Hamel often received a delegation of the Kiwanians at City Hall during the Saint Patrick's Day festivities. At various times they were accompanied by the Carnaval Queen and Duchesses.

Photos Oesterwinter Prints Pierre Cayer

The 1957 Saint Patrick's Day Mass, one of the last in the Old Church on McMahon street.

Photo Michèle V

Photo François Vézina

The last Saint Patrick's Day Mass in the Grande Allée church was celebrated in 1988. The most recent Saint Patrick's Day Mass was celebrated in the de Salaberry Church in 1990.

THE QUEBEC MERCURY.

THURSDAY MARCH 15, 1838.

MORES ET STUDIA ET POPULOS ET PRÆLIA DICAM. Virg. Georg. IV. 5.

VOLUME XXXIV. NUMBER 32.

ST. PATRICK'S DINNER.

TICKETS to be had at the bar of the ALBION HOTEL

Quebec, 8th March, 1838.

ST. GEORGE'S SOCIETY.

IT having been unanimously resolved, at a SPECIAL GENERAL MEETING, held on the 13th instant, to accept the invitation of the ST. PATRICK'S Society, the Members of the ST. GEORGE'S Society are requested to assemble at the ALBION Hotel, on ST. PATRICK'S Day, SATURDAY next, the 17th instant, at the hour of NINE, A. M.,—there to meet their Irish brethren, and to join the procession to be formed on that occasion.

A full attendance of the Members is requested.

J. C. FISHER,
Secretary St. G. S.

Quebec, 15th March, 1838.

ST. ANDREW'S SOCIETY.

THE St. Andrew's Society having been invited by the St Patrick's Society to accompany them in procession to Church, on St. Patrick's Day; and the invitation having been *unanimously* accepted—the Members are particularly requested to meet on SATURDAY next, the 17th instant, at *Half-past Eight* o'clock, A. M., at the ST ANDREW'S SCHOOL-HOUSE, from thence to proceed to the Albion Hotel, to join the procession.

(By Order.)

JAMES GILLESPIE,
Secretary.

15th March, 1838.

CALEDONIAN SOCIETY.

THE Members of the above Society are particularly requested to assemble at Mr. ROBT. LAFONTAINE'S, City Hotel, St. Anne Street, on SATURDAY next, the 17th inst., at NINE o'clock, A. M. precisely, to join ST. PATRICK'S SOCIETY in procession to Church.

By order,

JOHN FREW, Secretary.

Quebec, 13th March, 1838.

NOTICE.

To the Members of St. Patrick's Society

THE Silver and Metal Badges ordered by Mr. CULLEN, for the Members of said Society, are now ready and may be had at the shop of the subscriber.

JAMES SMILLIE,
No. 16, Mountain Street.

14th March, 1838.

Photo Oesterwinter Print Pierre Cayer

Irish Protestant Benevolent

SOCIETY.

THE ANNIVERSARY SERVICE OF THIS Society will be held at the WESLEYAN CHURCH, on next TUESDAY EVENING, the 12th Inst., at Half-Past Seven, when the REV. DR. IRVINE, of Montreal, will preach a Sermon, and a collection will be taken up in aid of the funds of the Society.

JOHN STOREY,
Secretary.

Quebec, March 9, 1867. 2-58

1867

THE ANNUAL CHURCH SERVICE

of the
Irish Protestant
Benevolent Society
will be held at
TRINITY
ANGLICAN CHURCH
15 St. Stanislas Street
Sunday, March 18th.
at 8.30 p. m.

All members are requested to attend

Members of Sister Societies are also cordially invited to attend

J. E. WEST,
Secretary.

1956

ANNIVERSARY SERVICE.

THE ANNUAL SERMON ON BEHALF of the IRISH PROTESTANT BENEVOLENT SOCIETY will be preached by the Reverend P. WRIGHT, in CHALMERS' CHURCH, on THURSDAY EVENING, the 16th instant.

All who sympathise with the benevolent objects of the Society are cordially invited.

The Service will commence at half-past SEVEN o'clock, and a collection will be taken up in aid of the Charitable Fund.

THOS. DAVIDSON,
Secretary.

March 14, 1876. 0

1876

"Members of St. Andrew's Society are invited to attend the Annual Church Service of The Irish Protestant Benevolent Society to be held in Trinity Church, St. Stanislas Street at 8.30 on Sunday evening March 18th. They are to meet in the Parish Hall under the Church at 8.00 p.m."

S. R. SMITH, Hon. Secretary
St. Andrew's Society.

1535 Boulevard de l'Entente,
Quebec 6, P..Q

1956

THE ANNUAL CHURCH SERVICE

of the
Irish Protestant
Benevolent Society
will be held in
TRINITY CHURCH
15 St. Stanislas Street
on Sunday March 18th
at 8.30 P.M.

Members will meet in the Parish Hall at 8.00 P.M.

A. E. WILLIAMS,
Secretary

1956

The Sister Societies celebrated well into the latter half of the 20th century. In 1959, the Centenary Dinner and Dance of the Irish Protestant Benevolent Society was held at the Saint Louis Hotel on Friday, March 13th.

Annual Soirée at the Palais Montcalm, where the performers played to a standing room only crowd.[8] On the 15th, the Kiwanians had joined with city hall officials for their Saint Patrick's Day luncheon at the Château Frontenac, where the guests of honour were the Carnival Queen and Duchesses. They were later invited to a reception at City Hall by Mayor Wilfrid Hamel.[9]

The Saint Andrew's and Saint George's Societies were guests at the 1956 anniversary service of the Irish Protestant Benevolent Society on Sunday the 18th. The choir's traditional rendition of the anthem "The Breastplate of Saint Patrick" was a feature of the evening. In 1957, the 17th itself fell on a Sunday, and the service was held at 8:30 in the evening, in Trinity Church on Saint Stanislas street. The president of the Society, choirmaster and organist Alfred E. Millar, presided a reception held in the Parish Hall after the service, attended as usual by members of the Protestant Sister Societies.[10]

The second highlight came in 1958. In addition to the usual celebrations, the 1957 festivities were also to have included the inauguration of the new Saint Patrick's Church, which had been in use as a basement church since 1915. A fire in August of 1956 had set its final construction schedule back a year, but 1958 saw the realisation of the community's dream. A dual liturgical celebration was held that year. In the morning, in a three hour ceremony, the auxiliary bishop of Québec, Monsignor N.A. Labrie, presided at the blessing of the new Grande Allée church and the dedication of its altars. In the afternoon, the traditional feast-day High Mass was sung in the Old Saint Patrick's Church on McMahon Street for the 125th time, the last of the Saint Patrick's Day masses to be held there.[11] Then at 5:30, the first High Mass was celebrated in the new church, followed by a civic reception at City Hall, hosted by Mayor Wilfrid Hamel. The evening's annual Soirée was followed by a dance and get together in honour of the day. The general feeling in the community was one of optimism. In his sermon at the High Mass, Father Arthur Ryan, Redemptorist provincial, remarked that the new church was the result of the vision of "the early people of Saint Patrick's Québec", whose convictions had been "amply fulfilled".[12]

Another centenary was celebrated in 1959, the 100th anniversary of the Irish Protestant Benevolent Society. Over seventy Society members and guests attended a banquet and dance on March 13th at the Hotel Saint Louis. The chairman was Dr Donald W. MacMillan, and among the guests were A.E. Williams, of the Saint George's Society, and Iain McGregor, representing the Saint Andrew's Society.

Mrs William Reid, from Antrim, Ireland, gave a recital of Irish songs, accompanied by the Society president, Alfred E. Millar. The latter also gave an organ recital of Irish Airs at the special anniversary service held on Sunday evening the 15th, at eight o'clock in Saint Matthew's Anglican Church.[13] The Society continued to hold its annual service for many years, but its numbers gradually diminished to such an extent that it eventually ceased its activities.[14]

The Quiet Revolution of the 1960s saw the beginning of a decline in the formerly strong anglophone influence in Québec culture and politics. This was accompanied by a gradual exodus of English and Irish young people to Montréal or to the English speaking provinces. At the same time, the city began to expand into the surrounding semi-rural areas. In spite of the political climate, however, the Saint Patrick's Day celebrations never faltered. The Mass was still the focus of the feast-day, attended by the Archbishop or the Cardinal and the Cardinal's councillors, representatives of other ethnic groups and denominations, and important civil authorities. Archbishop Maurice Roy, Lieutenant Governor Paul Comtois, Premier Jean Lesage and Mayor Wilfrid Hamel were among those present at the 1962 service. In 1966, a concelebration of the Pontifical High Mass by Maurice Cardinal Roy and six other priests was a first for the holiday celebration. The Cardinal was again the celebrant of the Canadian Centennial Year Mass the following year.

During the decade, several variations continued to find their way into the festivities, as the Irish community once more adjusted to its changing circumstances. The Annual Soirée finally went the way of the Matinée; the last performance at the Palais Montcalm was in 1965. The following year, the only shows remaining were those attached to the banquets and dinners, as well as the newly revived Shannon Show. As the influence of the metropolitan area widened during the 1960s and 1970s, the latter slowly began to take the place of the Soirée in the cycle of Saint Patrick's Day activities.

By 1961, the banquet of the Ancient Order of Hibernians was felt to have become too much of a financial drain on the society.[15] It was replaced by a tea given by the Ladies Auxiliary of the A.O.H. at the Château Frontenac, on the Sunday afternoon nearest Saint Patrick's Day. For many years the Auxiliary sponsored an Irish Essay Contest on such themes as "The Irish Contribution to North America", for the students in the different schools of the area. The essay of the 1962 winner, Moira Lonergan, was published in the newspaper on March 17th.[16] In 1964, the Auxiliary celebrated with a buffet social on Sunday, March 15th. Mrs John Kiley was president,

The O'Gallagher clan with friends and relatives at the 1948 Saint Patrick's Day Banquet at the Château Frontenac. Clockwise from the head of the table: Dermot O'Gallagher, Norma O'Gallagher, Tony Conway, Marianna O'Gallagher, John O'Gallagher, Eileen Conway, Tim Burke, May Donovan, Bill Hurley, and Ethel Rigger.

At their 1964 reception, the Ladies Auxiliary of the Ancient Order of Hibernians paid tribute to May Derouin for her many years of service to the community, particularly for the organisation of the Matinées and Soirées. Among those present were Mrs. H. McMahon, Mr John Kiley, Dr Howard McMahon, speaker, Mrs John Kiley, president of the A.O.H., Brother Raphael of Saint Patrick's High School, Mrs Geraldine Egan Gagnon, Miss May Derouin herself, and Mrs Keenan, National A.O.H. vice-president.

Photo Edwards

Photo Edwards Print Pierre Cayer

Saint Patrick's Day Banquet in 1972 at the Château Frontenac: J. Larkin Kerwin, Mayor Gilles Lamontagne, Millie Monaghan, Mgr. Falardeau, guest speaker Leo McCullen, James H. Monaghan, presiding, Father L.C. McAuley, Vivian McCullen, Tom Byrne, and Lupita Kerwin.

Guests at the 1962 Killarney Club Dance at the Château Frontenac included Austin Edwards, Frances Martin Edwards, Mayor Wilfrid Hamel, Helen Martin Haberlin, alderman David Burns, and Majella Haberlin, president of the Killarney Club.

Killarney Club

Join the fun
TUESDAY
MARCH 17th
It's our big St. Patrick Celebration

At the
Chateau Frontenac

Attend one, or both, of these two great events which will take place consecutively in the

MAIN BALLROOM

7:00 p. m.	9:00 p. m.
DINNER	**DANCE**
$7.50 (all inclusive) per person	GERALD BOUDREAU ORCHESTRA
	9:00 P.M. Refreshments available in Main ballroom foyer.
	10:00 P.M. Orchestra starts
	$5.00 per couple
Dress: Black tie or business suit	Dress optional
	(DANCE PROCEEDS: CAMP KILLARNEY)
No tickets sold at door	Adults only. Tickets at door or:

TICKET DEPOTS

St. Patrick's Rectory 140 Grande Allée East	St. Vincent's Rectory 2833 l'Isle Dieu
H. W. McKenna Inc. 1183 St. John St.	W. B. Edwards Inc. 819 St. John St.
Le Pub Bois Brulé 2766 Ste. Foy Road	The Chien d'Or 8 du Fort St.

Get your tickets now for a grand and glorious St. Patrick's Day

1970

and the guest speaker, Dr Howard McMahon, gave a slide presentation of his journey around Ireland. After the talk, Mrs T.J. Kerwin presented awards for the literary competition to Susan Montgrain, Catherine O'Keefe, Lena Fitzmorris, and Allan Bowles. Mrs Geraldine Egan Gagnon paid a special tribute to Miss Mae Derouin for her years of service to the community. Piano music accompanied the buffet, and the occasion ended with a sing song of Irish airs.[17] The entertainment was slightly more elaborate in 1966, when the Glee Club, composed of children from the elementary and the high school, gave a short concert following the speaker.

Saint Patrick's Parish replaced the Annual Soirée on Thursday the 17th in 1966 by a dinner at the Cambrai Curling Club, followed by a Saint Patrick's Day spectacular, a sing song and a dance, all under the direction of Father George Delaney. The performers were children from Saint Patrick's, Saint Vincent's, and Saint Stephen's schools, accompanied by Bonny Pike and Joan Halton on the piano, with music by pianist Euclide Gaudet, and Gerry Boudreau and his orchestra.[18] The following year at the Cambrai Club on the 17th, the students from the Girls' Elementary school put on an even more elaborate programme, under the direction of Mrs Nancy Copeman Pike.

Another popular event was the Killarney Club's Saint Patrick's Day dance at the Château Frontenac. At first it followed the Soirée, getting under way around eleven p.m. and continuing into the early hours of the morning, as it did in 1962, when the 17th fell on Saturday. Later it was held more or less in conjunction with the Saint Patrick's Parish supper at the Cambrai Club, which replaced the Soirée. On the 17th in 1967, the Cambrai Club dinner began at 7:30 in the evening, while the Killarney Canadian Centennial Year dance began at nine o'clock. People were able to attend both, if they wished, as the latter went on into the early hours of the morning.

Many activities were scheduled simultaneously during the 1960s, as there were enough people at each function to justify separate events. In 1967, Saint Vincent's P.T.A. and C.W.L. held their annual dinner and dance on the evening of the 17th at the Holiday Inn. While the Shannon Show took place on Saturday the 11th, Saint Joseph's C.W.L. also held a dinner and party on the 17th at the Shannon Hall. That same evening there was another dinner dance at Valcartier, sponsored by the Saint Gabriel C.W.L. As the Irish and anglophone population declined, however, a greater effort was made to avoid conflicting arrangements, in order that people might participate in as many activities as possible during the festive period.

During this time, different groups continued to give an Irish flavour to their activities around Saint Patrick's Day. At the March 15th meeting in 1961 of the Alliance Canadienne at the Château Frontenac, Father Edward Myers was invited to speak on the life of Saint Patrick. In 1966, many members of the Legislative Assembly wore green in honour of the day, while greetings were received from Premier Jean Lesage and opposition leader Daniel Johnson. Entertainment for the 1967 luncheon of the Kiwanis Club on the 16th was furnished by the girls of Saint Vincent's Elementary. The Québec Athletic Club still held its annual dinner. The Victoria Curling Club held its Saint Patrick's Day luncheon on Saturday the 18th, while the former "Ireland versus the World" matches had been replaced by the "Ladies Shamrock Bonspiel". Another sporting event that Saturday was the Saint Patrick's Day hockey match between Saint Patrick's High and Quebec High schools, followed by a game between the teachers of the two schools.

While a discreet consumption of alcohol was obviously part of the feast-day luncheons and dinners, the boisterous drinking traditionally associated with festive revelry found an outlet at Noonan's "Le Chien d'Or" tavern on du Fort street, for many, a not-to-be-missed venue on Saint Patrick's Day.[19] It was acquired by the senior William Noonan in 1917, and many a dispute was settled there in the old days during the "fine donnybrooks" that patrons were assured of during the Saint Patrick's celebrations. For a long time, Catholic Irishness was a condition of entry on the day itself: "if a Protestant came in those doors, they'd kill him."[20] Even French speakers of Irish descent were challenged if they had a non-Irish-sounding name. The tavern theoretically seated seventy, but on the 17th in 1961 there were approximately 140 seated and 150 standing during the day. It was a place where Irish tunes were heard and sung to the accompaniment of good-natured brawling, games of skill,[21] and laughter. In 1967 it had been feared that the tavern would be closed for repairs, but fortunately for tradition, it was open on Saint Patrick's Day.[22]

Seventies and Eighties

As Québec moved into the 1970s, many institutions surrounding the Irish and anglophone community underwent important changes. The English language daily newspaper, the *Quebec Chronicle-Telegraph*, was transformed into a weekly, appearing every Wednesday. The Old Saint Patrick's Church on McMahon

Photo. kindness of Bill Noonan.

Around 1917, a horse drawn wagon from Boswell's Breweries delivers supplies to the historic Chien d'Or on du Fort Street.

Photo Chronicle-Telegraph Print Pierre Cayer

1962

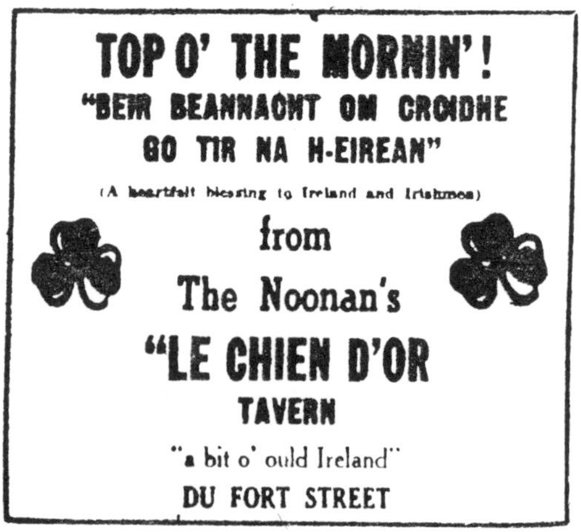

1955

1956

Historic Chien D'Or on du Fort street — Irishmen's Mecca on the 17th.

street, abandoned during the 1960s, was destroyed by fire in 1970.[23] Although deploring the disappearance of this landmark, as well as of the decorated streets, arches, parade, Matinée and Soirée, the March 15th editorial in 1972 was optimistic, pointing out that

> Times and customs have changed over the years, but the vigor and vitality of descendants of the Auld Sod remains undiminished, as brought out by their widespread activities on Saint Patrick's Day.[24]

The decentralisation of the various activities continued throughout the 1970s. Each school had its own show and celebration, while the Shannon Show at Sainte Catherine's Hall was gathering momentum. By 1975, it would be held in the new Shannon Recreation Center. Saint Vincent's parish had its own dinner dance in Sainte Foy, while the Saint Patrick's banquet had moved to the Château Frontenac, where the Killarney Club continued to have a dance for the benefit of its Camp Killarney.

In the wake of the Saint Patrick's Society and the Ancient Order of Hibernians, Saint Patrick's Parish Social Committee took over the annual dinner held on Saint Patrick's Day itself, a responsibility it assumes to the present day. The guest speaker of 1972, native Québecer Leo McCullen was typical of the era. He took as his theme the Matinées and Soirées of the middle of the century, in which he had often been a leading performer. His hopes for the development of the talents inherent in the young people of the Irish community, seem to have been partly fulfilled by some of the performers in the musical entertainment which rounded out the dinner. The four numbers by duo Richard Leahy and Barry Neville were followed by two songs from "Finian's Rainbow" by Janice Coull. Father Clark McAulay was prevailed upon to sing two of the Irish ballads for which he was well known. The piano accompanist was Euclide Gaudet, while Barbara Smith was Mistress of Ceremonies, leading a final sing-along which closed the performance. Those who wished could then attend the Killarney Club dance, held in the Chateau's main ballroom. Refreshments had been served there earlier for those who had not attended the banquet, and the dancing began at ten p.m., to the music of Gerald Boudreau and his Orchestra.[25] This was the pattern for many a dinner during the 1970s. The speakers were for the most part respected members of the community or former members who had gained prestige in other parts of Canada, such as the 1973 speaker, Montréaler Denis Kindellan, Corporate Manager of Imperial Oil, a "native son" of Québec. The speaker usually chose as his topic childhood memories of Saint Patrick's Day in Québec, often coupled with thoughts about the contribution of the Irish to Canadian life and history.

The Ladies Auxiliary of the Ancient Order of Hibernians held their 1972 reception in the same ballroom of the Château Frontenac on Sunday the 5th. Mrs Geraldine Egan Gagnon introduced the speaker, Father Martin Foley, pastor of Saint Richard's parish in Montréal. A native of Québec City, he recalled marching in the last parade as a member of the Cadet Corps, as well as his participation in the Matinées and Soirées. The entertainment included songs by Mrs Helen O'Hagan from Verdun, and an Irish Jig by Sister Sheila O'Connor of County Cork. They were accompanied by Sister Mary Mediatrix, who had also played Irish Airs during the "high tea". Prizes for their winning essays were awarded to Susan McCauley, Miriam Saville, Linda Murphy, and Suzanne Rousseau. The reception concluded with the usual sing song, led by M.C. John Monaghan.[26] By the end of the 1970s, however, the Ancient Order of Hibernians, as well as its Ladies Auxiliary, had been dissolved. They are remembered for the positive influence they had on Irish culture in Québec, especially on the young school-children of their day. Their reception had also been an alternative activity for those who did not wish to participate in the evening celebrations.[27]

The 1972 Shannon dinner dance was held on Friday the 17th. However, Saint Vincent's buffet dinner and dance that year had not conflicted with the other events. It was held at the Motel Carillon in Sainte Foy on Saturday the 18th and attracted over 150 people. Another dinner was held by the Ladies Auxiliary of the Army and Navy Veterans. The annual Ladies Shamrock Bonspiel was held on the weekend at the Cambrai Curling Club. It was organized that year by Suzanne Goyette, Thérèse Côté, Doris Germain and Maureen Malenfant. In 1984, a team from Rimouski led by Gladys Burgess won the Rourke trophy at the 25th anniversary of the Shamrock Bonspiel, which was held at the Curling Club of the Association des Employés civils.

By the 1980s, more substantial changes had tested the endurance of the Irish community. Little by little, Irish and anglophone institutions became less imposing in the de Salaberry-Grande Allée area. The first important change was the relocation of Saint Brigid's Home from the corner of de Salaberry and Grande Allée to Saint Louis road in Sillery in 1973, and the limiting of its residents to the older generation.[28] Then in 1987, as a result of the continuing decline in numbers of English speaking Catholics and the requirements of the language laws, the decrease in the English speaking school population necessitated combining the four existing schools into two. Katimavik High in Sainte Foy was incorporated into Saint Patrick's High School on Maisonneuve street, while the elementary youngsters were relocated at Saint Vincent's in Sainte Foy. The old Saint Patrick's Boys' school and the "Leonard" Girls' school passed into history. The latest upheaval was the 1990 closing of the Ladies' Protestant Home on Grande Allée, and the transfer of many of the residents to Saint Brigid's Home.

The turning point for the community came with the 1988 sale of Saint Patrick's church and monastery on Grande Allée. More than anything else, this signalled the end of the era which had seemed so promising when the "new" church was inaugurated on Saint Patrick's Day in 1958. Now, exactly thirty years later, the last Saint Patrick's Day mass was celebrated there in 1988. On March 2nd the sod was turned for a new and smaller church on de Salaberry, not far from the former Saint Patrick's Boys' School, and on the 25th, the demolition of the older church began. The vitality of the Irish community was far from being sapped, however. A year later, on Saint Patrick's Day 1989, the feast-day Mass saw a record crowd turn out for the inauguration of the newly-completed church.

The Saint Patrick's Day Mass in the latter decades of the 20th century remains the most stable of the festive events. The Archbishop of Québec, civil authorities and representatives of other churches and religious denominations, as well as community dignitaries, parishioners, relatives and friends, regularly attend. In 1985, the attention given to the visit of the American president on the 17th, prompted the filming of parts of the feast-day Mass, which took place on Saturday the 16th, for airing on the national evening news. Archbishop Louis Albert Vachon was the principal celebrant, assisted by five other priests; the Lieutenant Governor, Gilles Lamontagne, and Mayor Jean Pelletier and Mrs Pelletier were among those present. The music was furnished by a special Saint Patrick's Day choir, with a solo by Colleen Bilodeau. A reception was held in Saint Anne's chapel after the service.[29] Cardinal Vachon was the main celebrant of the concelebrated feast-day Mass on Monday the 17th in 1986. He also gave the sermon, using Saint Patrick's missionary activities as his theme. Over 500 people filled the church, among them senior clergy of the Anglican Cathedral, the United Church, the Presbyterian Church, the Salvation Army, and the Port Chaplain. The choir, directed by Helen McCauley, sang Irish music, accompanied by Lise Proulx on the organ. A coffee reception followed the Mass.[30] The last feast-day Mass held in the Grande Allée church also took place at five o'clock in the evening. It was followed at six-thirty by the festivities at the Château Frontenac.

The tradition of holding the Saint Patrick's parish dinner and dance at the Château Frontenac was put in abeyance during the years 1978 to 1987. During that time, it was held alternately at the Hilton Hotel, at Laval University, and finally at the Concorde Hotel. In part, this was due to difficulties in long-term scheduling, often arising from the presence of international congresses at the Château. In addition, the 1985 festivities had to be planned around the "Shamrock Summit" meeting of Prime Minister Mulroney and American president Reagan in Québec on March 17th. Those who attended the annual dinner dance at the Concorde Hotel had to run the security gauntlet set up to protect the heads of state, who were themselves dining at the Château Frontenac, and then attending a gala at the Grand Théâtre, not far from the Concorde. By 1987, the difficulties had been resolved, and the Château has once more become the preferred location for the annual feast.

Since the Killarney Club no longer held its annual dance, Saint Patrick's Parish Social Committee, long spearheaded by Rita Brown and Patricia Fitzpatrick Kiley, evolved a format combining a reception, dinner and dance. It begins with a Happy Hour, usually from six to seven in the evening, followed by the banquet itself. For some years, the tables could be reserved ahead of time, allowing families and friends to celebrate together. This has been discontinued, as not everyone always showed up exactly as planned. There are always at least 250 to 300 people present at the banquet.[31] After the dinner itself come the tributes and presentations, the equivalent of the speakers of the past. People are honoured for various contributions to the parish and to the Irish community. Rolande Drolet, organist at Saint Patrick's for many years, received a special presentation in 1985. In 1986, Father William Murphy received a plaque, honouring his sixty years as a Redemptorist. Certificates of merit were presented to Brendan O'Gallagher, Guthrie Scott, and Sister George Francis in 1987, as well as a plaque for community services to David Cannon.

The presentations are followed by a sing-along, led by the Master or Mistress of Ceremonies, in which the whole audience participates.[32] The songs include classic favourites, such as "A Great Day for the Irish", "When Irish Eyes Are Smiling", "Galway Bay", "The Band Played On", "Peg o' My Heart", "The Rose of Tralee", "Peggy O'Neil", "Has Anybody Here Seen Kelly", and "My Wild Irish Rose". During a short intermission, the tables are cleared and pushed back to make room for the dance and entertainment that follow. Music for the dancing may be furnished by an orchestra, such as that of "Irishman" Earl "O'Leblanc" in 1985, or the "Lucky Seven", Carmen Turpin Vallières and friends in 1987. Entertainment over the years has included the "Pub" section from the Shannon Show, organist and singer Jean Guy Dufresne, and selected numbers from the various High School shows. The entertainers tend to be drawn from talented amateur and semi-professional members of the community, alternating with the occasional professional musician or performing group.

For many years, pots of live shamrocks have decorated the altars of the parish church and the tables at Saint Patrick's Day parties and banquets. These do not come from a florist's, but are grown from hand-picked seeds by Hugh Bullock, head gardener and care-taker of Saint Patrick's Cemetery for fifty-eight years. Those sown on the 15th of October in 1985 yielded over 200 plants in March of 1986, to complement the green ribbons, balloons, streamers, and other decorations during the Saint Patrick's celebrations.[33] The participants in the various festivities never miss "the wearing of the green", as can be seen by the profusion of green dresses, ties, coats, hats, and corsages which are displayed on the day.[34]

Although many of the older social organisations have disappeared, they have been replaced in recent years by other groups, particularly those with a high proportion of anglophone members, who have come to regard Saint Patrick's Day as an occasion for festivity. The Kiwanis Club held its Saint Patrick's Day luncheon in 1986 at noon on the 17th at Le Pub. In 1988, the Newcomers Group cancelled its regular monthly luncheon in order to hold a Saint Patrick's Day Tea on March 17th. The Fifty Plus Club in Sillery holds an annual luncheon or dinner during the festive period, usually a day or two before or after the 17th, taking care not to conflict with the other major activities. Another organisation is the Ladies Auxiliary of the Army, Navy, and Air Force Veterans Unit 33, who hold a traditional "Irish" Lamb and Beef Stew supper at the Veterans' Club on Calixa Lavallée street, usually on the Friday or Saturday nearest Saint Patrick's Day. An evening of music and the distribution of door prizes complete the entertainment.

One of the last of the formal events of the festive period is the annual Saint Patrick's Day tea of the Saint Patrick's Council of the C.W.L. It is held on the Saturday or Sunday of the week following Saint Patrick's Day, to allow the members who have been busily participating in the activities to finally relax and look back with satisfaction on the season's accomplishments.

The more informal celebrations usually center around festive drinking. Various pubs and taverns in the city have been known in the past for their liveliness on March 17th, particularly in Old Québec. By the late 1970s, however, the tavern celebrations at the Chien d'Or were no more; the brasserie La Meunerie in Sillery had become the scene for as lively but less males-only oriented celebrations. Tickets for the Saint Patrick's Day evening were free, but had to be reserved in advance through Carmen Turpin Vallières, who was responsible for the entertainment. Green beer, paper hats and streamers were furnished by the management, and clusters of green balloons hung from the ceiling, to be released over the heads of the crowd at an advanced stage in the proceedings. Irish traditional melodies and sing-alongs enlivened the dancing and merrymaking, which went on until closing time. In 1983, the French language radio station, CHRC, broadcast its morning "Point de Vue" programme live from La Meunerie on the morning of Saint Patrick's Day. Carmen Vallières and her friends were the special guests during the 6:30 to 9:30 programme. Free coffee and doughnuts attracted many local and suburban merrymakers, many on their way to the feast-day Mass. The station extended its coverage of the event until noon in 1984. In 1986, the Saint Patrick's Day festivities at La Meunerie, now renamed La Bulle, were still well attended, with waiters and waitresses dressed in green serving the Sunday brunch. Yet in 1987, though the brasserie was gone and a restaurant chain had taken its place, Carmen and her friends were still going strong in the neighbourhood, at the "Pub" at Saint Brigid's Home.

In 1984, the Noonans' celebration had again moved, this time to their Brasserie Le Pub in Sainte Foy, where Saint Patrick's Day begins at noon, often with the Kiwanis Saint Patrick's Day luncheon, and continues with drinking and merrymaking into the early hours of the morning. The 1984 entertainers were country and western singer Roger Lamont from Valcartier. Le Pub offered its green beer for only a dollar in 1987. Various other taverns and bars have advertised Saint Patrick's Day specials through the years. In 1984, the Omnibus offered an "Irish Snow Ball" and "Irish Coffee", with traditional Irish music on Saint Patrick's Day. The Café l'Alibi, not far from Saint Patrick's church, proposed a celebration to begin "after Mass" and continue until closing time. The following year, they opened after the Sunday morning mass to serve Irish coffee throughout the day. In 1986, the Café Bar l'Ordinaire offered green beer and Irish music to its customers from March 13th to 17th. Thomas Dunn's pub, across from the Gare du Palais in Lower Town, lives up to its

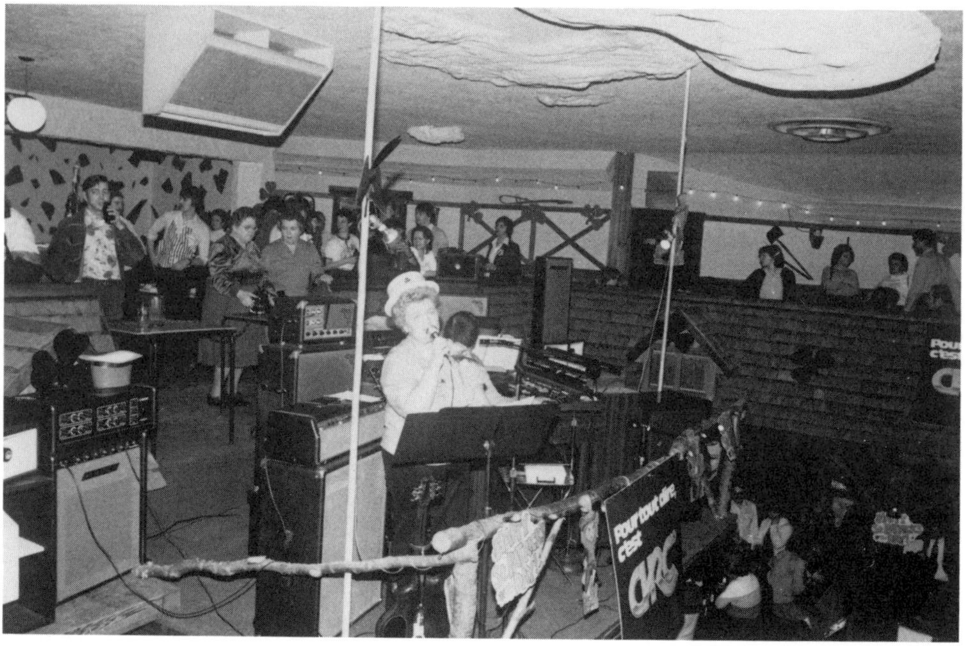

Photos Ross Corcoran Prints Edwards

Like mother, like daughter — Carmen and Lynn Vallières at La Meunerie, 1984.

Photos Ross Corcoran Prints Edwards

Part of the crowd of merrymakers at Le Pub and La Meunerie, 1984, 1985.

EVERYONE IS GOING TO THE

Special **ST. PATRICK'S** Day

DANCE

MARCH 17th. AT THE SHAMROCK

- Wonderful Orchestra !
- Irish Party Favors !

THE **SHAMROCK** RESTAURANT

MAKE UP A PARTY!

2950 LAURIER BLVD. RES.: MU 3-4269

1959

St. Patrick's Day March 17, 1988

Mass *St. Patrick's Church* 5:00 p.m.

Château Frontenac

Irish Happy Hour 6:30 p.m.

Dinner 7:30 p.m.

Irish Sing Song 8:30 p.m.

Dance 9:30 p.m.

Entertainment by: Members of the Royal 22nd Dance Band

Tickets for the dinner must be purchased in advance.

Sponsored by the St. Patrick's Social Committee

72 **St. Patrick's Day** 72

Loew's Le Concorde Hotel

March 17th 1986

Irish Happy Hour	6:00 - 7:00 P.M.
Dinner	7:00 - 8:15 P.M.
Irish Sing Song	8:15 - 9:15 P.M.
Dance	9:30 - 12:30 A.M.

Dress Informal Price: $20.00 per person

St. Patrick's Day

Château Frontenac

March 17, 1989

Mass (St. Patrick's Church)	5:00 p.m.
Irish Happy Hour	6:30 p.m.
Dinner	7:30 p.m.
Irish Sing Song	8:30 p.m.
Dance	9:30 p.m.

Entertainment by: Members of the Royal 22nd Dance Band

Dress informal Price $30.00 per person

Tickets must be purchased ahead of time. For information call 527-5252.

Photo François Vézina

Photo Stephen Monfette

Saint Patrick's Parish banquets bring community members together. The Pastor and Trustees of Saint Patrick's entertain distinguished friends of the parish at a festive table in 1990. The Fifty Plus Club shared a table at the 1989 banquet.

Photos M. O'Gallagher

Leo McCullen, Geraldine Egan Gagnon, Rita Brown and Patricia Fitzpatrick Kiley, in 1990, longtime participants and upholders of Saint Patrick's Day festivities.

Irish reputation with shamrock decorations and green hats, furnished by the brewers of Harp and Guinness for Saint Patrick's Day. The Sherlock Holmes pub, behind the National Assembly buildings near Grande Allée, goes in for lavish green decorations and also serves the traditional green beer. Le Merlin on Cartier avenue, and two pubs on Saint Jean street, Saint Alexandre and Le Refuge continue to attract older members of the Irish community.

Saint Patrick's Day Today

As the 20th century moves into its final decade, Saint Patrick's Day in Québec still rallies the remaining members of the Irish community and those most closely involved with it.[35] The new Saint Patrick's parish church, like a phoenix rising from its ashes, continues the tradition of the feast-day Mass in its third incarnation. Louis Albert Cardinal Vachon gave the homily at the 1989 inaugural Mass, which again preceded the banquet at five o'clock in the evening. In 1990, as retiring Bishop of Québec, the Cardinal concelebrated the feast-day Mass, which had reverted to its usual time of ten-thirty in the morning on Saturday the 17th. An estimated four hundred people, including representatives from the other churches, filled the church to overflowing on both occasions, with standing room only, even with extra seating in the vestibule. At both services, director Helen McCauley led the choir and congregation in the singing of the traditional feast-day carols, the opening hymn "Hail, Glorious Saint Patrick", and the recessional "Hibernia's Patron Saint, All Hail".[36] The 1990 Mass was followed by "Irish Coffee" and doughnuts in the Parish Hall, to the enjoyment of all present.[37]

The annual banquet in 1989 sponsored by Saint Patrick's parish at the Château Frontenac was attended by over two hundred and fifty people on Friday the 17th, following the inaugural Mass in the new church. Telegrams and letters from those unable to attend were read, and certificates of merit were awarded to Tim O'Connor, Mary McPeak and Eddy Walsh, while Harry Hannon received the Saint Patrick's plaque for his years of dedication to the community. The entertainment consisted of a presentation by the dance troupe Manigance, who performed Irish dances, traditional and soft shoe, from their production "Let Me tell You About Ireland".[38] A much appreciated finale of their performance was their invitation to the audience to join in the traditional dancing. The band of the Royal 22e Régiment played for the social dance which began at ten.[39]

More than two hundred and fifty people again filled the Château ballroom for the 1990 banquet on Saturday the 17th. Certificates of merit were awarded to Helen McCauley, Gertrude Edwards Grogan and Geraldine Egan Gagnon, while the plaque for outstanding service went to Yolande O'Neill. Because of the warm reception accorded the entertainment the previous year, the Manigance dance troupe was invited back to perform their Irish dances and to dance square dances with members of the audience. The final offering added a traditional Québécois quadrille, with the dancers costumed in old-fashioned dresses and overalls. The banquet continues to represent an important part of the Saint Patrick's Day celebrations for a significant proportion of the Irish community.

The Fifty Plus Club celebrates Saint Patrick's Day either with a luncheon, such as the one held at noon on Wednesday, March 15th in 1989, or alternately, a dinner, as they did the following year on Wednesday evening the 14th. In 1989 and 1990, the Army, Navy, and Air Force Veterans Club Ladies Auxiliary held their Lamb and Beef Stew supper, with the usual trimmings. The modest but enjoyable entertainment consists of a sing-along, with piano accompaniment, and the awarding of the usual door prizes.[40] The annual Saint Patrick's Day tea of the Saint Patrick's Council of the C.W.L. was held, exceptionally, on March 12th in 1989, but reverted to its traditional date of Sunday, March 25th in 1990.

There has been a recently renewed effort to favour the centralisation of certain activities by avoiding conflicting schedules wherever possible. This is often more natural than artificial, as certain institutions diminish in scope or vanish altogether. The regrouping of the school populations has resulted in there being only one show prepared by each level, elementary and secondary. The diminution of the interested population means that many of the same people are involved in the preparation of different events. However, when the feast-day itself occurs on a Saturday, as it did in 1990, a certain amount of overlapping is inevitable. People find themselves obliged to choose between activities, which they manage to do without missing too much. For many, it keeps them on their toes, as they bustle from one event to the other.[41]

The various brasseries and pubs continue to attract those who insist on "drowning the shamrock". In 1989, several disco bars on Grande Allée offered green beer at half price to those patrons dressed in green or green and white on the 17th. The Sherlock Holmes, la Grande Hermine, and Thomas Dunn's held somewhat subdued but colourful festivities, although green beer and hats and decorations were much in evidence in many public drinking places in both 1989 and 1990. Green beer was free in 1990 at the Merlin on Cartier avenue. The rallying point for most of the singing crowd was quite certainly the Noonans' Pub on chemin Sainte Foy. In 1990, Carmen Vallières was there with her band, to lead the singing in her usual style.

A typical pub circuit on Saint Patrick's Day usually begins early at Le Pub, particularly when the feast-day falls on a Saturday, as it did in 1990.[42] By noon, the celebration was well under way, with green beer flowing and the distribution of complimentary buttons carrying Irish sentiments. Then it was on to Thomas Dunn's later in the afternoon, where some of the merrymakers were obliged to furnish their own music, for which they had come prepared by bringing a cassette of Irish music with them. In most places, even though green beer and decorations abound, the tendency is away from Irish traditional music and toward the usual pub music sound, disco or otherwise. After supper, there was dancing at Dunn's, until the group decided to move on to Le Refuge on Saint Jean street, where some older relatives were reminiscing over more green beer. Finally, they gravitated back to Le Pub, where green beer flowed until "midnight and beyond, as young and old drank a toast to Old Ireland and anything else".[43] As a member of the group commented, "As long as we're having fun, we keep on."[44]

In addition to the public celebrations, many members of the Irish and anglophone community hold private parties with friends and neighbours. For those whose birthday falls on the 17th or 18th (and there are more than one would suspect), there is an additional inducement to celebrate.[45] The Shannon Show performers continue the party at the community centre far into the night, after the Soirée has come to an end, and some even come into town to add to the celebration at Le Pub. No matter how they choose to mark the feast, the important thing for the Québec Irish in the 1990s is to take part in the festivities, wherever they may be.

Notes

1. Their collaboration helped swell the numbers of participants, since the Irish community was estimated at only about 6 000 at this time. *Le Soleil*, 17 mars 1950, p. 28.
2. *Quebec Chronicle-Telegraph*, March 17, 1955, p. 3.
3. *Quebec Chronicle-Telegraph*, March 18, 1955, p. 5.
4. *Quebec Chronicle-Telegraph*, March 18, 1959, p. 1; March 13, 1959, p. 3.
5. *Quebec Chronicle-Telegraph*, March 17, 1955, p. 3.
6. *Le Soleil*, 19 mars 1950, p. 30.
7. *Quebec Chronicle-Telegraph*, March 17, 1955, p. 3.
8. *Quebec Chronicle-Telegraph*, March 19, 1956, p. 2-3
9. *Quebec Chronicle-Telegraph*, March 16, 1956, p. 4
10. *Quebec Chronicle-Telegraph*, March 16, 1957, p. 6.
11. Father Clark McAulay celebrated the last mass held in the Old Church on May 28, 1967.
12. *Quebec Chronicle-Telegraph*, March 18, 1958, p. 6.
13. *Quebec Chronicle-Telegraph*, March 14, 1959, p. 1.
14. In 1981, the Irish Protestant Benevolent Society was dissolved when it turned its remaining funds over to the Citadel Charities group, thus terminating its existence as a separate charitable organisation. The Saint George's Society had done the same in 1976, and the Saint Andrew's Society in 1977. Information from John McGreevy, 1990. Since these societies had been formed for the purpose of raising money for charity, they had no longer any reason to exist, unlike the Saint Patrick's Societies, whose primary raison d'être was to organize Saint Patrick's Day activities.
15. Dermot O'Gallagher, *Quebec Chronicle-Telegraph*, March 17, 1961, p. 11.
16. *Quebec Chronicle-Telegraph*, March 17, 1962, p. 10.
17. *Quebec Chronicle-Telegraph*, March 17, 1964, p. 6.
18. *Quebec Chronicle-Telegraph*, March 15, 1966, p. 3, and March 18, p. 5.
19. "You see the old ones, they come only once a year but they want to be here on Saint Patrick's Day." Bill Noonan, *Quebec Chronicle-Telegraph*, March 17, 1962, p. 17.
20. Bill Noonan, *Quebec Chronicle-Telegraph*, March 17, 1962, p. 17.
21. One feat was to stand on one's head in the center of a table ringed with glasses of brew. If unsuccessful, the loser had to empty all the glasses.
22. *Quebec Chronicle-Telegraph*, March 17, 1967, p. 14.
23. The McMahon street fire occurred on October 13, 1970.
24. *Quebec Chronicle-Telegraph*, March 15, 1972, p. 4.
25. *Quebec Chronicle-Telegraph*, March 8, 1972, p. 17; March 22, p. 3.
26. *Quebec Chronicle-Telegraph*, March 15, 1972, p. 7.
27. Leo McCullen, interview 1978.
28. Until then, it had also sheltered orphaned children. See chapter V for a description of Saint Brigid's celebrations.
29. *Quebec Chronicle-Telegraph*, March 20, 1985, p. 7.
30. *Quebec Chronicle-Telegraph*, March 19, 1986, p. 1 & 6.
31. Saint Vincent's no longer holds a separate dinner dance.

32. The green song leaflets which are distributed at this point in the evening are furnished by Saint Patrick's Parish Social Committee, and are a complimentary printing of the *Quebec Chronicle-Telegraph*.
33. Hugh Bullock, interviewed by Colleen Bilodeau, *Quebec Chronicle-Telegraph*, March 19, 1986, p. 8.
34. The community today depends mainly upon Archer's Florists to furnish the personal decorations typical of the feast-day, including green carnations and sprigs of shamrock with the usual green ribbons.
35. General background for this chapter was also furnished by persons not referred to elsewhere who were interviewed by the researchers in 1978 and 1979. These include Mrs Edwin [Geraldine O'Hearn] Burridge, Doctor William Delaney and Mrs Rosemary Power Cannon, Joan Kane, Maurice LeBon, Dorothea Mulroney Kane, Mary Kenny McGrath, Miles O'Farrell, Gary Ouellet, Ross Rourke, Brian and Patrick Turpin, and David Walsh. Among those interviewed in 1990 were Rita Brown, Geraldine Egan Gagnon, Micheline Gravel, Elmar Kane, and Gerry and Kevin McNulty. Marie Claude Bonniot Cabanac also collaborated in fieldwork in 1989 and 1990.
36. These hymns are characteristic of the Catholic service, while "Saint Patrick's Breastplate" is generally considered a Protestant hymn, in spite of its origin. See above, p. 3-4.
37. The closest thing to the Saint Patrick's Day storm: "Saturday's rain and fog did not stop the Irish from celebrating Saint Patrick's Day." *Quebec Chronicle-Telegraph*, March 21, 1990, p. 1.
38. The Manigance dancers are trained by Montréal Irish dance professor Bernadette Short, who has also trained the Shannon dancers since 1981.
39. *Quebec Chronicle-Telegraph*, March 22, 1989, p. 1.
40. Madame Thérèse Galichan, interview 1990.
41. For some examples of this practice, see the *Quebec Chronicle-Telegraph*, March 21, 1990, p. 2.
42. When it falls on a weekday, particularly a Friday, as in 1989, those who do not have an official holiday, such as the teachers in the "Irish" schools, take the afternoon off work if they can, in order to properly respect the feast-day.
43. *Quebec Chronicle-Telegraph*, March 21, 1990, p. 2.
44. Unnamed informant, interview 1990.
45. These include members of the community such as Patrick Turpin, and James (Bev) Wetmore. For many years, an elderly American from Portland, Maine, Philip McCaffery, came to Québec to celebrate his Saint Patrick's Day birthday. He was a well-known guest at the parish banquet.

Overleaf:

Quebec Chronicle-Telegraph

March 15, 1956

THE BUSINESS FIRMS BELOW SEND GREETINGS TO ALL THEIR IRISH FRIENDS AND CUSTOMERS WITH BEST WISHES FOR A MOST SUCCESSFUL SOIREE

Terreau & Racine Ltd.
196 St. Paul St. — Phone: 4-5181

Librairie Vachon
Phone: 5-7064

St. Lawrence Paper Bag Co. Ltd.
875 Des Prairies — Phone: 4-8078

Henri Gagnon
Tobacconist
56 Palace Hill — Phone: 2-4286

The Quebec Savings Bank
La Banque D'Economie de Quebec
HEAD OFFICE: 21 St. John Street

Claire Fontaine Ltee. (7-Up)
Abraham Hill — Phone: 2-8171

Turnbull Auto Service Reg'd.
18 Turnbull Avenue — Phone: 4-1244

G. & G. Bros. Ltd.
Charest Blvd. E. — Phone: 5-4701

John Millen Quebec Ltd.
27 Place Jean Talon — Phone: 4-8864

The John Ritchie Co. Ltd.
Shoe Manufacturers
St. Vallier St. E. — Phone: 5-6128

Power, Kieffer & Power
Lawyers
10 Du Fort Street — Phone: 3-0619 - 4-1084

H. J. & W. O'Brien
SILLERY — QUEBEC

J. L. Drolet Automobiles Ltee.
Your GM Dealer Chevrolet Oldsmobile
350 Blvd Charest E. — Phone: 5-4681

Mark & Ross Drouin, Q.C.
Lawyers
200 St. Joseph St. E. — Phone: 2-1881

Restaurant Marine
34 Dauphine St. — Phone: 2-0076

Chouor Ltee.
The Friendly Department Store
St. Joseph St. E. — Phone: 2-8661

Laval Dairy
Milk - Cream - Ice Cream
875 - 4th Avenue — Phone: 4-8661

Canadian Import Company
Coal & Fuel Oil
Dalhousie St. — Phone: 2-1221

SATURDAY, MARCH 17th
ST. PATRICK'S DAY
SOLEMN HIGH MASS
McMAHON STREET CHURCH
10.00 A. M.
His Excellency Bishop Omer Garant assisting in the sanctuary
Sermon: Very Rev. Father R. Macdonald, Rector
Organist: Miss Cecile Jensen
St. Patrick's Boys' and Men's Choir
Directed by Rev. Bro. Norbert, F.S.C.

ST-PATRICK'S DAY CENTENARY — SOIREE

1856 100th ANNIVERSARY OF... 1956

ST-PATRICK'S PARISH — SOIREE — ST-BRIGID'S HOME

Dances & Songs from each decade!

BALLET — "Patricia, My Patricia"

Dolly Sisters — "Daughter of Rosie O'Grady"

CHARLESTON — "My Wild Irish Rose"

RECITATION — "Trimmings of the Rosary"

SOFT SHOE — "Did anyone ever tell you, Mrs. Murphy"

JITTERBUG — "It's an Irish Lullaby"

Gay Nineties — "Dare tread on the tail O' me coat"

POLKA — "When Irish Eyes are Smiling"

WALTZ — "It was only an Irishman's Dream"

Cha-Cha-Cha — "Kerry Dance"

SONG — "Galway Bay" & "O'Donnell Aboo"

IRISH JIG — "Irish Washerwoman"

The Patrician Players

PRESENT

"WHEN IRISH EYES ARE SMILING"

ONE PERFORMANCE ONLY

SATURDAY MARCH 17th
8.00 P.M.
PALAIS MONTCALM
Doors open 7.30 — — Overture 7.55 P.M.

Cast of play as they appear:

Rita Madden as	Mamie
Ina Macdonaldd as	Eileen
Joseph Thomas as	Harry Riner
Dorothy Doherty as	Lou
James Peacock as	Pat Geraghty
Cullen Keane as	Tim Casey
Mickey Fiset as	Mrs. Mulroney
Beatrice Henderson as	Mrs. Feinberg
Harold Dionne as	Jimmie Duggan
Bernadette Griffin as	Mary Mulroney
John Monaghan as	Bob Geraghty

CHOREOGRAPHERS: **VE VE & PAT KELLY** — PLAY DIRECTOR: **STEVE PROSENYAK**

THE BUSINESS FIRMS BELOW SEND GREETINGS TO ALL THEIR IRISH FRIENDS AND CUSTOMERS WITH BEST WISHES FOR A MOST SUCCESSFUL SOIREE

Samson & Filion Ltee.
General Hardware — Wholesale & Retail
343 St. Paul St. — Phone: 2-2871

Madden & Son Co. Ltd.
Coal Dealers
624 Blvd Charest E. — Phone: 4-3578

Dominion Corset Co. Ltd.
"Gothic" — "Lily of France" "Barong" — "Nu-Back"
450 Dorchester St. — Phone: 5-8151

Lauri's Ltd.
Ladies Wear
51 St. John St. — Phone: 2-0883

Ste-Marie Plywoods Inc.
INDUSTRIAL CENTER No. 5
QUEBEC, P. Q.

Genevieve Morel
287 St. Joseph St. E. — Phone: 2-8500

Hetherington Bakery Inc.
336 St. John St. — Phone: 2-2061

Carrier & Goulet
Meats
120 Bridge Street — Tel.: 2-5291

Theo. Berns Reg'd.
Tobacconists
65 Buade Street — Tel.: 2-0034

Maguire Electric Ltd.
Television Sales & Service
1280 Maguire Avenue, Sillery — Tel.: 7-3401

W. G. McCauley & Son Reg'd.
General Stevedores
40 St. Paul Street — Tel.: 2-6712

Chinic Hardware
55 St. Peter St. — Tel.: 5-4861

W. E. Bégin
The Sanitary Markets — Quality Meats Only
436 St. John Street — Tel.: 4-5271
142 de la Salle Street — Tel.: 5-8196

Marquette Electrique Reg'd.
"Appliances & Record Bar"
123 St. John St. — Phone 5-2114

Victoria-Cambrai-Classic-Sillery
Your Neighborhood Theatres
HAROLD VANCE, Mgr.

P J Evoy — Bookseller - Stationer
Fine selection of St. Patrick's & Easter Cards
A great day for the Irish ... A great day for us
86 years in business on March 17th
141 St. John Street — Tel.: 2-7501

BOX OFFICE
TOMORROW MARCH 14TH
at
PALAIS MONTCALM
10 A. M. to 5.30 P. M.
Orchestra & Balcony
Section "A" $1.25
Orchestra & Balcony
Section "B" $1.00

CHAPTER V

Matinées and Soirées

Theatricals have always held a prominent place in Québec society, both French and English.[1] As early as 1817, English amateurs, under the direction of Thomas Carey, founder of *The Quebec Mercury*, were putting on plays, including Shakespeare, Sheridan and others, in The Royal Circus Theatre, behind what is now the Hotel Manoir Victoria on Côte du Palais. They even went so far as to bring in professionals from New York.[2] Artists of international reputation performed at The Haymarket Theatre on the corner of des Jardins and Sainte Anne streets[3] between 1806 and 1825, as well as at the Près de Ville Theatre on Champlain street, from 1852 until its demolition in 1914. These were but a few of the Theatres and Music Halls to be found in Québec during the last century.

The Nineteenth Century

The Théâtre Royal, which became the Music Hall, and finally the Academy of Music, on Saint Louis street, saw many a Saint Patrick's Day Soirée from its inception in 1853 until its destruction by fire in 1900. After 1849, the former Wesleyan chapel on Sainte Anne street became known as the Lecture Hall, then the Victoria Hall, and finally, when it was acquired by the Saint Patrick's Literary institute in 1876, as the Tara Hall. The Auditorium de Québec, now the Capitol Theatre, inaugurated in 1903, and later the Palais Montcalm, both in Carré Youville, were also the scene of numerous Saint Patrick's Day Matinées and Soirées. On the 28th of December 1852, the Saint Patrick's Catholic [Literary] Institute was founded "for the benefit of the members of the Saint Patrick's Church congregation".[4] The Institute's first Soirée was held on the 17th of March 1856 in the Saint Patrick's church hall. The Literary Institute would continue to sponsor the Matinée and the Soirée of the 17th of March for over a hundred years.

For the first few years of its existence, the Literary Institute was not alone in sponsoring theatrical performances around the feast-day. In 1867, Saint Patrick's Day fell on a Sunday and the Soirée was put off until Monday evening. On Saturday the 16th, the Dramatic Club of the 30th Regiment, under the patronage of Colonel T.H. Pakenham, performed Dion Boucicault's two-act "Popular Drama": "Andy Blake or The Irish Diamond", followed by Richard Brinsley Sheridan's two-act comedy, "Saint Patrick's Day or The Scheming Lieutenant". The orchestra was formed by the string band of the regiment, who also performed on the 18th for the "Musical Soirée" sponsored by Saint Patrick's Catholic and Literary Institute.[5] In 1875, there was a division in the ranks of the Catholic and Literary Institute. The separatists became incorporated under the title of the Saint Patrick's Literary Institute.[6] By the end of the century, however, only the Saint Patrick's Literary Institute continued to exist.

The programmes of the events reveal a mixture of speeches, solo, and choral performances, with the later addition of a melodrama or musical, with the usual performances interspersed between acts. Often there were several speakers, and the speeches could be long ones. The Soirée of 1872 offers a good example.

> The annual Irish musical soirée, under the auspices of the Saint Patrick's Catholic and Literary Institute, came off on Monday evening last, at the Music Hall. As has been the case ever since the inception of these soirées, the Hall was crowded even to the inability of finding standing room. The doors were opened at half past six, and at seven there was not a seat to be had. In point of appearance, we may safely say that a finer assemblage has never been witnessed on any similar occasion. The opening address was delivered by the President, Mr Foley, whose sentiments were very appropriate and were enthusiastically received. The Musical portion of the entertainment was under the superintendence of Mr F.W. Mills, assisted by the members of the Septuor Haydn Club, who kindly lent their valuable services. The choruses were very well rendered, and the solos were all faithfully and well executed, in most cases repeatedly encored, and obligingly complied with. It is unnecessary to mention names, where all performed so well; the performance was equal, if not superior to any we have ever yet been privileged to attend. At the opening of the second portion of the entertainment Mr Gahan delivered an address on "Home Rule". His remarks were well received, and at the conclusion the speaker took his seat amidst loud applause. The entertainment was varied by the performances of two bands—one, the Hibernian, and the other that of the 9th Battalion. The band of the 9th was ably directed by the brothers Vézina, and performed their part, especially the Pot Pourri of Irish airs, with remarkable taste and skill. The band of the Hibernians have made wonderful progress since we had the pleasure of hearing them last, and do infinite credit to themselves and their bandmaster. On the whole, we must say the soirée was a complete success, and was a pleasing termination of one of the most orderly and pleasant celebrations of Saint Patrick's

St. Patrick's Catholic Institute.

ST. PATRICK'S DAY.

A SOIREE, under the auspices of the SAINT PATRICK'S CATHOLIC INSTITUTE, will be held at the HALL of the INSTITUTE, on MONDAY, the 17th MARCH.

The Chair will be taken at SEVEN o'clock precisely.

Several Gentlemen will deliver appropriate addresses.

J R. MAGRATH, Esq., Organist of St. Patrick's Church, will preside at the Piano, assisted by a few Ladies and Gentlemen, who have kindly consented to sing some IRISH MELODIES.

Mr. LINDENBERG will attend with a full Orchestra.

TICKETS—1s. 3d. each; may be procured from Messrs. D. Maguire, Jr., St. Peter Street; John Nolan, Diamond Harbor; Carey Brothers, Booksellers, St. John Street; and at the door.

By order of the Council.

M. F. WALSH,
Recording Secretary.

Quebec, March 15, 1856. 2

Temperance Meeting

ON

PATRICK'S NIGHT.

A PUBLIC MEETING will be held by ST. LAWRENCE DIVISION, SONS OF TEMPERANCE, on

TUESDAY,

The 17th inst., at the TEMPERANCE HALL, St. FRANCIS STREET, when it is expected several Gentlemen, favorable to the cause, will address the Meeting.

A CHOIR of VOCAL MUSIC will be in attendance.

A Collection will be taken up at the close of the Meeting.

Doors open at 7½, Chair to be taken at 8 o'clock precisely.

Quebec, March 14, 1857. 3

St. Patrick's Catholic Institute.

SECOND

ANNUAL CELEBRATION

OF

ST. PATRICK'S DAY.

THE ANNIVERSARY of IRELAND' PATRON SAINT will be celebrated by a

LITERARY & MUSICAL SOIREE,

under the auspices of SAINT PATRICK'S CATHOLIC INSTITUTE, at the

MUSIC HALL,

ON

TUESDAY EVENING, 17th instant.

During the evening appropriate Addresses will be delivered by several gentlemen.

An efficient Choir, composed of Ladies and Gentlemen who have kindly consented to lend their assistance, will sing several of the NATIONAL MELODIES.

C. W. SABATIER, Esq., Knight of the Legion of Honor, Organist of St. Patrick's Church, &c., will preside at the Piano Forte.

M LAVIGUER, Professor of Music, has kindly consented to perform some pieces on the VIOLIN.

By the kind permission of COL. COCKELL and the OFFICERS, the BAND of H. M. 16TH REGT. will be in attendance, under the direction of MR. CARR.

ADMISSION—Gentlemen 2s. 6d.; Ladies 1s. 3d.; Children under 12 years of age, 1s. 3d.

Tickets may be had at Messrs Carey Brothers, St. John Street; Mr. P. Lawlor's, St. Rochs; Mr. P. Shee's, Lower Town; Mr Jno. Nolan's, Diamond Harbour; at the Hall of the Institute, and from Members of the Council.

Chair will be taken at SEVEN o'clock

By order of the Council.

M. F. WALSH,
Recdg. Secy.

Quebec, March 11, 1857. 4

St. Patrick's Soiree

THIS EVENING,

REFRESHMENTS may be had in the REFRESHMENT ROOM of the MUSIC HALL, furnished by

J. GRACE,
Confectioner.

Quebec, March 17, 1857. 1

The Morning Chronicle

MUSIC HALL.

30th Regiment.

BY THE KIND PERMISSION AND under the patronage of Colonel T. H. Pakenham. Commandant, and Officers, the Dramatic Club of the above Regiment will

PERFORM

IN THE ABOVE HALL, ON

ST. PATRICK'S EVE,

MARCH 16th:

Dion Bourcicault's POPULAR DRAMA, in Two Acts, entitled

ANDY BLAKE

—OR—

The Irish Diamond;

And Sheridan's BRILLIANT COMEDY, in Two Acts, entitled

ST. PATRICK'S DAY,

—OR—

THE SCHEMING LIEUTENANT.

THE STRING BAND OF THE REGIMENT Will form the Orchestra, under the Conductorship of Herr Standhaft, B M.

PRICES OF ADMISSION.—Reserved Seats, 50 cents; Gallery, 37½ cents; Pit, 25 cents.

Box Plan can be seen at Mr. Holiwell's, (opposite the Post Office). Tickets can also be had at the doors.

Doors open at 7 30 P. M. To commence at 8 prompt.

Carriages may be ordered for 10.45

☞ For further particulars see programmes.

God Save the Queen.

Quebec, March 15, 1867 63

The Quebec Mercury

ST. PATRICK'S DAY, 1867.

ANNUAL CELEBRATION.

The Anniversary of Ireland's Patron Saint will be Celebrated by a

MUSICAL SOIREE,

Under the Auspices of the

St. Patrick's Catholic & Literary INSTITUTE,

—AT THE—

MUSIC HALL

ST. LOUIS STREET,

—ON—

MONDAY EVENING

NEXT, 18th MARCH.

MR. F. W. MILLS, F.C.O., will preside at the Piano.

A Choir of Ladies and Gentlemen will sing the National Melodies.

By the kind permission of Lieut.-Colonel Pakenham and Officers, the BAND of the 30th Regiment will attend, under the leadership of Mr. Standhaft.

ADMISSION.—Gentlemen, 50 cents; Ladies 25 cents. Members and Subscribers, who are not in arrears, will be admitted free.

TICKETS may be procured at R. Morgan's Music Store, St. John Street; at C. E Holiwell & Co.'s News Depot, opposite the Post Office; from the Members of the Council of the Institute, and at the door of the Music Hall on the evening of the Soiree.

Doors open at half-past SIX.

The chair will be taken at half-past SEVEN o'clock precisely.

The Piano to be used on this occasion is from the celebrated manufactory of Messrs Steinway & Co., and is kindly furnished by Mr. Robt. Morgan, Music Dealer, St. John Street.

WM. H. LAROCHE,
Recording Secretary.

Quebec, March 14, 1867. 3-63

MARCH 16, 1876.

1876 1876

ERIN GO BRAGH

Music Hall.

TWENTIETH

ANNUAL MUSICAL SOIREE

— ON —

St. Patrick's Night,

UNDER THE AUSPICES OF

ST. PATRICK'S
Catholic and Literary Institute,

And the able management of

SIMON PETERS, Esq.,

President of St. Patrick's Choir.

R. H. WATSON, Esq., Royal Academy of Music, Organist of St. Patrick's Church, will preside at the Piano and Organ, and will be assisted by WENTWORTH PETRY, Esquire, (late Organist).

PROGRAMME:

PART FIRST.

ST. PATRICK'S DAY.............................BAND.
Introductory remarks by the President.
Address..............Rev. Father Burke, O.S.S.R.
1. Chorus—The Minstrel Boy............Moore.
2. Song—Believe me if all those..........Moore.
Miss Ross.
3. Song—The Harp that once..............Moore.
Mr. Chamberlin.
4. Solo and Quartette—Eilleen Allanna.........Thomas.
Miss McNaughton.
5. Song—The Shamrock.....................Moore.
Mr F. M. Duggan.
6. Song—I Saw by the Beach..............Moore.
Miss Lennon.
7. Duet—Irish Airs.......................................
Euphonium and Organ.
Messrs. McKernan and Watson.
8. Song—The last Rose of Summer......Moore.
Miss Dessane.
9. Song (Comic)—Paddy's Dream........ Lover.
Mr. Watson.

PART SECOND.

Address.................Richard Alleyn, Esq., Q.C.
1. Overture—Tancredi.......................Rossini.
Organ and Piano.
Messrs. Watson and Petry.
2. Song—My Molly Asthore................Lavenus.
Miss A. O'Connell.
3. Solo and Quartette—Kathleen Mavourneen Crouch.
Specially arranged by Mr. Watson.
Mr. T. Nelson.
4. Song—Don't go Molly Darling..Whittymore
Miss Delany.
5. Chorus—The meeting of the Waters..Moore
Specially arranged by Mr. Watson.
6. Song—Terrence's Farewell...Lady Dufferin.
Miss H. Verina.
7. Song—Where is the slave so lowly...Moore.
Old Air, Sios Agus Sios Liom.
Mr. P. E. Lane.
8. Song (Comic)—The Low Back Car....Lover.
Mr. Chas. Murray.
9. Band...

The Band of St. Patrick's T. A. Society will be in attendance, under the able leadership of Mr. H. J. McKernan.

Mr. R. Morgan has kindly lent for the occasion one of Steinway's Pianos, and also a magnificent Organ by Mason & Hamlin.

ADMISSION—Gentlemen 50 cents, Ladies 25 cents.

Tickets can be procured at the stores of Messrs. C. E. Holiwell, Wright & Co., R. Morgan, and J. Barrow, and from the members of the Council.

Doors open at 6.30.

Curtain Rises at 8 SHARP.

By order,

J. M. KENNEDY,
Recording-Secretary.

March 16, 1876. mch13

☞ For the accommodation of Parties in Levis desirous of attending this Soiree, the Association has made arrangements, through the courtesy of J. Chabot, Esq., for the Ferry-Boat to make a special trip at midnight.

SAINT PATRICK'S
Catholic and Literary Institute,

GRAND REHEARSAL.

A GRAND REHEARSAL FOR THIS SOIREE, takes place THIS (Thursday) EVENING, at 7.30 P.M., *sharp*, in Mr. R. Morgan's Music Rooms.

All the Ladies and Gentlemen taking part in the Solos and Choruses, are particularly requested to attend.

By order,

J. M. KENNEDY,
Recording Secretary.

March 16, 1876. A

The Morning Chronicle

1876. ERIN GO BRAGH 1876.

TWENTIETH

ANNUAL SOIREE

UNDER THE AUSPICES OF

The St. Patrick's Literary Institute,

The proceeds to be devoted to the Funds of the

St. Bridget's Asylum

TO BE HELD IN THE

INSTITUTE HALL,

ST. ANN STREET,

— ON —

17th instant.

THE MANAGEMENT AND MUSICAL direction is kindly undertaken by

ADOLPHE HAMEL, Esqr.,

who has secured the assistance of the leading Artists and Amateurs.

The Orchestra and Chorus will consist of

One Hundred and Twenty Performers and Singers,

which is freely admitted to be the GRANDEST and STRONGEST ever practised for any National Concert in this city.

The SEPTUOR HAYDN will kindly perform some New Compositions, which they have specially arranged for the Soiree, and will also perform with the Grand Orchestra L'UNION MUSICALE.

Through the kind permission of Colonel Strange and Officers of "B" Battery, their splendid BAND will render its choicest selections of Irish Airs, and newest pieces.

PROGRAMME:

PART I.

1. ST. PATRICK'S DAY...Band B Battery, C.A.
2. Unveiling Picture of Late Reverend Mr. O'Doherty, by the Lady Mayoress.
3. Address by the President.......................... Mr. John Lane.
4. Grand Chorus from "Christopher Columbus"—F. David. with full Band and Orchestra accompaniment.
5. Song—Kathleen Aroon..................T, Att. Miss Owen.
6. Chorus—The Minstrel Boy......arranged by F. Mills. Solo by Mr. John P. Stafford.
7. Song—This Happy Day......... .....Evarest. Madame Lyon.
8. Selection—Si j'etais Roi..... ....Adam. Band B Battery, C.A.
9. Song—The Harp that once thro' Tara's Hall—Moore. Mr. P. Plamondon.
10. Duet—The Merry Bells..............Glover. Miss Coote and Mrs. J. J. Fitzpatrick.
11. Cornet Solo—Fantaisie Brilliante—Pietro il grande—Arban. Mr. Ernest Lavigne with Orchestra and Piano accompaniment by Mr. Jules Lemoine.
12. Song—Killarney..... ....Balfe. Miss Miller.
16. Chorus—Silver Threads among the Gold... with B Battery Orchestra accompaniment, Solo by an Officer of B Battery, C.A.
14. Address..............Reverend Mr. Connolly.

PART II.

15 Grand Fantaisie—"Erin"... ..... Basquit, Band B Battery.
16. Grand Sacred Chorus—Inflamatus—Rossini Solo by Mrs. Cauldwell. with full Band, Orchestra and Piano accompaniment. (under the leadership of Mr. Gustave Gagnon)
17. Song—Believe me if all those endearing young charms. Mr. A. Gourdeau.
18. Song—Sad will be Kathleen...........White. Miss Deegan.
19. Song—The last Rose of Summer...Flotow. Mrs. J. J. Fitzpatrick, (with Orchestra accompaniment.)
20. Grand Valse de Concert—La sensitive.... By the full Orchestra, Piano accompaniment by Mr. Jules Lemoine.
21. Song............ .... Mr. Wm H. LaRoche.
22. Song—Kathleen Mavourneen.. ......Moore. Mrs. Cauldwell.
23. Song—Cruiskeen Lawn..............Dalkers. Captain LaRue.
24. Address......................Mr. P. C. Murphy.
25, Grand Chorus from "Christopher Columbus"—F. David. by the members of L'Union Musicale and Gentlemen Amateurs, with full Orchestra and Band, and Piano accompaniment by Mr. Gustave Gagnon.

FINALE.

The Piano to be used on the occasion is one of the celebrated manufacture of PLEYEL kindly loaned by Mr. A. Lavigne, Sole Agent, Quebec.

Concert will commence at 8 o'clock, precisely.

Doors open at 7.15.

TICKETS—Gentlemen 50cts., Ladies 25cts., for sale at Mr. R. Morgan, Mr. Lavigne, Messrs. Vezina Bros., Music Stores, and at Messrs. Wright & Co's Book-Store. Also at the Store of Mr. J. Giblin, Champlain Street, and at the Door of the Hall on the night of Concert.

THOMAS COOLICAN,
Secretary.

March 15, 1876. Mch14

The Morning Chronicle

ERIN GO BRAGH

SECOND ANNUAL SOIREE

UNDER THE AUSPICES OF

THE

ST. PATRICK'S SOCIETY

—OF—

ST. COLUMBA

TO BE HELD IN THE

NEW ST. PATRICK'S HALL,

—ON—

The 17th Instant.

Monday, 20th inst.

MISS E. McCAULEY, - - - - - MUSICAL DIRECTRESS,

PROGRAMME.

PART I.

Opening Address by the President, J. Cantillon, Esq.

1. Selection of Irish Melodies..................
Violin and Piano.
2. Address by His Lordship Bishop Persico,
Honorary President.
3. Ode to Pius IX ....Rossini
Solo, Dr. Rochette.
4. Song......The Land of the West......Lover
Mr. Kennefick.
5. Song......Wild Norah's Lament......Lady Dufferin
Miss Rockett.
6. Song.........Ailleen My Darling..................
Mr. John.
7. Duett...O'er the Hill, o'er the Dale...Lover
Mrs. J. Power and Miss M. A. Cantillon.
8. Song......Kathleen Mavourneen.....Crouch
Miss Fitzpatrick.
9. An Address...
Rev. Mr. Paquet.
10. Chorus......The Harp that once......Moore
Solo, Miss A. Power.
11. Piano Solo......The Fairy......LeBoutillier
Mr. J. LeBoutillier.
12. Duett......La Croix des Bois...................
Mr. and Mrs. Rochette,
13. Song...Dreaming of Home and Mother...
Miss Rosemary Connolly.
14. Song...The Irish Emigrant's Lament......Lady Dufferin
Mr. H. McCauley.
15. Chorus..........Away, Away............Auber
16. Comic Song.......................................
Mr. T. Lane.

PART II.

1. Address...
Rev. Mr. O'Farrell.
2. Chorus.............My Erin, Oh..................
Solo, Mr. J. Power.
3. Song...........Katey's Letter...........Lover
Miss McNeil.
4. Song............Erin Machree...................
Miss Jackle,
5. Song......Sad will be Kathleen......White
Miss Gray.
6. Address...
Rev. Mr. Audet.
7. Song...Beautiful Isle of the Sea...Cooper
Miss Bogue.
8. Song...While there's Life there's Hope.....Howard
Mr. F. Winter.
9. Song...The Meeting of the Waters...Moore
Miss Hennessy.
10. Address...
Charles Fitzpatrick, Esq.
11. Song........Bells of Shandon........Mahoney
Mrs. J. Power.
12. Selection of Irish Airs—Violin and Piano
Miss McCauley and Mr. O'Malley.
13. Humorous Duett...................................
Miss S. McCauley and Mr. H. McCauley.
14. Grand Finale Chorus—
"ST. PATRICK'S DAY."

The Piano to be used on the occasion is kindly loaned by Mr. R. Morgan.

Concert will commence at 8 o'clock, P.M. Doors open at 7 o'clock.

Admission 25cts ; Reserved Seats 50cts. Tickets to be had at Mr. Morgan's Music Store, and from any of the members of the Committee.

PATRICK LAMBERT,
Secretary.

March 18, 1878.

The Morning Chronicle

1880 ST. PATRICK'S DAY. 1880

ERIN GO BRAGH

TWENTY-FOURTH GRAND ANNUAL SOIREE, under the auspices of ST. PATRICK'S LITERARY INSTITUTE, in the

VICTORIA HALL,

Under the Management of MR. VEZINA, Bandmaster "B" Battery, on

Wednesday Evening, 17th March.

PROGRAMME:

PART I.

ST. PATRICK'S DAY, Union Musicale Band.

1. Overture..Band.
2. Address by the President,......................
   Owen Murphy, Esq.
3. Chorus—"Let Erin Remember"...............
   Union Musicale and Lady and Gentlemen Amateurs.
4. Song—"My dear little Colleen"...............
   Miss O'Regan.
5. Song—"Rose of Kildare"...
   Miss Gallagher.
6. Song..
   Mr. James Lawler.
7. Duet—"Kerry Dance"...........................
   Misses Hardman and Jessie Martin.
8. Song "Harp that Once"...
   Miss Finn.
9. Song—"Aileen Mavourneen"....................
   Miss Ross.
10. Song..
    Mr. John Morkill.
11. Song..
    Miss Hetherington.
12. Song—"You'll soon forget Kathleen".......
    Miss Treggett.

PART II.

1. Selection Irish Airs........................Band.
2. Address—R. J. Bradley, Esq., President St. Patrick's Society.
3. Song—"Kathleen Mavourneen"...............
   Miss Boisvert.
4. Song—"Dear little Shamrock"..................
   Mr. Chas. Veasey.
5. Song—"Dermot Asthore"...
   Miss Lafrance.
6. Duet—"Believe me of all"...........................
   Misses Hardman and Jessie Martin.
7. Selection..Band.
8. Song—"Minstrel Boy"...
   Mr. Eugene Belleau.
9. Song—"Rose of Erin"...
   Mrs. R. J. Bradley
10. Song..
    Mr. Ed. Gingras.
11. Song—"Beautiful Girl of Kildare"...............
    Miss O'Malley.
12. Chorus—"Away, Away"...
    Union Musicale and Lady and Gentlemen Amateurs.

GOD SAVE IRELAND.

JOHN KILEY,
Secretary.

ST. PATRICK'S DAY

1880. 1880.

ERIN GO BRAGH

THE

GRAND ANNUAL SOIREE!

—UNDER THE AUSPICES OF—

The St. Patrick's Catholic and Literary Institute,

—WILL TAKE PLACE IN THE—

MUSIC HALL

—ON—

WEDNESDAY, 17th March,

UNDER THE MANAGEMENT OF

CALIXA LAVALLÉE, ESQ.,

(Organist of St. Patrick's Church)

Assisted by Lady and Gentlemen Amateurs of this City, the Quatuor Vocal de Quebec, the united Choirs of St. Patrick's Church and the Emerald Independent Band, under Mr. McKernan's leadership.

Addresses will be delivered by the Honorary President, Revd. Father HENNING C.SS.R., the President, Mr. W. McDONALD and Mr. JOSEPH K. FORAN, Laval University.

TICKETS to be had at the Presbytery, Capt. C. F. Hollwell's, R. Morgan's, Wright & Co.'s, J. E. Walsh's, A. Lavigne's, and at the Door of the Hall on the night of the Soiree.

Admittance—Gentlemen, 50 cents.
Ladies........25 cents.

Doors open at 7 o'clock. Concert will commence at 8 o'clock precisely.

The Piano is kindly furnished by Mr. A. Lavigne.

GOD SAVE IRELAND.

THOS. KELLY,
Secretary.

March 16, 1880. B

1880. 1880

ERIN GO BRAGH

ST. PATRICK'S DAY

St. Patrick's Literary Institute

THE TWENTY-FOURTH

GRAND ANNUAL SOIREE

Under the Auspices of the above Association will take place at the

VICTORIA HALL

ANN STREET,

—ON—

ST. PATRICK'S NIGHT,

WEDNESDAY, 17th MARCH, 1880

UNDER THE MANAGEMENT OF

Mr. VEZINA.

(Bandmaster "B" Battery,)

—ASSISTED BY—

The Union Musicale. (Choir and Band,) and a large number of leading Lady and Gentlemen Amateurs.

ADDRESSES will be delivered by the President of the Institute,

OWEN MURPHY, Esq.

—AND—

R. J. BRADLEY, Esq.

President St. Patrick's Society.

TICKETS to be had at Messrs. Wright & Co.'s, (Mountain Hill,) and Lavigne's Music Store, St. John Street.

Admittance—Gentlemen, 50c.; Ladies, 25c.

Doors open at 7 o'clock, Concert to commence at 8 o'clock precisely.

JOHN KILEY,
Secretary.

March 13, 1880.

> Day we have ever witnessed in this good old city. A very commendable feature connected with the entertainment, was a well-arranged programme containing the words of the various songs, got up with very great taste; for which the president and committee of management deserve the thanks of all.[7]

Songs, poetry and instrumental performances were offered by men and women, boys and girls. Occasionally a visiting artist performed, but in general it was local talented amateurs. Even when it was possible to have a visiting singer of note, however, people were often lukewarm, preferring to see their own family members or friends perform.[8] The presence of international artists on the Québec theatrical scene no doubt encouraged the players in the Matinées and Soirées to adopt the costumes and manners of the international artists, but the contents of the concerts were Irish, particularly in the choice of the songs, and later of the themes treated in the plays and melodramas.

The fervour for theatrical performances in the 1870s was such that in 1876 there were actually three full-scale Saint Patrick's Day Soirées, whose programmes were given in full in *The Morning Chronicle*. The shows of the rival Literary Societies, each announcing its own performance as the "Twentieth Annual [Musical] Soirée", were held on the 17th of March itself, while that of the Saint Patrick's Society of Saint Columba's, Sillery, although meant to take place on the 17th, had to be postponed to the following Monday, March 20th.[9] Saint Patrick's Catholic and Literary Institute's Soirée was held in the Music Hall. It was under the direction of Simon Peters, the president of the Saint Patrick's Church Choir[10], with accompanists R. H. Watson, oranist, and Wentworth Petry, former organist of the Church. Further musical accompaniment was furnished by the Band of Saint Patrick's Total Abstinence Society, under the direction of H.J. McKernan. Saint Patrick's Literary Institute held their Soirée in the Institute [Tara] Hall, "the proceeds to be devoted to the Funds of the Saint Bridget's Asylum". Their programme, under the direction of Adolphe Hamel, was the most imposing, with an Orchestra and Chorus of "One Hundred and Twenty Performers and Singers". The musical selections were accompanied by the Grand Orchestra with l'Union Musicale, the Septuor Haydn, the "B" Battery Band, and with Gustave Gagnon at the piano. The Saint Columba's offering was more modest, with a simple piano accompaniment for the songs, and a violin and piano medley.

There were at these three performances no regular full-scale dramatic presentations. Numerous speeches by prominent members of the community were still a major feature of the evening, though they would inevitably diminish in number when the long patriotic and nostalgic melodramas began to be common. At the Catholic and Literary Institute evening, after an opening address by James Creighton, the president of the Institute, the first item was a speech by Father Burke, the pastor of Saint Patrick's, while the Hon. Richard Alleyn gave the address that opened the second half. John Lane, president of the Literary Institute gave the first address, while Father John Connolly's speech closed the first part of the programme. The Saint Patrick's Society of Saint Columba's programme, while less imposing musically, had no fewer than five speakers: J. Cantillon, the president of the Saint Patrick's Society, Bishop Persico, the honourary president, Fathers O'Farrell and Audet, and the honourable Charles Fitzpatrick. These were interspersed with songs by Moore, Lover, Lady Dufferin, White and others. The song titles were typically Irish, as a sample will show: "My Erin, Oh", "The Land of the West" (Lover), "Sad will be Kathleen" (White), "Wild Norah's Lament" (Lady Dufferin). Thomas Moore's "The Harp that once through Tara's Halls" was on all three programmes, while his "The Minstrel Boy" and "The Meeting of the Waters" was on two of them. The Catholic and Literary Institute's audience were treated to no fewer than seven Moore favourites. "Saint Patrick's Day" was the opening selection at the that event, while it was used as the finale for the Saint Columba programme.[11]

The melodies of Moore, Lover, and others would continue to be popular. Melodramatic plays by Chauncey Olcott and various Irish or American authors appealed to audiences from Victorian to modern times. Plays were often written by the different directors of the Soirées. During the 1890s there existed the "Tara Dramatic Club", which would become "Saint Patrick's Dramatic Club" after the turn of the century, under the management of Richard Timmons. Dick Timmons was a wit, an actor and a dancer. He often wrote the plays that the Dramatic Club put on. Talent was attracted from all quarters, not just the Irish. The Union Musicale and the Septuor Haydn were often called upon for the musical accompaniment, and organists Joseph Vézina and Calixa Lavallée contributed their skills. The organisation of the 1895 show was another example. The musical director was Mr E. Batterton, and the leader of the orchestra was Professor Carbonneau.

By the 1890s, a tradition of two shows on Saint Patrick's day, incorporating plays, songs and solo performances for children and adults, was firmly established. For example in 1899, the "lovely matinée" for the children in the afternoon took place at the Tara Hall. The evening concert, or Soirée, held at the Academy of Music[12], included songs and recitations by "amateurs of the Irish Society" and a brilliant and witty oration by Father Grogan. These were followed by a "great

REHEARSAL.

THE FINAL REHEARSAL FOR THE ST. PATRICK'S NIGHT SOIREE, takes place THIS EVENING (MONDAY), at the MUSIC HALL.

☞ No person will be admitted without Ticket.

By order,

P. H. DUHIG,
Secretary

March 16, 1885.

St. Patrick's Day

St. Patrick's Literary Institute.

THE TWENTY-NINTH

ANNUAL SOIREE,

Under the auspices of this Institute, will take place on

Tuesday, 17th instant,

— AT THE —

MUSIC HALL.

Directress, MISS BURKE, assisted by MRS. E. FOLEY, by St. Patrick's Choral Union and the Institute Choral Class.

Admittance—Gentlemen, 50 cents.
Ladies, 25 cents.

Doors open at 7 o'clock. Concert to commence at 8 o'clock precisely.

Tickets to be had at Capt. C. E. Holiwell's, Messrs. Wright & Co.'s, Mountain Hill and St. John Street, Mr. J. E. Walsh's, John Street, Morgan & Co.'s, Buade Street, and Mr. A. Lavigne's, Fabrique Street, who will kindly loan the Piano for the occasion.

GOD SAVE IRELAND.

J. E. LEDDEN,
Secretary

March 16, 1885. B

ERIN GO BRAGH

The 39th Annual Soiree,

....UNDER THE AUSPICES OF....

St. Patrick's Literary Institute

WILL TAKE PLACE IN THE

Academy of Music,

— ON —

Monday Eve'ng, 18th inst.

When will be produced by Lady and Gentlemen Amateurs, the Drama entitled :

"A BIT OF BLARNEY,"

BY FITZGERALD MURPHY.

Interspersed with Vocal and Musical Selections

An Address will be delivered by Rev. B. McManus, C.SS.R.

Tickets for sale at Mr. L. Kerwin's, Buade street; Mr. Mark Tucker's, Champlain street, and at Mr John E. Walsh's, St. John street, where the Box Plan is on view.

Prices of Admission :—Gallery, 35c. ; Parquette, 50c. ; Orchestra Chairs, 75c. ; Opera Boxes, $6.00.

Doors open at 7 o'clock. Performance commences at 8 o'clock.

J. E. DELANY,
Secretary, St. P. Lit. Inst.

March 14, 1895.

TARA HALL.

Grand Matinee and Farce

IN THE ABOVE HALL,

On MONDAY, 18th Instant,

AT 2 30 P.M.

Admission :—Adults, 20c. ; Children, 10c.
Tickets for sale at the door.

J. E. DELANEY,
Secretary, St. P. L. Inst.

March 14, 1895.

The Morning Chronicle

Performers at the Soiree

R. TIMMONS
Director

JOHN H. KELLY, M. P. P.,
Orator of the Evening.

P. GRAHAM

Miss BRIDGEFORD

MISS FREDA O'CONNELL

Miss MAY SWINDELL

D. O'GALLAGHER

J. TIMMONS

W. P. MACNAMARA

D. GRIFFIN

M. J. HANRAHAN

The 1912 souvenir programme for St. Patrick's Day, 24 pages in length, gave a brief history of many of the existing Irish societies, along with portraits of their officers, and of the cast of the play

Programme—*Continued*

..The Irish Rebel..

A Romantic Play of the Days of '98, in Three Acts,

....By....

BERNARD FRANCIS MOORE

—— CHARACTERS ——

FATHER O'DWYER—A beloved Soggarth Aroon	Mr. D. O'GALLAGHER
HARRY RICHARDSON—A deep-dyed villain	M. J. HANRAHAN
DICK MASSEY—A young Irish Rebel	P. GRAHAM
DAN MULLIGAN—A Rambling Irish Bouchal	J. TIMMONS
CLAUDE SIMPSON—Richardson's accomplice	W. P. MACNAMARA
SERGEANT HICKMAN—An English Soldier	D. J. GRIFFIN
ETTA O'DWYER—Father O'Dwyer's niece	Miss MAY SWINDELL
LITTLE KATHLEEN—Father O'Dwyer's grand niece	Miss F. O'CONNELL
MOLLY O'CONNOR—Father O'Dwyer's ward	Miss BRIDGEFORD
ENGLISH SOLDIERS	

SYNOPSIS.

Act FIRST—Father O'Dwyer's home	The Arrest
Act SECOND—The Prison	The Escape
Act THIRD—The Mountainside	The Pardon

—— GOD SAVE IRELAND ——

The following songs will be introduced in the play:—

"TAKE OFF YOUR HAT TO OLD IRELAND" ....

Miss FREDA O'CONNELL, as Kathleen.

"THE DUBLIN DAISIES" ....

Mr. J. TIMMONS, as Dan Mulligan   Miss BRIDGEFORD, as Molly O'Connor.

In 1935 the Saint Patrick Players put on "The Heart of Paddy Whack". The cast included Frank Webster, Helen Brown, Mike Thomas, Doris McNaughton, Leo McCullen, Jack Berrigan, Joyce McNaughton, Gerry (Geraldine) O'Hearn, Doris Wyse, Kenny Alleyn, and the young Jack "Bumps" Walsh. The picture was reprinted in *Le Soleil* in 1950.

Photo kindness of Leo McCullen

Irish drama" in four acts entitled "Innisfail". The 1900 offering, "Savourneen Deelish", a presentation of the "Saint Patrick's Literary and Dramatic Club", was an Irish melodrama of the time of the "Peep O' Day" Boys. The principal roles were played by P.H. Graham, R. and J. Timmons, W.P. McManamy and the Misses E. Brady and A. Maguire. They and others would also appear in the 1903 production. From 1901 to 1904, after the destruction of the Academy of Music, both the Matinée and the Soirée were held in the Institute's Tara Hall.[13]

The Twentieth Century

Besides the address of welcome by the president of the Literary Institute, there was for a long time still at least one featured speaker at the Soirée, who was alternately a political or civil dignitary, or a member of the clergy. The main attraction of the 1901 Soirée was the Honourable Charles Fitzpatrick, Solicitor General, whose speech was "greatly appreciated."[14] He would again be the speaker in 1915, when he had become Chief Justice of the Supreme Court of Canada. In 1908, the speaker was D'Arcy Scott, the mayor of Ottawa[15] and in 1912, J.H. Kelly, M.P.P. for the Magdalen Islands. The 1916 address was E.B. Devlin, M.P. In 1904 and 1907, Father M. Gannon was the invited speaker, and in 1910 the address was given by Father Thos P. Heffernan, pastor of Saint Thomas Aquinas Parish in Montréal. The 1913 speaker was Father Turner, whose topic was "The Cross and the Shamrock", and in 1914, a Father Murphy. In general, these were Redemptorist Fathers from various Canadian parishes, who had been invited to preach the sermon at the Saint Patrick's Day Mass.

From the beginning, patriotic Irish themes dominated the dramatic offerings of director Richard Timmons: in 1902, the play was "Captain Jack or the Irish Outlaw"; in 1903 and 1907, J.F. Murphy's the "Shamrock and Rose", a play about the troubles in Ireland; in 1904, Bernard Francis Moore's three-act drama "Faugh-a-Ballagh or The Wearing of the Green", and in 1910, "Robert Emmett". The cast of the 1912 drama, B.F. Moore's "The Irish Rebel", included Messrs D. O'Gallagher, M.J. Hanrahan, P. Graham, J. Timmons, W.P. Macnamara, D.J. Griffin and Miss Bridgeford, Miss May Swindell, and the young Freda O'Connell[16]. The following year, 1913, there was no play, and the programme was composed entirely of variety acts, as in the past. The First World War did not affect the Matinée and Soirée as greatly as it had the parade; the programmes went on much as usual. During the war years, however, lighter melodramas began gradually to replace the more tragic ones.[17] The 1916 Matinée, under the direction of L.A. McCauley and Edith Davis, presented vocal selections and a one-act comedy called "Madcap Geraldine". In 1919, the comedy was "The School in Turkey Hollow". The Matinées were directed by Miss McCauley with various assistants, until 1923, when Mrs Hasting and the "Sarsfield Minstrels" were the central offering.

The 1916 Soirée featured a two-act comedy, "O'Halloran at His Wit's End", under the direction of Richard Timmons. The 1918 three-act play, "Virtue Conquers" or "The O'Dwyers of Ivy Hall" was both written and directed by Richard Timmons. The name of May Derouin appears in the 1919 offering, "The Romance of Athlone", as a member of the "Ladies". In 1921 both Irish and French-Canadian artists interpreted the comedy "My Irish Molly O". In 1920, "A Limerick Frolic", a two-act musical comedy, was under the direction of Mr and Mrs Harry S. Quart[18], who also wrote, directed and staged the 1924 offering, "Larry-O". The 1924 programme also included 18 variety acts, among them "Flippety, Floppety, Flappers", directed by William McNamara. Taking part in the various groups, "Flappers", "Tin Cans", and others, was again Mae Derouin, who would take over the direction of the Matinée and Soirée the following year, and continue to do so for the next quarter of a century. A teacher at Saint Patrick's School, she had studied dramatic arts at Columbia University in New York. Rather than pursue a career on the stage, she preferred to devote her talents to her community. She is remembered with pride and fondness by all who ever participated in the Saint Patrick's Day shows in Québec during those many years.[19]

The 70th anniversary of the annual performances came in 1926. The Matinée that year featured gymnastic exercises by the boys, under the direction of Sgt-Maj L.E. Bouchard, a comedy, "Handy Andy", directed by Mae Derouin, and a little tots' sketch, under the direction of Mr J. McDermott. At the Soirée, the guests of the evening were the Sons of Ireland hockey team, and a capacity house enjoyed the classic melodrama,[20] "Mick Murphy's Home Town",[21] which was written, staged and directed by Mr and Mrs Albert Adams. The players were Misses Joyce McNaughton, G. Fusk, Mary Grannary, and Mary Frawley, and Messrs John Peacock, Harry Quart, William McMahon, J. Farrell, William O'Reilly, J. Thomson, G. Getty, Jack Berrigan, and M. Mulroney. Selections within and between acts included choral song numbers, solos, clog dances and jigs, and the finale "God Save Ireland".[22] Many of the same actors were also featured in the 1930 production of "The Daughter of Mother Machree".

In the early 1920s, other groups had begun to offer Saint Patrick's Day concerts, among which the most successful for many years was that of the Ladies Auxiliary of the YMCA. The format was similar to the Institute's productions, featuring songs, dance numbers, recitations and instrumental solos. Their 1935 concert gives a good idea of what was offered. It was held on March 14 in the Association Hall of the YMCA, under the presidency of T.A. Begley. The programme opened with "Bless the House" and "The Little Pigs", sung by Ayton Lennon, accompanied on the piano by Sydney Martin. A piano solo by William Ross was followed by Miss McIlroy, singing "The Irish Colleen" and another "Irish Song". Irving Little gave a monologue, "Nothing at All". Muriel Hall then sang a selection which included "Kathleen Mavourneen", Rimsky-Korsakov's "Chant Hindou", "Danny Boy", "Believe me if all those endearing young charms", and "Since you and I were young, Maggie". William O'Reilly sang "The Rose of Tralee" and "I hear you calling me". A reading, "The Forsaken Merman", and a dance number by Vera Watt rounded out the performance. The president of the Ladies Auxiliary, Mrs G.D. Jackson, was in charge of the arrangements, and her committee included Mrs Campbell Amaron, Mrs Harold LeMarquand, Ruth Miller, Patricia Newton, and Mrs Maurice Parker. Candy was sold during the intermission for the benefit of the funds of the Auxiliary.[23]

The Depression era did not inhibit participation in the Matinées and Soirées. People pulled together, finding ingenious ways of fitting out the productions at little expense, even when members of large families participated. Acting roles were coveted, and many a star of a Soirée performance began his or her career by capturing a speaking role in various Matinées.[24]

The shows often featured families that performed together, like the Kelly sisters and the Adams. Mae Derouin organized the whole parish, beginning rehearsals after Christmas.[25] It became almost second nature for the children in the Matinée to go directly from school to the Literary Institute on Sainte Anne street and practice until supper time. Then the people performing in the Soirée would come in and practice until 11 or 12 o'clock at night. Sometimes if an older brother or sister had been in the shows, the younger ones would take it up automatically as they grew up. At other times, only one person in a family might participate. No one need feel left out, however; anyone who wished was given a part, at the very least in a choral number if not a solo.[26]

The 1935 Matinée and Soirée were the last ones held in the Auditorium, by then the Capitol Theatre[27]. The following year the performances moved to the recently completed Palais Montcalm, where they would continue to be held until the 1960s.[28] A Matinée performance could last for almost four hours, from two o'clock until six, according to the length of the speeches. Patricia Fitzpatrick Kiley's reminiscences describe the atmosphere that prevailed.

> About a quarter to two, we were all prepared. The play started at two. Then you'd hear the band and the goose-bumps started. Their uniforms were navy blue with white braid, but they'd put a green stripe on Saint Patrick's Day, with big bunches of shamrocks and green ribbon that went down to their knees. And they'd come down the aisle playing the Irish national anthem. Well, you'd have to be made of stone; there wasn't a dry eye in the place. And they'd march right up on the stage. The curtain would be open. We'd all be in our places ready and they'd play. Well, your heart would be beating furiously. And when they had finished their numbers, they'd march back down and then they'd just play with muted drums.
>
> Then the curtain would close and the president of the Ancient Order of Hibernians would go out and greet them. He was always a very imposing man. [The presidents] would say a few words of Gaelic, "a hundred thousand welcomes". They were supposed to speak no more than ten minutes, but some of them spoke for half an hour, which meant that the Matinée finished at six and the Soirée was at eight. While [the speaker] was doing that, we were all in the back and the Father would come and bless us and we'd all have to say, "Our Father, Hail Mary", and he'd bless us and wish us good luck. In those days, they didn't say "break a leg". Then we'd take our places. I was so nervous, I was shaking. The minute the curtain went up and I saw the crowd, that was it. I was at home. We were sorry when it was all over.[29]

The 1935 Matinée brought together what was practically the entire population of the Irish schools at that time, in a full and ambitious programme.[30] The first number was an Opening Greeting by the Saint Patrick's High School Cadet Band, under the direction of Brother Gerald and band instructor F. Unwins. This was followed by an Overture, "Memories of Erin", by Professor Léonce Crépault on the organ. The first variety number featured the "Tiny Tots" in "The Runaway Fairy", the story of a runaway, played by Nora McDermott, who was rescued by gnomes and restored to fairyland. The groups were made up of Lantern Fairies, Sunshine Fairies, Shadows, Gnomes, and the act included a Russian Dance solo by Constance Lecouvie, a Soldiers number, a song by Arline Baribeau, a solo dance by Nora McDermott, another group, The Forests and a solo song by Ruth Ledden.

Next came "The Krazy Kat Symphony" featuring songs, clog and novelty dancing: a waltz clog, an Irish jig, choral numbers for junior and senior girls, character clogs, and two solos, a Spanish dance and a novelty dance. The last number before the intermission exploited the theme of "The Rehearsal", a fictive "last practice before Saint Patrick's Day", to bring in more choral numbers, solos, Irish songs and dances, a tableau representing "Killarney", in which the "Maids of Erin" were Gertrude Dollard, Veronica Sutcliffe and Charlotte Fitzpatrick. A final medley chorus by the entire company closed the first half of the performance. After the intermission, the boys came into their own with a number featuring the "Irish Minstrels".[31] Ken Gudgeon was the minstrel boy, Hally Evans, Kenneth Savard, Hartland Brown, Dan Kane, Michael Delaney, John Farago and Jim Brady were the end men, while Arthur Keane, Roderick Bilodeau, Fred Farago and John Walsh were the soloists. An exhibition of Indian club swinging, an Irish jig and a banjo selection brought the performance to a close, amid enthusiastic applause from the appreciative audience of relatives, friends and members of the community.

The 1935 Soirée featured the Saint Patrick Players, also under the direction of Mae Derouin. The play was J. Hartley Manners' "Peg O' My Heart". Doris Wyse was "Peg", Quentin Delaney was "Jerry", the footman was played by William Jones, and Jean [Geraldine] Egan was the "demure maid". The theme song, "Peg O' My Heart", sung by Theodore J. Carbray, was repeatedly encored.

The following year, 1936, the 80th annual Soirée featured Chauncey Olcott's three-act comedy, "The Heart of Paddy Whack", for which the 1830s period costumes were brought from New York for the occasion. The cast included Doris Wyse, Doris McNaughton, Joyce McNaughton, Geraldine O'Hearn, Helen Brown, Jack Berrigan, Leo McCullen, Kenneth Alleyn, Michael Thomas, Frank Webster, and Jack Walsh. The proceeds went to benefit Saint Brigid's Home. The afternoon performance featured the youngsters in "A Dream of Toys", while the older performers put on a two-act comedy, "The Bird of Saint Patrick". These longer plays were Mae's way of preparing the young people for future Soirée performances.[32] In 1937, the Soirée offering, "Kathleen Mavourneen", boasted a cast of ten.[33] Chauncey Olcott's "The Rose O' Kildare" was the 1938 offering, and 1939 saw another ambitious production by Mae Derouin and the Saint Patrick Players: Ann Nichols' "Abie's Irish Rose". Leo McCullen played Solomon Levy, Kenneth Alleyn was Abie, with Joyce McNaughton as his wife; Hartland Brown played the neighbour, Mary Maidens was the neighbour's wife, while Frank Halpin, Ray Mathieu and Maureen O'Reilly rounded out the cast. The 1939 Matinée included the usual drills, Irish jigs, reels, and songs, with another play, "A Daughter of Erin", featuring Patsy Fitzpatrick, Joseph Fitzpatrick, Jeanette Malloy, George Madden, John Peacock, M. [Bill] Mulcair, Herman Dawson, and George Bryson.

The 17th of March fell on Palm Sunday in 1940, and, exceptionally, the 84th Matinée and Soirée took place on Wednesday, April 3rd. Participation, however, was undiminished.

The 1941 Matinée included a particularly interesting influence of the media on the shows' contents. The variety number, "Marionettes on Parade", was a character group number based on Walt Disney's Pinocchio: Jiminy Cricket was played by Albert Paquet, Mark Heitshu was Pinocchio and the Good Fairy was Arline Baribeau. Generally speaking, though, the programmes were more influenced by the forms of entertainment popular in different eras, such as drills and clog dances, than by the content. The Irish themes easily predominated, since the audiences had ample access on other occasions to non-Irish forms of entertainment.

As the Second World War progressed, the absence of many adult members of the community caused the shows to be composed principally of school children, and the Soirée programme was often little more than a slightly modified version of the Matinée performance. At this time as well, teachers in the schools began to take a larger part in the preparation of the shows. The Matinée and Soirée of 1943, "A Grand Irish Pageant", was staged by the girls of the Leonard School and the boys of Saint Patrick's, under the direction of Brother George. Among those in charge of the sale of candies and programmes were Mae Derouin, Anna Burridge, Winnie Brown, Gertie Edwards, and Peg Fitzpatrick. The Soirée was under the patronage of the Lieutenant-Governor, and included Kerry Dancers Emily Fitzpatrick and Louise Verge. Marianna O'Gallagher played the Irish King and Jean Valiquette, Patricia White, Mary Adams and Teresa Kokesch played the Companions in one of the skits. The 1944 afternoon programme featured Clark and Strickland's operetta "Kathleen", while Grubb and Penn's "The Lady of the Terrace" was added to the evening performançe by the older performers. The shows were under the responsibility of the professors at Saint Patrick's School. The 1945 shows were billed as the "6th wartime and 89th Grand Annual" Matinée and Soirée. The two programmes were practically identical, featuring Carrington's two-act operetta "Bits of Blarney", under the direction of the Sisters of the Leonard School. The school orchestra, under the direction of William Murphy, played selections between the acts and at the intermission. "Hundreds celebrated", and "in spite of the weather, there was not an empty seat."[34]

Mae Derouin continued to organize the Soirée for some time after the Sisters from the school took over the Matinée, but by the 1950s she finally retired, leaving to others what, while a labour of love, had

Photo kindness of Pat Fitzpatrick Kiley

Photo kindness of Leo McCullen

The dashing hero "Tim Maloney", as played by Joe Fitzpatrick in the Matinée of 1939. Joe Fitzpatrick, pictured here outside the Palais Montcalm, was killed at Hong Kong before the year's end.

Leo McCullen and Frank Halpin in a scene from "Abie's Irish Rose", the main attraction of the Soirée for 1939.

Mae Derouin and an assistant surrounded by the boys and girls of the parish, about 1939 or 1940. Ve Ve and Pat Kelly appear in the top row costumed for a "Skaters' Waltz."

In the 1940s the Literary Institute gradually handed over the direction of the Matinée to the Sisters of Charity at the Leonard School. This picture illustrates the accepted 'colleen costume' of the day. A small orchestra is present, trained and directed by William Murphy.

Photo Edwards, kindness of Mary Kenny McGrath

The children of Saint Patrick's parish were directed in the 1945 Matinée at the Palais Montcalm by the Sisters of the Leonard School. During the late 1940s Sister Mary Teresina and Sister Joan Conway were two of the teachers frequently involved in the production of the Matinées.

March 17, 1947: "The Luck of the Irish" drama presented at the Soirée at the Palais Montcalm. The players were Bill Bantey, Pete Poulin, Ed Bantey, Mary Maidens, Jack Maroney, Maureen Walsh, Pat Fitzpatrick, Michael Coss.

Photo Edwards, kindness of Pat Fitzpatrick Kiley

The Ravanello Choral Society performed at many functions, including the March 17th show. Brother Anthony here directs the choir at the Palais Montcalm, 1947, accompanied by Léonce Crépault, organist at St Patrick's Church.

Photo kindness of Charlotte Pichard

Photo Chronicle-Telegraph

The ever popular Irish jig was performed by Diane Kenyon, Charlotte Jones Pichard and Ursula Oliver in the 1947 Matinée at the Palais Montcalm. Green skirt, black velvet bodice and white blouse comprised the conventional costume for the jig in those days.

Ve Ve and Pat Kelly did the choreography for the 1956 Centenary Soirée at the Palais Montcalm.

The twelve dancing daughters of Billy John McMahon: Anne Marie, Isabel, Eileen, Connie, Carol, Sylvia, Norma, Alice, Carmen, Rita, Teresa, Grace, at the Palais Montcalm, March 17, 1958. Photo Oesterwinter, Chronicle-Telegraph

been nevertheless a tremendous amount of work. During the post-war period, the Irish population began to be dispersed among the various sectors of the city, rather than being concentrated around the Montcalm area. It became more and more difficult to bring the children together from the several schools for the type of rehearsals which had been possible up until the 1940s. As a result, between 1954 and 1956, the Matinée was at last given up as a single public performance and was replaced by individual performances particular to each school and district. The Soirée, however, regained much of its pre-war flamboyance, encompassing performances by both adult and younger members of the community. The 1947 performance of "The Luck of the Irish" saw spirited performances by Jack Maroney, Patricia Fitzpatrick, Michael Coss, Mary Maidens, Bill and Edward Bantey, Peter Poulin, and Maureen Walsh. André Jacques accompanied Vincent Munro in a selection of Irish airs, while Brother Anthony directed the Ravanello Choral Society, accompanied by Léonce Crépault. The traditional Irish Jig was performed by Charlotte Pichard, Ursula Oliver and Diane Kenyon.

On March 13, 1954 a two-page spread in the newspapers announced the "Patrick's Day Grand Annual Entertainment". The Patrician Players presented "Princess O'Toole", a comedy in three acts by Edith Loring at the Palais Montcalm on Wednesday, March 17 at 8:00 p.m. The director was James Peacock, with choreography by Veronica and Patricia Kelly and a musical score arrangement by Gerard Montreuil. Besides the play, a group of "Irish Variety numbers" was offered, which included a dream waltz, "It was only an Irishman's Dream", an Irish reel, the perennial "Irish Washerwoman", a soft shoe song and dance, "Mickey, Pretty Mickey", "Four Fellows" doing "Phil the Fluter's Ball", an Irish polka, "When Irish eyes are smiling", the "Irish Rockettes" doing "Saint Patrick's Day Parade", the Debbie Sisters doing a Song and Dance: "Has anyone here seen Kelly" and Marlene Angers singing "Danny Boy". This was offered both as a Matinee and a Soirée, with prices for the Matinée at 90¢ and 85¢, and the Soirée at $1.25 and $1.00. The Patrician Players were high school youngsters, but the whole event drew the community at large and was generally a huge success. The show was presented one evening only, but acts and performers for the show also "did their stuff" at the weekly Optimists' Club luncheon. Eight little girls from Saint Brigid's Home, accompanied by Mae Derouin, presented two numbers which were roundly applauded.[35] This grand performance was followed in 1955 by a repeat of the 1935 offering: "Peg O' My Heart", reduced to a single evening performance at the Palais Montcalm. "Peg" was played by

Florence McGrath, who had also played Princess O'Brien in the previous year's "Princess O'Toole".

On March 16, 1956, a poem in the newspaper by a local author regrets the passing of the Matinée, while giving a pertinent description of the elements that remained in people's memories.

Vanished Matinee
(Slievenamon)

I wonder in what place of bliss
The songs of children fill the air;
In what green valley little miss
In gold-starred dress that fairies wear
Proclaims how Ireland is so fair;
Two years have blown them all away,
And little colleens, none so rare.
Where are the plays of yesterday?

Say where the Maids of Erin walk
Strumming a plaintive harp, and where
The precious poems in baby talk,
Or green bows tying youthful hair;
Where minuet and dances square;
Some wind has blown them all away.
And what of an old Irish air.
Where are the ties of yesterday?

Where is the Queen-of-Ireland-scene,
And tableaux of Mayo and Clare;
By what strange sea does John, Eileen,
With Jimmy and Lauretta share
Our children's sorrow and despair:
No more rehearsals, none to care;
Where the ideals of yesterday?

Alas for culture, gone, and where
The stage-kiss children wiped away;
The side-wings where they pair by pair
All vanished with the Matinee.

Desmond Lonergan[36]

That same year, another two-page spread[37] announced the Saint Patrick's Day Centenary: the 100th Annual Soirée, the 100th anniversary of Saint Patrick's Parish and of Saint Brigid's Home. The Patrician Players' presented "When Irish Eyes are Smiling", under the direction of Steve Prosenyak, with "Ve Ve" and Pat Kelly as choreographers. The cast was composed of Rita Madden, Ina Macdonald, Joseph Thomas, Dorothy Doherty, James Peacock, Cullen Keane, Mickey Fiset, Beatrice Henderson, Harold Dionne, Bernadette Griffin, and John Monaghan.

Photo Oesterwinter

Photo Edwards

A highstepping chorus line in a number at the 1959 Soirée on Sunday, March 15th, was made up of girls from Saint Patrick's parish: Faye Burridge, Ellen Clare O'Gallagher, Maureen O'Reilly, Lucy Lefebvre, Mimi Lapointe, Connie Desmarais, Madeleine Pagé, and Jeannette Filion.

Nancy Pike, Donna Perks, Marion Mercier, France Richard, Louise Marman, Sandra Lamontagne, and Louise Angers rehearse a soft-shoe number for the 106th annual Soirée at the Palais Montcalm on Saturday, March 17, 1962.

Photo: Roland Dore, kindness of Charlotte Pichard

An enterprising photographer lined up one of the acts of the 1960 Irish show at the Palais Montcalm, and got this pleasing array: Nancy Copeman and her brother Robert at the top; Wendy Quart and Heather Kirkwood in the centre with two unnamed girls on either side; Anne Pichard and her sister Mary Lou (daughters of Charlotte Jones Pichard); and the Gorman twins: Donna and Debbie. Choreography in 1960 was by Geraldine Savard.

Photos W.B. Edwards

John Lamb, Kevin Ryan, and Larry Saville perform a song in the 1962 Saint Patrick's Day show. Pat Kiley and Sheldon Phaneuf were the principals in 1962's "A Mad Breakfast".

Audience at the last Saint Patrick's Soirée in 1965 at the Palais Montcalm.

Photo Chronicle-Telegraph

In addition to the play, the programme contained a variety of dances and songs meant to be typical of each decade:

WALTZ: "It was only an Irishman's Dream
POLKA: "When Irish Eyes are Smiling"
GAY NINETIES: "Dare tread on the tail o' me coat"
BALLET: "Patricia, My Patricia"
DOLLY SISTERS: "Daughter of Rosie O'Grady"
CHARLESTON: "My Wild Irish Rose"
RECITATION: "Trimmings of the Rosary"
SOFT SHOE: "Did anyone ever tell you, Mrs Murphy"
JITTERBUG: "It's an Irish Lullaby"
CHA-CHA-CHA: "Kerry Dance"
SONG: "Galway Bay"
"O'Donnell Aboo"
IRISH JIG: "Irish Washerwoman"

The 1956 festivities added a slightly new touch: the program of Irish songs, dancing and music prepared by the children of Saint Brigid's Home under the direction of Miss Geraldine Savard was aired on a special television programme at noon on Friday the 17th. While the 1955 and 1956 productions were given once only in the evening, in 1957, Harry Delf's three-act farce "The Rooney Family" was again performed as both a Matinée and a Soirée presentation.

For almost another decade, the Soirées would continue with much the same format, drawing on the talent of the Patrician Players, with directors James Peacock and Jack Maroney. Veronica and Patricia Kelly continued to choreograph many of the dances, and the music was furnished variously by Jean Marc Legrand on the organ or, when possible, an orchestra. The 1958 Soirée, staged in the High School auditorium,[38] was followed by a parish social, with dancing and an orchestra. One interesting highlight of that year's programme was a single dance number by the twelve daughters of Mr and Mrs William John McMahon, whose ages ranged from five to nineteen.[39] In 1959 the Soirée was back in the Palais Montcalm on Sunday evening the 15th. Jean Kerr's three-act play, "Jenny Kissed Me", featured players Robert Torpey, Louise Brown, Audrey O'Reilly, Yvonne Martell, Brian Watson, Jack Maroney, Doreen Warren, Patricia O'Donnell, James Noonan, Viola Lewin, and Denise Cole. The 106th Soirée in 1962 included two one-act plays, Peg Lynch's "The Income Tax", and Isabel McReynolds Gray's "A Mad Breakfast", plus a variety of singing and dancing acts. It was sponsored by the parish, under the direction of Father John Corkery. The Patrician Players included performers Pat Kiley, Ken Morgan, Joan Brown, Sheldon Phaneuf, and Doreen Warren. Louise Angers and Joyce Drouin directed the dancers: twins Donna and Deborah Gorman, the Pichard Sisters, Anne and Mary Lou, and "The Irish Steppers". The singers were Nancy Pike, Carol Doherty, Nancy Monaghan, Barbara Smith, Linda Davis, Denis Doucet, Harry Griffin, John Lamb, Kevin Ryan, and Larry Saville.[40] The 1963 performance of "Rise and Shine" was the last offering by Jack J. Maroney and the Patrician Players.

In 1964 and 1965, Louise Angers, who had choreographed the dance numbers in previous Soirées, and her brother, Arnold Angers, co-directed what were to be the last Grand Annual Soirées at the Palais Montcalm. The 1964 offering used the musical comedy format with the theme of a "Dress Rehearsal", presenting such acts as Harry and Duey, the Accordionaires, Donna and Debbie Gorman, with backup music by Marius Fleury's Orchestra. There were numbers by the Saint Patrick's high school glee club, under the direction of Sister Joseph Anthony and the Saint Lawrence College guitar group, "The Originals".[41] In 1965, the 109th, and last, Soirée featured variety numbers from calypso to twist, with Irish jigs got up as Russian hopaks, twists and, finally, as proper jigs. The Irish Double Eight chorus, with a medley of Irish songs and singers Wendy Angers, Mary Quinn, and Joanne Wright, were complemented by dancers Katy Angers, veteran troupers the Pichard Sisters, as well as folksingers Jocelyne Triganne, Mike Gauthreau, Gary Ouellet, and Larry Saville.[42]

In 1966, the Soirée was reduced to a combined banquet and show at the Cambrai Curling Club, under the auspices of the parish. The performers at the show were students from the various elementary schools, including, however, such veteran performers as the Gorman twins. A new era had begun.[43]

During the 1950s, the musical and theatrical selections had continued to be heavily influenced by what was available within the scope of general North American Irish culture, centered on the eastern United States and Canada, particularly Toronto, Montréal, New York and Boston. As travel outside North America became more common, during the 1960s and 1970s, more Québec City Irish began to visit Ireland and to become familiar with contemporary Irish productions. This led to a more balanced selection of traditional Irish as well as Irish-American content for the different shows and entertainment. By the time of the demise of the Grand Soirée at the Palais Montcalm, various other manifestations had already become established, such as the shows in the various schools, which were often repeated either in institutions, such as Saint Brigid's Home or the Jeffery Hale Hospital, or at other celebrations, such as the different dinners and banquets during the festive period. These smaller-scale productions permitted

Photo W.B. Edwards

Photo Ross Corcoran. Print Pierre Cayer

March 16, 1962, Variety Show by Saint Patrick's elementary school pupils. The show was opened by the Grade One children.

Saint Patrick's Elementary School children performing in the show in 1985.

Photos W.B. Edwards

Saint Vincent's school dancers Anne Baller, Margaret Ann Cook, Shirley Kuzminski, and Joyce Tremblay do a jig and reel at the Cambrai Club soirée in 1966. Anne and Mary Lou Pichard were part of the 1966 Saint Stephen's elementary school show.

Photos W.B. Edwards

The 1964 Variety Show staged by Saint Vincent's Elementary School gave many children an opportunity to shine in some dramatic activity: acting, dancing or singing.

Photos W.B. Edwards

The 1964 Show by the children of Saint Vincent's School included a short play. Many parents and other friends attended.

the inclusion of a variety of participants as well as a diversification of appreciative audiences.

School Celebrations

Wherever Irish Catholic children went to school, there was feasting on Saint Patrick's Day. The convent boarding schools in and around the city marked the day, sometimes with a concert or other stage presentation, frequently with something special at table—the gift of parents who wanted notice taken of the day as special for children of Irish descent. For example, in 1914, the students of the English class of the Saint Roch convent school gave a patriotic show, which included a two-part reading of the life of Father T.N. Burke, national Irish music, and the usual recitations. All the young girls were dressed in white and wearing the "dear little Shamrock". At the end, they were congratulated by Father Lagueux as well as one of the Fathers from Saint Patrick's. Their French classmates joined them in singing "God Save Ireland". At the reception for the parents of students in 1918, some of the French girls also took part in the programme.[44]

From the point of view of the authorities of the schools, for the most part religious communities, there was no lack of awareness of the feast, for there were many Irishwomen in the ranks of the religious of Québec. The Séminaire de Québec also celebrated the feast in a variety of ways during its long history. Frequently there was a solemn High Mass in the morning, celebrated by the Superior himself, and concerts, as for example in 1947, when a special musical programme was prepared for the Mass by the Seminary Chorale.[45] The Irish boarders were allowed special meals, and were often excused from classes for the day. If there were no special Mass on the day itself, the students had permission to attend the Mass at Saint Patrick's, and were sometimes given the rest of the day as a holiday in order to celebrate with the community.[46]

Irish and other English speaking Catholic girls were obliged to frequent the various French convent schools until the establishment of the Leonard School in 1935, while the boys had had their own schools since the middle of the 19th century. While the schools were grouped together in the de Salaberry-Maisonneuve area, it was easy for the children to participate in the parish-oriented activities, which included the Matinées. With their disappearance, the children and young people continued their celebrations within the context of the various schools themselves. Over the years, the preparation of an annual Saint Patrick's Day show in both the elementary and high schools has thus continued to be the responsibility of members of the teaching staff.

The elementary school pupils usually prepare two performances: one within the school itself, for the rest of the students, the other for parents and friends, either in the afternoon or the evening. The young people also put on all or part of the show elsewhere, during the festive period, according to requests from different groups in the community. For example, in 1967, the students from Saint Patrick's Girls Elementary school, under the direction of Mrs Nancy Pike, put on their show for the dinner dance held at the Cambrai Curling Club. Colleen Bilodeau, Linda Bédard and Mary Rémy were the soloists, accompanied by Bonnie Pike on the piano. Mrs Pike herself performed a selection of traditional Irish songs. Other participants included Barbara Smith and Cheryl Griffin, local television personalities of the time. Also in 1967, the Saint Vincent School Girls performed for the Kiwanis Club dinner which was held at the Château Frontenac at noon on Saint Patrick's Day. They then appeared on television in the evening, and went on to dance for the Saint Vincent's parish dinner at the Holiday Inn. The Saint Vincent's Girls School put on a three-act operetta, "The Jig is Up", in the school auditorium on the evening of March 12th, 1969. In 1972, Saint Vincent's production was called "The Children of Ireland Today", and included a certain amount of social commentary: the Northern Irish child was portrayed with a gun, while the child from Eire was a happy colleen. The different ethnic groups were portrayed as tourists from different countries.

In 1984 and 1985, Saint Patrick's Elementary's traditional annual show had as its guests, besides parents and friends, the students from Saint Vincent's Elementary. The shows included poems, songs, dances and a play. Portions of the show were also presented to the residents of Saint Brigid's home and the patients in the chronic ward at Jeffery Hale's Hospital. In 1986, the same "public" performances of the show had to be postponed to the 20th and 21st because of the "Saint Patrick's Day Storm". Today, after the merging of the elementary schools, Saint Vincent's School continues the tradition of the annual show as firmly as ever.

The Saint Patrick's High School shows have retained a format similar to the old Soirées, with songs, dances, instrumental selections and short plays. They are sometimes built around a unifying theme. Among others, in 1972, 1973 and 1984 this was based on the always popular formula of "Paddy's Pub". The 1972 show was produced and directed by five students: Kevin and Glen O'Farrell, Thomas Quigley,

Photos Frank Scardina

The Saint Patrick's High School boys' chorus in 1979 was trained by Joe Lonergan, who accompanied them together with student Barry Maher. The stage set was created by art students under the direction of Frank Scardina. The whole school chorus filled the stage for the finale, "A Nation Once Again." Control and creation of the right light and sound effects give other tasks to the many students who wish to take part in the Show.

Photos Frank Scarding

High stepping dancers and choral singers show off their hard-earned skills in the 1979 high school show.

David Ross and Kevin Saville. "The Shillelagh Pub" of 1973 presented twenty-one numbers, including Irish jigs, reels, and songs, with chorus, band, and orchestra. It was directed by Peter Maher and co-ordinated by Sister Mildred Wallace. In 1979, the programme entitled "Travel With Us Around Ireland In Song" was under the direction of Sister Marianna O'Gallagher, assisted by Joseph Lonergan.[47] The master of ceremonies was James O'Farrell, the dancers were taught by Geraldine O'Shea and Louanne McGrory, students from Shannon[48], and the musicians were teachers Roger Colleret and Joe Lonergan, with Shannonite Barry Maher. The songs were varied: songs from the Irish American repertoire, regional Irish songs, such as "Donaree", "The Boys of Armagh"; marching songs, war songs, a song in Gaelic, "Fanny Power"; Irish romantic and nostalgic ballads, and the patriotic "The Wearing of the Green" and "A Nation Once Again". The dancers performed a six hand and a three hand reel, while the skit was based on a traditional Irish tale, "The Leprechaun's Revenge"[49]. The 1980 performances, scheduled for Friday the 14th, had to be put off until the following Tuesday, the 18th, because of the "Saint Patrick's Day Storm"!

The 1984 and 1985 shows were emceed by the team of Kevin McNulty and Jocelyne Slattery. Singers Richard Dalpé, Mario Gingras, Jimmy McLean, Tommy O'Neill, and Réjean Rouleau in 1984, and Marco Anctil, Nancy Brennan, Maureen Corrigan, Helen Dalpé, Brian Fiset, Shannon Gauvin, Ruth O'Brien, Esther Paradis, and Philip Trudel in 1985, among others, were a good example of the Irish/French composition of the school. The High School shows continued throughout the 1980s under the direction of teachers Marianna O'Gallagher, until her retirement, and Joe Lonergan, who is in charge of them at the present time. The programmes contain skilful variations and combinations of Irish songs, Irish dancing, the Irish harp, flutes, guitars, and plays with Irish themes. The 1990 one-act play was Lady Gregory's "Spreading the News", which was directed by Sister Frances Timmons. "God Save Ireland" is always an appropriate inclusion, particularly in view of the present situation in Northern Ireland. The evening performance is always attended by an appreciative audience of parents, former students, friends and members of the community. They also bring a slightly modified version of the performance to the residents of Saint Brigid's Home, on one of the afternoons during the festive period. The students are, as always, a mixture of Irish, French and other ethnic origins, but, what is most important, all seem to enjoy showing that they are "Irish on Saint Patrick's Day".[50]

These school shows are limited to the English Catholic school system.[51] The Protestant elementary and high schools have no organized festivities, although individual teachers may utilise the theme in classroom activities during the month of March.[52]

Saint Brigid's Home

Where an institution did not have sufficient numbers of Irish or other residents interested in the feast, the Irish and their friends went to the High Mass at the old church and joined the festive Irish that way. For example, the Grey Nuns at Saint Brigid's Home were sure, for many years, to receive a visit from six or seven of the Irish Sisters from the Motherhouse on Saint Patrick's Day.[53] Their visit coincided with that of the Cardinal celebrant of the High Mass. It appears that part of the duty of the celebrant and guest preacher, besides officiating at Mass, was to visit the orphans and the elderly at Saint Brigid's Home. The children were trained to read little speeches, to present bouquets and to request a holiday of their visitors. The visits of Cardinals Rouleau, Bégin and Villeneuve are thus recorded for several Saint Patrick's Days. When Saint Patrick's Literary Institute put on the Matinée and Soirée, the proceeds went to the Home. The children in the Home would also put on performances over the years, but since the building of the new Saint Brigid's in Sillery in 1973, the residents have been limited to the older generation.

For the last few years, the main event during the Saint Patrick's Day festive period has been the Saint Brigid's Guild's "Irish Pub". It is usually one of the earliest celebrations to take place, and has come anywhere between the 6th and the 13th, so as not to conflict with any of the other events. This was particularly true in the middle 1980s, when there was a proliferation of celebrations by different groups. The Home is decorated with shamrocks, streamers and ribbons, while the residents wear corsages of "green" flowers, besides the usual shamrock and ribbon rosettes. The members of the Guild serve green beer and other refreshments. There are between sixty and a hundred attendance prizes, which are donated by local merchants and friends of the Home. The entertainment usually consists of sing-alongs, jigs and reels, to the music of Carmen Turpin Vallières and her band: Carmen, Lynn, Paule Vallières, Bruce Turpin, and Gilles Lefevre.[54] In 1987, they were joined by Gary Fleming, Renée Deschamps, Sister Eleanor Keller, and Gilbert Darisse, and in 1990, Yves Robitaille and Hélène Gagnon also

PARISH PREPARES FOR A BIG DAY

Children at Saint Brigid's Home, dancers, actors, singers and other performers, preparing for the 1956 Centenary variety show.

Photo Chronicle-Telegraph

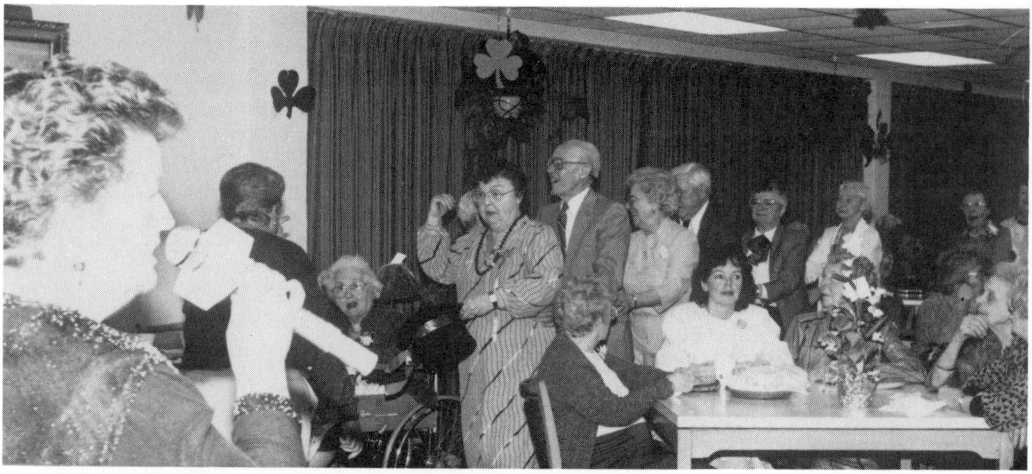

Scenes from the 1988 Saint Brigid's Home party for Saint Patrick's Day. Familiar leaders and participants appear: Carmen Vallières, Rita Brown, Pat and Howard Kiley. The delightfully joyful conga line in the second picture is led by Eileen Kelly. Allen Copeman, the piper, was a welcome performer at Saint Brigid's Home in 1990.

took part. Another feature of the 1990 celebration was a bagpipe performance by piper Allen Copeman.

Saint Brigid's Home furnishes a link between performances past and present. Many of the residents were themselves participants in the long-ago Matinées and Soirées, and they have not lost their enthusiasm for the various presentations of the Shannon Pub, the high school choral groups, and their own Guild-sponsored event. The Home is a crossroads for the different age groups in the community during the festive period.

The theatrical aspect of the Saint Patrick's Day celebrations seems thus to be alive and well as the Québec Irish community moves toward the 21st century.

Notes

1. See George Gale, *Historic Tales of Old Quebec*, p. 256-268, for an overview of theatrical activity in Québec during the 19th century.
2. George Gale, *Quebec 'Twixt Old and New*, p. 136.
3. Where the Hotel Clarendon now stands.
4. Gale, *Quebec 'Twixt Old and New*, p. 246.
5. *The Quebec Mercury*, March 15, 1867. The band was under the leadership of Band Master, "Herr" Standhaft.
6. Quebec Chronicle-Telegraph, eds., *100th Anniversary: Saint Patrick's Parish*, booklet, p. 14.
7. *The Quebec Gazette*, 20th March 1872.
8. On one occasion, the Literary Institute brought in Griffin, a well-known singer, but the idea was not particularly appealing to people. Hugh Kane, formerly a president of the Literary Institute, interview 1978.
9. While the announcements from March 15th to 17th in *The Morning Chronicle* gave the date for Saint Columba's Soirée as the 17th, the advertisement on the 18th gave notice that the parade and Soirée were postponed because of the "howling gale".
10. Gale, *Quebec 'Twixt Old and New*, p. 247.
11. *The Morning Chronicle*, March 18, 1876.
12. This hall, inaugurated in 1853, was variously known as the Theatre Royal, then the Music Hall and finally the Academy of Music. It caught fire on March 17th, 1900, just as the Saint Patrick's Day Soirée was ending. Although the Hall was totally destroyed, the calm behaviour of the manager, Edward Varney, and the set director, Charles Auburn, as well as the actions of the firemen, resulted in the complete evacuation of spectators, actors and even of the Varney family with no loss of life.
13. The Auditorium was inaugurated in August of 1903.
14. *Le Soleil*, 18 mars 1901, p. 1.
15. *The Quebec Chronicle*, March 18, 1908, p. 4.
16. Freda O'Connell died at Saint Brigid's Home on May 28, 1990, at the age of 89. Information, Saint Brigid's Home.
17. For the 1927 Matinée, May Derouin did attempt Lady Gregory's farce-comedy, "The Rising of the Moon", but quickly returned to lighter productions.
18. Josie Dinan Quart was delegate to the United Nations in 1957, and was a Senator from 1960 until her death in 1980.
19. *Quebec Chronicle-Telegraph*, March 15, 1972, p. 1. Mae died at Saint Brigid's Home on December 26, 1975, at the age of 90: Marianna O'Gallagher, *Saint Brigid's, Québec*, p. 65.
20. "The English landlord threatens eviction and the Irish lad returns from America with the money needed." Leo McCullen, interview 1978.
21. The town was Enniscorthy, County Wexford.
22. *Quebec Chronicle-Telegraph*, March 18, 1926, p. 1 & 9.
23. *Quebec Chronicle-Telegraph*, March 15, 1935, p. 3. In 1937, they also put on a play, "Mrs Maloney's Infirmity".
24. Patricia Fitzpatrick Kiley, interview 1978.

25. "It was quite a part of our school life. The Boys' Choir rehearsed for three months in advance." Hugh Kane, interview 1978.
26. Patricia Fitzpatrick Kiley, Doris Coveney, Mildred Wallace, interviews 1978.
27. It was named the Capitol Theatre after its acquisition by Famous Players in 1929, and was turned into a cinema in 1935.
28. The city furnished a grant to the parish to cover the cost of the use of the Auditorium/Capitol, but upon completion of the Palais Montcalm, the grant was replaced by free use of the latter. The change came about, therefore, for financial reasons, since the Capitol was preferred as a nicer place for the show. Patricia Fitzpatrick Kiley, interview 1978.
29. Patricia Fitzpatrick Kiley, interview 1978.
30. The Matinée included the population of the schools, and the names of the participants in the 1935 Matinée give a good idea of the composition of that population. All had their names in the paper, and some more than once, according to their participation in one or more numbers, as chorus or solo. **Girls**: Arline Baribeau, Helen Brown, Doreen Burgess, Mildred Byrne, Norma Copeman, Alexis Corbett, Rita Corcoran, Marie Coss, Pat Coss, Mary Deakin, Olive Delany, Vivian Delany, Louise Deny, Gertrude Dollard, Mary Donnelly, Celina Doyle, Mary Doyle, Antoinette Fitzpatrick, Charlotte Fitzpatrick, Patricia Fitzpatrick, Margaret Frezell, Antoinette Gilbert, Gemma Gilbert, Pauline Goulet, Drusilla Hewitt, Irene Hogan, Charlotte Jones, Dorothea Kane, Yvette M. Laferriere, Constance Lecouvie, Ruth Ledden, Evelyn Luckman, Evelyn Lyons, Nora McDermott, Barbara McLaren, Doreen McMahon, Patricia McMahon, Rita McMahon, Jeanette Molloy, Lillian Morissette, Mignonne Myrand, Kathleen Oliver, Ursula Oliver, Theresa Peters, Lorraine Power, Norma Power, Doris Quinn, Gladys Roberts, Frances Robinson, Mary Ryan, Helen Shirley, Veronica Sutcliffe, Yvette Trudel, Doris Tupper, Inez Tupper, Lorna Tupper, Marjorie Walsh, Mildred Walsh, Patsy Walsh, Joan Watters, Joan Whitely. **Boys**: Walter Adams, Paul Ahern, Edward Alleyn, Maurice Alleyn, Robert Anger, Bob Angers, E. Angers, Ted Angers, A. Bailey, Gerry Berrigan, Roderick Bilodeau, Jerry Blondeau, L. Boulet, Desmond Brady, James Brady, Paul Brault, Art Brown, Fred Brown, Hartland Brown, Paul Brown, George Bryson, Frank Bussieres, Maurice Cadoret, George Cooper, William Cooper, Patrick Corcoran, Ray Corcoran, Charles Cosgrove, Philip Coudert, Ken Coughlin, Frank Couture, Gordon Dale, Kevin C. Davis, F. Dawson, Herman Dawson, William Dawson, Paul Deakin, Charles Delaney, Michael Delaney, Philip Delaney, R. Delisle, Gerry Dempsey, Paul Derouin, Maurice Doherty, Frank Dollard, William Donnelly, M. Douglas, Earl Dundon, Austin Edwards, Maurice Edwards, Hally Evans, Fred Farago, Jack Farago, Joseph Fitzpatrick, Robert Fleury, Edward Fox, G. Gagnon, G. Gauvreau, Willy Genois, Jack Golden, Ernie Gorman, James Gorman, John Gorman, A. Gudgeon, Eric Gudgeon, Kenneth Gudgeon, Rodney Gudgeon, Julian Guntensperger, George Hacket, James Halpin, Louis Hanrahan, Gerry Healey, James Hewitt, Edward Hobbs, John Houde, A. Jacques, H. Jacques, Bill Kane, Dan Kane, Hugh Kane, John Kane, Arthur Keane, Lindy Keane, Gerry Kelly, Charles Kent, Larkin Kerwin, Gilbert Kirkwood, P. Langevin, Brian Laurie, Ernie Laurie, Ian Laurie, L. Laurie, J. LeBlanc, Adrien Leger, Bryce Mackasey, K. Mackay, Frank MacManus, George Madden, Raymond Madden, Gerry Marcoux, Harvey Marier, Jacques Marion, William McCauley, Edward McDermott, James McGarretty, Gerry McNeal, Jack McNicholl, Harold McPeak, Jim Monaghan, Bernard Morris, William Mulcair, Frank Mullally, Vincent Munro, Hubert Murphy, Mervin Murphy, Eugene [Jeep]

Neal, Curtis Neale, Frank Noonan, R. O'Brien, Tim O'Connell, John O'Connor, Reggie O'Donnell, Colin O'Neil, Desmond Paquet, D. Patterson, James Peacock, James Pelletier, Leo Petitpas, John Poliquin, Gerry Power, Gerry Quart, Harry Quart, Cyril Quinn, Bill Reid, Doug Reid, Milton Reid, Edward Richards, Gordon Rioux, Gerry Robitaille, R. Ruel, Ken Savard, Charles Shanahan, James Shanahan, Joseph Shirley, Bob Tessier, R. Thivierge, Alphonsus Thomas, James Trainor, Lorne Trainor, Ronald Tupper, Archie Vezina, Dick Vezina, C. Vieu, Desmond Wallace, Raines Walling, F. Walsh, Henry Walsh, John Walsh, George Watters, Roger Watters, and Joseph Woods.

31. Since the girls' and boys' schools had different schedules, boys and girls practised separately and could only come together occasionally to permit the coordination of the whole performance. Patricia Fitzpatrick Kiley, interview 1978.
32. Patricia Fitzpatrick Kiley, interview 1978.
33. They were Joyce McNaughton, Michael Delaney, Margaret Foley, Kenneth Alleyn, Ray Mathieu, Doris McNaughton, Harry Alleyn, Joseph Thomas, Ray Corcoran, and Gerald Healey.
34. *Quebec Chronicle-Telegraph*, March 19, 1945, p. 3.
35. *Quebec Chronicle-Telegraph*, March 18, 1954, p. 9.
36. Saint Patrick's Verse. Editorial Page, *Quebec Chronicle-Telegraph*, March 16, 1956.
37. *Quebec Chronicle-Telegraph*, March 13, 1956, p. 6-7.
38. After the fire in the Grande Allée basement church, the new school auditorium had been used for religious services. The opening of the new church allowed the auditorium to be used again for other community activities.
39. *Quebec Chronicle-Telegraph*, March 17, 1958, p. 1.
40. *Quebec Chronicle-Telegraph*, March 19, 1962, p. 3.
41. *Quebec Chronicle-Telegraph*, March 16, 1964, p. 3.
42. *Quebec Chronicle-Telegraph*, March 18, 1965, p. 3.
43. *Quebec Chronicle-Telegraph*, March 15, 1966, p. 3 and March 18, p. 5.
44. *Le Soleil*, 17 mars 1914, p. 10: "dear little Shamrock" and "God Save Ireland" are in English in the text. Also *Le Soleil*, 18 mars 1918, p. 8.
45. Articles in both *L'Action catholique*, and *L'Evénement-Journal*, 18 mars 1947.
46. Father Honorius Provost, interview 1978.
47. Joe Lonergan is a grandson of turn-of-the-century actor and Soirée director, Richard [Dick] Timmons.
48. See chapter VII.
49. This traditional folktale, Aarne-Thompson tale type 503, "The Gifts of the Little People", is a widespread tale in Irish folklore.
50. Throughout the history of the Matinées and the school shows, there has always been a good mixture of French and Irish among the participants. This is borne out by a look at the names of the performers and crew of the 1990 high school programme: Baller, Bédard, Bélanger, Bérubé, Bouchard, Boucher, Bowles, Cameron, Casolino, Claveau, Cloutier, Corrigan, Cossette, Coulombe, Crawford, Delaney, Desrosiers, Drolet, Dubé, Gagnon, Garon, Gauvin, Giguère, Gingras, Godbout, Goodyer, Gravel, Haché, Hodgson, Hunter, Joncas, Julien, Kack, Kelly, Kilganan, Labar, Labrie, Langlois, Legroulx, Mainguy, McDonald, McEnaney, McKenna, Miville-Dechêne, Monaghan, Moreau, Morin, Mulholland, Murphy, O'Connell, O'Connor, O'Doherty, Perrin, Peters, Poirier, Poulin, Pouliot, Rochette, Royer, Sanfaçon, Seto, Soucy, Thériault, Trudel, Tuppert, Vo, Walsh, and Wong. French family names comprise about 53%, little different from 1979, when they

were 60%. Saint Patrick's High now includes the entire English Catholic secondary population since the merger with Katimavik. Bill 101 having limited access to English language schools, this would indicate that one or both French parents would have received their own primary education in English.

51. Though Irish Protestant children might not go the the Matinées, they sometimes did go to school wearing green ribbons on Saint Patrick's Day. Ross Rourke, interview 1979.
52. Unnamed informant, Holland School, 1990.
53. *Annales de l'Asile Sainte-Brigitte.*
54. Carmen Turpin Vallières and her band have been together since 1975. She made her own singing début as a youngster under Mae Derouin in the Matinée.

Overleaf:
Map by N. Schmitz

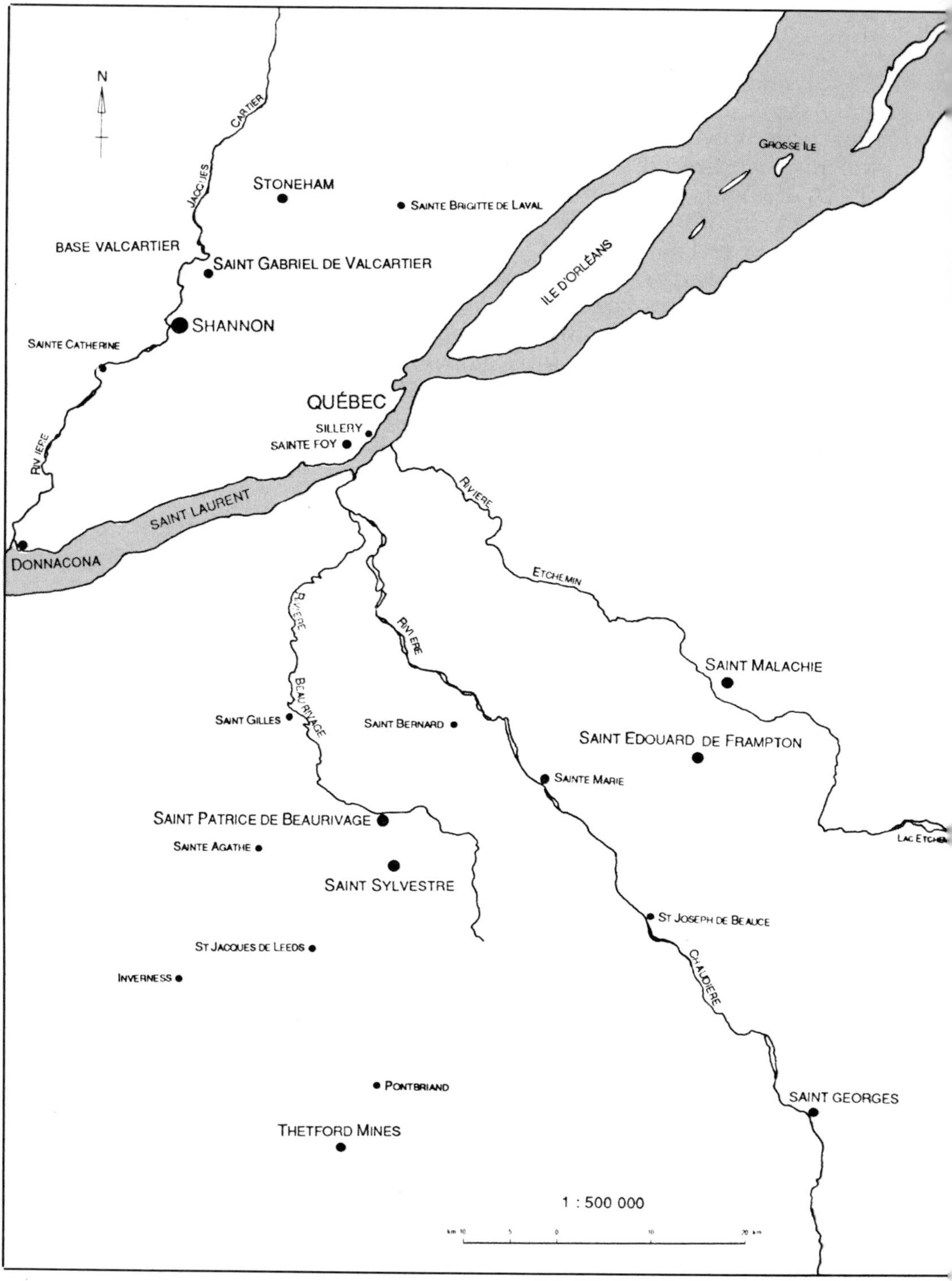
N
JACQUES CARTIER
STONEHAM
SAINTE BRIGITTE DE LAVAL
GROSSE ILE
BASE VALCARTIER
SAINT GABRIEL DE VALCARTIER
ILE D'ORLÉANS
SHANNON
SAINTE CATHERINE
QUÉBEC
SILLERY
SAINTE FOY
RIVIERE
SAINT LAURENT
DONNACONA
RIVIERE ETCHEMIN
RIVIERE BEAURIVAGE
RIVIERE
SAINT MALACHIE
SAINT GILLES
SAINT BERNARD
SAINT EDOUARD DE FRAMPTON
SAINTE MARIE
SAINT PATRICE DE BEAURIVAGE
SAINTE AGATHE
SAINT SYLVESTRE
ST JOSEPH DE BEAUCE
CHAUDIERE
ST JACQUES DE LEEDS
INVERNESS
PONTBRIAND
SAINT GEORGES
THETFORD MINES
1 : 500 000

CHAPTER VI

Rural Communities

While members of the Irish population of the smaller rural communities surrounding Québec City participate in various city-centered festivities, they also hold local celebrations of their own. Not all these communities, however, consider themselves within the direct sphere of influence of Québec City. For geographical or historical reasons, or both, several are more oriented toward the Eastern Townships region or the Trois Rivières and Montréal region. The villages mentioned here are those peripheral to the city, on both the north and south shores of the Saint Lawrence River, whose celebrations are representative of the immediate rural area, and whose interests are, or have been in the past, tied to those of Québec City's Irish community.[1]

These rural communities were mainly settled by Irish immigrants who arrived ahead of the flood of famine immigration during the second half of the 19th century. The Irish who arrived via Grosse Ile during the famine years did not settle in Québec in very great numbers, but merely transited here, moving on to the United States or to western destinations in Canada.[2] As McQuillan and others have pointed out:

> The earlier and more important migration was spread over three decades, from about 1814 to 1844, with peak years in the mid-1820s and the early 1830s. The Irish immigrants in these decades were frequently tenant farmers who had operated small farms in Ireland. They were ambitious individuals, anxious to escape the constraints of tenant farming and to improve opportunities for their children. These were the Irish immigrants who fanned out and settled in pioneer communities along the fringes of the Saint Lawrence valley in the 1820s and 1830s.[3]

The Irish population of these rural areas diminished greatly at the beginning of the 20th century and has done so even further since the 1980s, yet in most areas some form of a Saint Patrick's Day celebration continues to exist.

The North Shore

Irish settlement can be found principally in communities from Sainte Brigitte in the east to Donnacona in the west. Westwards from Donnacona, however, the emphasis shifts toward the Trois Rivières/ Montréal-Laurentian area and away from Québec City's influence. Of the north shore communities examined here, by far the most important is Shannon, which has come to dominate the region in recent years, while the decrease in their Irish population has caused some of the other communities to give up organizing local events. It will be necessary to treat the Shannon event in a separate chapter in order to properly appreciate the significance of its impact on the celebrations in Québec and in the rural areas as a whole.

Donnacona

The Irish population of this shoreline village[4], some forty kilometres to the west of Québec City, was principally drawn to the area because of the presence of the Domtar (now Daishowa) pulp and paper mill industry situated at that time at Donnacona. As a company town, the community was fairly heterogeneous, composed of English and Irish Protestants, Irish Catholics, administrators and workers. On Saint Patrick's Day, apart from the Mass, the celebrations were mainly family-oriented. People wore shamrocks and green ribbons and took a "nip" in honour of the day. Members of Irish families would visit each other during the day, to play cards, drink Irish coffee and sing Irish songs.[5] It was a good excuse for a "gathering of the clans".[6] Various attempts were made to hold events bringing together the different English speaking groups in the community, as well as sympathetic French neighbours and relatives. Generally the forms of entertainment offered were not as appealing to the Irish themselves as the traditional music and singing,[7] in spite of the usual sentiment that everyone could feel themselves Irish on the feast day. As people in the other villages of the periphery did, the Donnacona Irish often took advantage of the activities in Shannon and in Québec City, such as the parade, in the old days, and school shows, when they had children who attended Saint Patrick's schools. By the early 1980s most of the Irish had left the community, for mainly economic reasons, and any who were left preferred to take part in celebrations closer to Québec City or in the city itself.

Saint Gabriel de Valcartier

Located to the east of Shannon, along the Jacques Cartier River, Saint Gabriel was originally situated where the Valcartier Canadian Forces Base is today. The 1914-1918 expropriations which enlarged the Base territory forced the inhabitants to move further east and to reconsolidate the parish in its present location. Together with Shannon, it originally formed part of the Seigneury of Saint Gabriel and of the Fief Saint Ignace, and its recent history is similar to that of Shannon.[8] The settler who had the greatest impact on its development was John Neilson, a Scot who came to Canada in 1791 to work for his uncle, William Brown, owner of *The Quebec Gazette*. In 1815, with Andrew Stuart, the lawyer Louis Moquin, and Nicholas Vincent, chief of the Hurons, Neilson bought up a large tract of land from the Jesuits, and opened up the area to colonisation. Another of its more well-known inhabitants was Alexander Wolff, a former adjutant of the 60th Regiment, who established himself there with his family in 1824, and also attracted his friends to settle in the area with him. The area was principally settled by Irish, English and Scots, both Catholic and Protestant: it contains Saint Gabriel Catholic Church, as well as Anglican, United and Presbyterian churches.[9] Today its population can be considered as anglophone-oriented, though members of all groups feel welcome to participate in the various festive activities.

Saint Patrick's Day in Saint Gabriel was originally a home centered celebration. When weather permitted, people would go to Québec City for the parade, until its disappearance at the beginning of the century. Celebrations organized by the Catholic Women's League were often held at Mont Saint Sacrement and at the Price Brothers'. The 1954 dinner was held at Valcartier Lodge on the evening of the 17th. The guest speaker was Dermot O'Gallagher, and the evening finished with an "Old-Time Dance".[10] In 1967, Valcartier joined Shannon in presenting the Soirée at the Sainte Jeanne d'Arc school on March 11th, while the Canadian centennial year dinner dance itself was held on the 17th at the Drouin Hall in Valcartier Village, the same evening as the Shannon, Saint Patrick's, and Saint Vincent's events.[11] Since the construction of the Valcartier Community Centre in 1973, the principal activity has been a Hot Roast Beef Supper,[12] followed by a "concert", related to but less elaborate than the Shannon show, or simply traditional singing and dancing by residents, with guests joining in. The evening ends with a dance to modern music or a disco. Since many of the same people who participate in the Shannon Irish Show also attend the Saint Gabriel celebrations, for many years now the two events have been planned so that they do not conflict.[13] Although the festivities are under the responsibility of the Saint Gabriel Council of the C.W.L., Saint Patrick's Day is celebrated by everyone, not just the Irish.[14]

The 1985 celebration was a typical one. The roast beef dinner in the Community Centre on Saturday, March 16th, was attended by some 450 people. The Hall was decorated with shamrocks, green streamers and other decorations with Irish themes. The food was cooked by the women of the C.W.L., the men cleaned off the tables and washed the dishes, while the young people helped with the serving of the meal. The dinner attracted people from Québec, Shannon, Sainte Foy, and elsewhere in the area. Even though not all were Irish, everyone was "Irish" for the occasion. Immediately following the meal there was traditional dancing to music provided by the quartet of accordionists Bernie Monaghan and Keith Corrigan, Eric Corrigan on the violin, and Helen Bureau on the piano. The square dancing finished up with Valcartier's favourite, the Lancers. Then the older people retired and the disco music came on, to allow the young people to celebrate in their own way.

The feast day Mass the next day, Sunday the 17th, was preceded by a violin recital given by Bernard Monaghan and Eric Corrigan, accompanied by C.W.L. president, Theresa Whealan, on the organ. Taking as his theme the hymn "Faith of our Fathers", Father Maurice Delisle's sermon traced the beginnings of Saint Gabriel's parish in 1839 to a group of Irish determined to maintain their faith. The server was Danny Johnston, member of an Irish family who has been in Valcartier for five generations. At the end of the service, the singing of "God Save Ireland", accompanied by the musicians, with the addition of Roger Lamont on the guitar, "almost lifted the roof right off".[15]

In Saint Gabriel de Valcartier, the celebration of Saint Patrick's Day with a Hot Roast Beef Supper and dance sponsored by the C.W.L. is still going strong, the most recent having been held on the 10th of March 1990.

Stoneham

Stoneham, Valcartier's neighbouring community, was set up as a township in 1800. The first settlers came around 1817 from the Connecticut region; the majority were Irish, followed by Scots,

Photos Carol Monaghan

In the 1977 Saint Gabriel de Valcartier concert, Eric Corrigan accompanies green-costumed dancers Kathleen and Brian Corrigan, Fern Boyd, and Nancy Adams. The younger generation filled the stage for their enthusiastic contribution.

Photos Carol Monaghan

Saint Patrick's statue in Saint Gabriel Church is given special attention on the feast-day. Lucienne Hamel and Helen Corrigan Bureau preside a table filled with feast-day offerings, including the traditional shamrock-decorated cake, at the 1984 Saint Gabriel de Valcartier Dinner.

English, Germans and others.[16] Owen Murphy, mayor of Québec from 1874 to 1877, was born in Stoneham. Traditionally there was never a very big celebration in Stoneham because of the difficulty of getting over the bad roads in winter. There was always a Mass, however, and people celebrated in their homes, usually with a special cake with green icing and at least a bottle of beer. All the Irish would wear a green ribbon, and sometimes some of the Scots would as well. In the early part of the century, people would go to Québec City for the parade. People also took advantage of the Valcartier festivities, and when celebrations began to be held in the Stoneham ski centre in the early 1970s, the two communities were careful to alternate the two events. Many French members of the community, as well as the senior citizens' group participated in the organisation of the Stoneham event.[17] The Catholic and Anglican churches of Saint Edmond's and Saint Peter's held a special Ecumenical Service in honour of Saint Patrick's Day on the evening of March 16, 1983, at Saint Edmond's. In 1985 and 1986, a Stoneham Irish Variety Show was held during the week after Saint Patrick's Day at the Recreational Centre of Lac Saint Charles. There was "square dancing, singing, an audience sing-along and lots of Irish Coffee".[18]

Sainte Brigitte de Laval

In the early 1830s, the first settlers to obtain land titles in Sainte Brigitte de Laval, some thirty kilometres northeast of Québec, were all of Irish origin. The first baptisms recorded in 1834 and 1835 were those of Peter Dawson, Catherine Dawson and Margaret Gough. It remained a predominantly Irish community until 1870. After that date, the Irish population diminished rapidly, until by the late 1940s it numbered less than one percent.[19] Sister Marie Ursule's extensive monograph on traditional customs in Sainte Brigitte in the late 1940s contains no information on Saint Patrick's Day celebrations, even though she was able to interview a number of English speaking Irish residents.[20] Evidently, those who wished to celebrate Saint Patrick's Day must have done so within the circle of celebrations in Québec City or other neighbouring communities.[21] In spite of the purely Irish origin of Sainte Brigitte, and probably due to its isolated situation, Saint Patrick's Day never seems to have been important enough to leave its mark on the calendar customs of the population. It has now become a completely French community.

The South Shore

Among the parishes on the South Shore of the Saint Lawrence historically noted for their Irish populations, four are particularly valuable for understanding Saint Patrick's Day celebrations in the area. These are Saint Patrice de Beaurivage, Saint Sylvestre de Lotbinière, Saint Edouard de Frampton, and Saint Malachie de Dorchester, all located in the region directly south of Québec City known as the Beauce. Each parish has its own character and maintains different forms of relationships with the other groups in the area.[22] Of these communities, those most directly oriented toward Québec City are those on the eastern side of the Chaudière River, Saint Malachie and Saint Edouard (or Frampton). Historically, the construction of the Craig Road along the western side of the Chaudière and Beaurivage rivers directed the interests of that region towards Mégantic County and the Eastern Townships. Thus the celebrations of the population of the sister parishes of Saint Patrice and Saint Sylvestre on the western side of the Chaudière have, in the long run, become more oriented towards Thetford Mines and its neighbouring communities of Leeds and Inverness, among others.

The Irish in the Beauce today are a minority within the francophone majority, in spite of the importance of their presence during the 19th century. The impact of Irish settlers upon the history of the region is most evident in the number of French speaking people with Irish surnames or an Irish ancestor, who in various ways, partly through their participation in Saint Patrick's Day celebrations, maintain and interpret Irish traditions. The feast could not be maintained without some francophone support, as is the case throughout the Québec City region.

The persons in the Frampton–Saint Malachie area who participate in Saint Patrick's Day celebrations are, for the most part, English and French speaking people of Irish descent, while the Beaurivage festivities include more anglophones of English and Scottish origin, both Catholic and Protestant. This group is composed principally of middle-aged or elderly persons, for whom leaving their region of origin is difficult or out of the question. Young people tend to go away to study or to find employment in urban Québec or elsewhere in Canada, especially Ontario. Some of the Irish families who have stayed in the region are those whose families have lived there over a period of five to seven generations, and who have remained for family reasons rather than economic advantage.

Saint Sylvestre and Saint Patrice de Beaurivage

Saint Sylvestre and Saint Patrice de Beaurivage are agricultural communities in Lotbinière County, about seventy kilometres south of Québec City.[23] Both originally formed part of the Seigneury of Saint Gilles de Beaurivage, first conceded in 1738. In 1782, it was acquired by Alexander Fraser, a former captain of the 24th Infantry. The first settlers to receive concession titles from Fraser were fifteen German colonists. Fraser's grandson, Walter Davidson, inherited the Seigneury, but when he died prematurely, the succession was given to his sister Jane and her husband, David Ross.[24] At the beginning of the 19th century, the Rosses encouraged colonisation by French, Irish, Scottish and English settlers, as well as the original Germans, and the Irish were soon in the majority in Saint Sylvestre. Around 1840, Ross settled a further 200 destitute Irish families sent him by immigration authorities. At that time, Saint Patrice was still part of Saint Sylvestre, which had been established as a parish in 1829. The distances the settlers had to travel to worship at Saint Gilles or Saint Sylvestre, as well as the presence of such a large Irish Catholic population, encouraged Ross to grant land for the founding of a chapel in Saint Patrice, and after many difficulties, it was established as a separate parish in 1871.

The early history of the Beaurivage parishes shows the Irish there to have been in greater conflict with their French neighbours than in other parts of the Québec area,[25] resulting in their isolation to a certain extent from both Catholic French and Protestant English. Today there are few Irish families remaining in Saint Sylvestre and Saint Patrice. The social life of the remaining Irish has become oriented towards the area to the southwest: Sainte Agathe, Leeds, Inverness, Pontbriand, and Thetford Mines, rather than towards Québec City.

For a time, early in the century, there was a parade held in Saint Sylvestre with horse-drawn floats and, once, a drummer from Leeds. The whole population of the village, Irish and French, participated. It ceased to exist, however before the First World War.[26] Until the 1950s, Saint Patrick's Day was "a great day for the Irish". At the convent boarding school, run by the Good Shepherd nuns with an English class for the Irish, there would be a special Mass in the morning, with singing by the girls' choir from the school, followed in the afternoon by a patriotic presentation by the students.[27] The show would include plays, acts, songs, step-dancing, and the singing of

"God Save Ireland". The presentation would have been prepared months in advance by the nuns, and it was much appreciated by the parents and Irish members of the community. The children would receive "candies and goodies" from the adults who attended the Mass and show; they would then be given the rest of the day off school. The Irish would wear something green for the celebration, an article of clothing, a necktie, a hat, a ribbon or bow, or a shamrock. These were the only formally organized events in the community. However, there was an informal round of activities. The mother of the household would prepare a special cake covered with green icing. In the evening there would be house parties, which would include card-playing, story-telling and jokes, singing, dancing, and — drinking.

> The Irish would get together, and if they had a little drink, they could be merry, and sing and dance on Saint Patrick's Day, if they had it.[28]

In Saint Patrice, celebrations also traditionally consisted of music and dancing. In former days, there would be an English Mass in the parish Church for Saint Patrick's Day, and in bad weather, there would be cake and tea served at the place where horses were left during the mass.[29] The children from Saint Patrice attended the convent school in Saint Sylvestre and participated in the show presented for their families. As in Saint Sylvestre, there would be house-parties in the evening. The main activities at these parties were square-dancing and singing, with music furnished by local musicians, such as fiddler Edgar Burns. Later the Irish had to make do with fiddlers who were not very familiar with Irish music, and these were less appreciated by the older members of the community. Generally the parties would be held if at all possible in spite of bad weather. By the end of the 1970s, the local Irish people had begun going to combined Saint Patrick's Day parties in neighbouring villages.

As the Irish population of Saint Sylvestre and Saint Patrice steadily decreased, so did the feast day activities. After the closing of the boarding school in the sixties, there were no more shows as such and house parties, except in rare cases, ceased to exist. There were no more English classes in Saint Sylvestre. The Good Shepherd Irish nuns returned to Québec City and the children were transferred to Québec City or Thetford Mines. From 1951-1964, the Canadian Forces operated a radar station near Saint Sylvestre, and during those years there was a Mass and school entertainment at the base on Saint Patrick's Day.[30] In 1979, an effort made to organize a separate party in Saint Patrice was not very successful, since half the people stayed and the other half went to Thetford Mines.

A Saint Patrick's Day Mass is still celebrated in the parish church at Saint Sylvestre, but the congregation is largely French. In Saint Patrice, it is scarcely noted. Since there are not enough Irish in any one village to warrant organizing major activities, the dance now rotates between the different villages in the region. It may draw as many as 300 people, since not only Irish, but also English, Scottish, and French people attend. Today the inhabitants of Saint Patrice, like Saint Sylvestre, join the combined celebrations within the Sainte Agathe–Thetford Mines circuit. At the 1990 Saint Patrick's Day dance on March 17th in Sainte Agathe, there were people from Saint Bernard, Saint Gilles, Saint Sylvestre, and Inverness. Green dress was very much in evidence, while people danced traditional square dances accompanied by local fiddlers and callers.[31]

Saint Edouard and Saint Malachie

The history of these two communities is similar to that of Saint Sylvestre and Saint Patrice. Saint Edouard and Saint Malachie[32] were originally part of the Seigneury of Lauzon, which was subsequently subdivided in part into the townships of West Frampton (Saint Edouard) and East Frampton (Saint Malachie). Saint Edouard is situated some sixty-five kilometres south of Québec City. It was named in honour of Edouard Desbarats, the founder of the township of West Frampton, who arrived around 1820. Today, it is simply known as Frampton. East Frampton was settled under the leadership of William Henderson, the organizer of the "Canada Fire Insurance Company" in 1818. His brother, Gilbert Henderson, bought up lots in East Frampton from his brother and from demobilized soldiers who were not interested in settling on the lands they had received as grants from the government after the War of 1812. After becoming seigneur of East Frampton in 1814, he encouraged the settlement of the area by Irish and Scots immigrants during the first half of the 19th century. Among the first Irish settlers were Connell, Corrigan, Cullen, Dillon, Doyle, Fitzgerald, Kennedy, Kilcullen, Kinsella, Lonergan, Lyons, O'Farrell, and Quigley. There was even a concession in East Frampton named Saint Patrick, though with the increase in French settlement in the area after the 1870s, it subsequently became known as "la Crapaudière".

The village of Saint Malachie was founded on the concession of Ballyporeen, where Irish immigrants had replaced the original

French owners of the lands. Like Saint Patrice, Saint Malachie was originally a mission area, served from Saint Edouard. The mission was founded in response to a need to bring the church closer to the inhabitants of the area. From 1841 to 1845, mass was celebrated in private homes. A chapel was approved and erected during this time, and was consecrated in December 1845, under the name of Saint Malachie.[33] Until 1855, all the parish priests of Saint Edouard had been Irish. The first French pastor was Father Odilon Paradis[34], who arranged for Saint Malachie to have its own parish priest, the first of whom was Father Louis Léon Rousseau, named in 1857. It became a canonical parish in 1874. By the beginning of the 20th century, there were about one-third Irish and two-thirds French families in the parish, since the Protestants tended to sell off their lands to French settlers. The construction of the railroad also brought a number of Italians into the Frampton–Saint Malachie area.

Saint Edouard de Frampton

At the end of the 19th century, there seems to have been a Saint Patrick's Day parade in Saint Edouard, but it was discontinued before the First World War. Traditionally Saint Patrick's Day was celebrated by a Mass, followed by an evening concert and a euchre party at the convent, where the Irish nuns tried to instill patriotic traditions in the children. There were also house parties, with square-dancing late into the night. People would wear green and try to outdo each other in the number of typical accessories, such as hats, bouquets and shamrocks they wore. By the end of the 1970s, only the euchre party remained. It was organized within the regular Church activities and attended by more French than Irish. The Irish presence is practically extinct today. In 1979, the Mass in honour of Saint Patrick was not even held. The last Irish parish priest, Father Humphrey, retired in 1966. The Irish did at least wear shamrocks at the regular weekday Mass on the feast day.[35] Both Irish and French interested in maintaining the festive tradition now join in the celebrations at Saint Malachie.

Saint Malachie de Dorchester

Saint Malachie itself has continued to affirm its Irish identity, in spite of the diminishing numbers of Irish within the French

Photos Sister Ann Travers

Saint Patrick's Day in Saint Sylvestre School in 1961 and in 1962.

Photo Monica Quigley

Photo Joan Quigley Blais

1961 Saint Patrick's Day at Lemire's Hotel in Saint Malachie. O'Farrells: uncles, fathers and sons: Bobby, John, Patrick, Joseph, Joseph Jr, Jimmy.

The new generation in Saint Malachie in 1979.

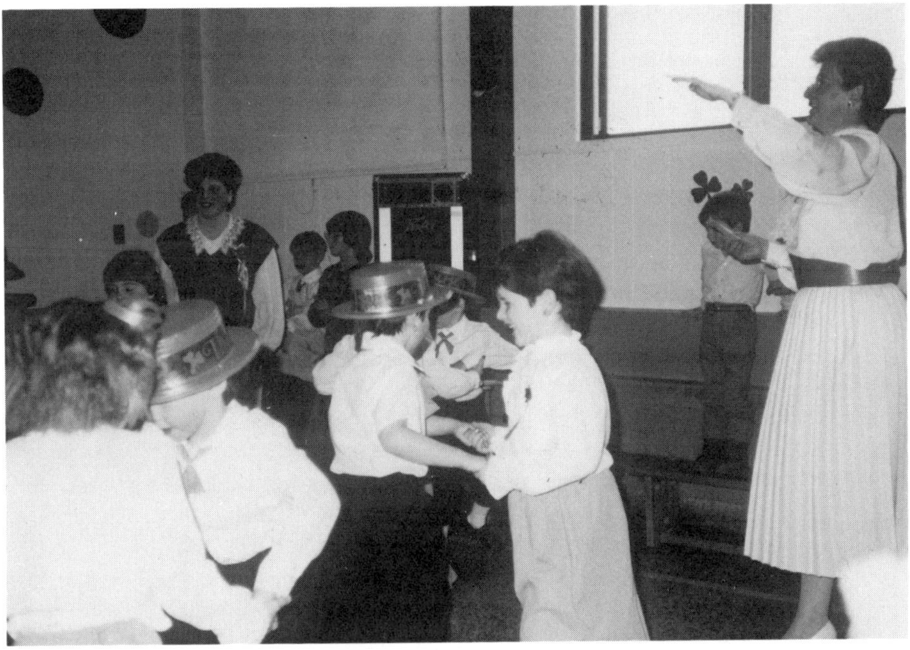

Photos kindness of Joan Quigley Blais

The Saint Malachie children are no strangers to square dancing. Here Joan Quigley Blais puts the performers through their paces in 1979.

Photos kindness of Joan Quigley Blais

Jim and Joan Quigley trained dancers and players for the 1979 Saint Malachie's show. Rehearsals were as much fun to watch as the actual performance itself.

population. During the late 19th century, Saint Patrick's Day was celebrated by card-playing and traditional singing and dancing. Around the beginning of the 20th century,[36] when the strictness of the Lenten observance caused the dance to be eliminated, the celebration consisted mainly of a dinner with invited speakers, followed by a card party. With the relaxation of this attitude, dancing once more became part of the celebration. Since 1935 the Saint Patrick's Day activities have been organized locally by the Saint Patrick's Society and are its principal activity of the year.[37]

The events begin with a Mass in the parish church, the only occasion during the year when the service is in English except for funerals of Irish members of the community. During the afternoon and evening, there are different activities which bring in all the members of the community, from children to adults. Over the years, these have varied slightly in content, but the idea of an all-day, whole community celebration continues to exist.

During the 1950s, the Mass was in the morning, attended by prominent members of the community, both French and Irish.

> We'd sing: 'Grace and Glory, Saint Patrick'. We would take the roof off the church.[38]

This was followed in the afternoon by a programme of movies and other treats for the children. The evening activities were mainly for adults, and included speeches by local dignitaries. One year the banquet was held at Lemire's Hotel.[39] At the 1955 service, the president of the Saint Jean Baptiste Society, Emile Fleury, together with Joseph O'Farrell, treasurer of the Saint Patrick's Society, took up the collection. That evening, the dinner speakers included Mayor J.A. Michaud and Francis O'Farrell.[40] In 1956, the feast-day fell on a Saturday and George Lafontaine,[41] president of the Saint Patrick's Society, with the other organizers took full advantage of the day. The festivities began in the morning with a Solemn High Mass in the parish church, celebrated by the pastor, Father Emile Bourassa. This was followed at one-thirty in the afternoon by an animated colour cartoon and games and treats for the children of the community, though adults were also welcome to attend. The social evening was preceded by a showing at seven-thirty of the film "My Wild Irish Rose", followed by an auction, and addresses by the mayor and other persons of note in the community. The climax of the evening was a programme of special entertainment, traditional numbers with a sing-along for the members of the audience, the whole accompanied by a popular dance orchestra.[42]

People would come from Québec City for the celebration, and as in Shannon and elsewhere, Saint Patrick's Day was an occasion for sons and daughters of Saint Malachie families who had left the community to come home for a festive reunion, provided the notorious "Saint Patrick's Day storm" did not prevent them. As elsewhere, green dress, shamrocks, ribbons, rosettes and Society badges have always been much in evidence.

By the 1970s, the programme had undergone some slight adaptations. The Mass was held around five-thirty in the evening, instead of in the morning, even though in 1979 Saint Patrick's Day again fell on a Saturday. The Mass was followed by a banquet in the parish hall. At the head table were seated the officers of the Saint Patrick's Society, the parish priest and members of the older families in the community. After the supper, there was music and singing,[43] speeches and "blarney", that is, Irish stories. The president of the Society would welcome the guests, the parish priest would say a few words, and there was often an invited speaker. The dance which followed would continue as long as the hall was open, or, as the saying went, "the party would last until Saint Joseph's Day."[44] It was attended by both French members of the community and English speaking people, including Irish Protestants, from the surrounding communities. Only about 400 people could be seated for the banquet, so that sometimes people had to be turned away for lack of space. As far as attendance at the banquet was concerned, the only requirement was to buy a ticket as quickly as possible. There was no distinction made between French and English, or Protestant and Catholic. In general, however, the banquet and the Irish traditional sing-along that accompanied it were favoured by the Irish members of the community, while French spouses and others would come along for the dance afterwards.[45]

Both the Irish and French in Saint Malachie took advantage of Saint Patrick's Day in 1985, to celebrate the 50th anniversary of the founding of the Saint Patrick's Society. The activities began with an Irish pub on Saturday, the 16th, at two o'clock in the afternoon in the Quatre Vents school. The show used as its framework Saint Malachie in olden times, and the programme was made up of Irish songs and dances, including traditional dancing by a group of children, some as young as four years old. An English Mass was said at five-thirty in the parish church, during which there was a special programme of singing. Following the Mass, a banquet was held in the Hall.[46] A special feature of the banquet was a huge birthday cake, covered with green icing and decorations. One of the Society's

Photo François Pouliot

Photo La Voix du Sud

Photo François Pouliot

Farrell Quigley, Irene Cassidy, Joan Quigley Blais, and Larry Quigley were in charge of the 1987 Saint Patrick's Day festivities in Saint Malachie. The 1988 show at the primary school was made up of patriotic sketches and songs by the school children, under the direction of English teacher Annie Quigley.

Quebec Chronicle-Telegraph

ST.P … DAY

DINNER

AT VALCARTIER LODGE

Sponsored by Valcartier Subdivision of the Catholic Women's League

WEDNESDAY, MARCH 17th at 7 O'clock

• Dinner to be followed by Old-Time Dance

Guest Speaker: **D. I. O'GALLAGHER**

Adults .. $2.00 —— Children .. $1.00

For reservations, please telephone

Valcartier Lodge — Loretteville, Que.

Phone VI 2-8007

People attending the dance may obtain tickets at the door.

1954

CELEBRATE

ST. PATRICKS DAY

WITH A **DINNER** AT

L'AUBERGE DES PINS

LAKE ST. JOSEPH

Sponsored by Valcartier Subdivision of the Catholic Women's League

THURSDAY, MARCH 17th at 7 P. M.

• Dinner to be followed by Old-Time Dance

People attending the dance may obtain tickets at the door.

Guest Speaker: **CHARLES WALSH**

Adults — $2.00 —— Children — $1.00

For reservations, please telephone

Mrs. HUGH KACK

LORETTEVILLE: VI-2-3369

BEST WISHES

From

CARRIER & GOULET

118 BRIDGE ST., QUEBEC

1955

CELEBRATE

St. Patrick's DAY

WITH A **DINNER** AT

L'AUBERGE DES PINS

LAKE ST. JOSEPH

Sponsored by Valcartier Subdivision of the Catholic Women's League

SATURDAY, MARCH 17th at 7.30 P. M.

• Dinner to be followed by Old-Time Dance

People attending the dance may obtain tickets at the door

Guest Speaker: **Dr. LARKIN KERWIN**

ADMISSION — — — $2.00

For reservations, please telephone

Mrs. HUGH KACK

LORETTEVILLE: VI-2-3369

BEST WISHES

From

CARRIER & GOULET

118 BRIDGE ST., QUEBEC

1956

original founders, Arthur Healy, its first secretary, was presented with a plaque in honour of the anniversary. After the dinner, people went upstairs and danced for the rest of the evening, to the music of Pat Métivier and his band. The children performed their dances again, this time accompanied by the adults[47].

Since 1986, the Saint Patrick's Day celebrations have continued to be held on the Saturday nearest the 17th, at the Quatre Vents primary school in the afternoon, and in the evening at the Parasol Hall. The 1987 show featured a skit at the afternoon performance, with players Marc and John Blais, Larry Quigley, Nancy Kilganon, and Stewart Humphrey. The 1988 choral group was directed by Annie Quigley, English teacher in the school. Another feature of the celebration for several years has been the presence at the festivities of a person costumed as Saint Patrick himself. The local member of parliament, Solicitor General Pierre Blais, was guest of honour on more than one occasion. While the feast-day Mass is now generally said in French, the hymns are sung in English. The regional dance troupe Manigance performed Irish dances at the dinner dance in 1989, fresh from their success the previous evening at the Saint Patrick's parish event in the city. The guests at the 1989 dinner came from as far away as Ireland and Norway, as well as from other regions of Canada. The 1989 and 1990 celebrations included a ski competition, the "Irish Cup", at La Crapaudière ski centre, in addition to the usual Mass and dinner dance. These occasions serve to reinforce the determination of Saint Malachie's citizens to continue to affirm their Irish heritage. They are resolved that their Saint Patrick's Day celebrations will still be going strong for many years to come.[48]

In the rural areas around Québec City, the Irish population has thus adapted itself with varying degrees of success to the changing demographic and social climate over the years. With the consolidation of the organisation of Saint Patrick's Day celebrations on the one hand, and on the other a continuing support of appropriate activities by the different ethnic groups, Saint Patrick's Day seems in no danger of disappearing from the calendar of festive occasions.

Notes

1. This section contains material based on interviews, during fieldwork in 1978 by the author and by Marianna O'Gallagher and in 1979 by field workers William Moss, Frances Slaney and Richard Stephani, of the following persons: Saint Gabriel de Valcartier: Helen Corrigan Bureau, Temple Clark, Clare Haberlin McBain, Derek McBain, Bernard Monaghan, and Joan Lamont Sheehan; Stoneham: Mr and Mrs Frank Corrigan and Jack Dunn; Sainte Brigitte de Laval: Marcel Marceau and Henri Mountain; Donnacona: Mrs Eddy [Patricia] Burke, Helen Burke, Mr and Mrs William Cleary, and Mrs Patricia Gurny St-Pierre; Cap Santé: David Berryman; Saint Sylvestre: Joseph and Marion Donahue, Edmund Hogan, Dennis Hooley, Mrs Frank [Mary] Hooley, Mrs McKinney, Mrs Eddie [Mary McCourt] Moran; Saint Patrice: Nelly Brown, Edgar Burns, Mary Burns, Bert and Pat Mulleavey; Saint Edouard de Frampton: Mrs Bernard Hennessey, and Mrs Elizabeth Courtney Kelly; Saint Malachie: Mrs Thomas [Helen O'Farrell] Quigley, John O'Farrell, and James Quigley.
2. A partial exception to this phenomenon was the adoption, and subsequent absorption by the French population, of a large number of Irish children orphaned by the various epidemics associated with the famine ships. M. O'Gallagher, *Grosse-Ile: Gateway to Canada, 1832-1937*, passim. See also Houston and Smyth, "Irish Emigrants to Canada: Whence They Came", p. 34.
3. D. Aidan McQuillan, "Beaurivage: The Development of an Irish Ethnic Identity in Rural Quebec," p. 264. See also John Mannion, *Irish Settlements in Eastern Canada*, p. 15-32.
4. Included in the Donnacona region are neighbouring Cap Santé and the village of Les Ecureuils.
5. Mrs Patricia Burke, interview 1979.
6. David Berryman, interview 1979.
7. Mr and Mrs William Cleary, interview 1979.
8. See below, p. 209-210.
9. Johanne Robinson et al., *St Gabriel de Valcartier*, p. 4-10.
10. Which probably included Valcartier's favourite "Lancers".
11. *Quebec Chronicle-Telegraph*, March 10, 1967, p. 5, and March 17, p. 10.
12. In the 1970s it began as a cold turkey supper. Helen Bureau, interview 1979.
13. See below, p. 214-215.
14. Johanne Robinson et al., *St-Gabriel de Valcartier*, p. 50; *Quebec Chronicle-Telegraph*, March 20, 1985, p. 7.
15. *Quebec Chronicle-Telegraph*, March 20, 1985, p. 7.
16. *Quebec Chronicle-Telegraph*, June 13, 1979, p.2.
17. Jack Dunn, interview 1979.
18. *Quebec Chronicle-Telegraph*, March 12, 1986, p. 8.
19. Sister Marie Ursule, *Civilisation traditionnelle des Lavalois*, p. 13-65.
20. Under the heading "Feast-days in the month of March", she mentions only the feasts of Saint Joseph and the Annunciation, and a novena in honour of Saint Francis Xavier. *Civilisation traditionnelle des Lavalois*, p. 78-79.
21. The 1979 research found no trace of a local celebration, nor could people interviewed in 1990 remember there having been one. Sainte Brigitte is included

here because of its proximity to Québec and the strength of its early Irish settlement.

22. See McQuillan, "Beaurivage," for an insight into these differences.
23. Historical material is taken from Julien Bilodeau, *Saint-Sylvestre se raconte: 1828-1978*, and André Nadeau, *Histoire de la paroisse de Saint-Patrice de Beaurivage: 1871-1946*.
24. The seigneurial line ended in the late 1940s when the seigneury was sold by Mrs W.A. [Dorothy Ross] Lewis, the great-granddaughter of David Ross.
25. For a discussion of the conflicts in the Beaurivage area, see McQuillan, "Beaurivage," passim.
26. Marion [Mrs Joseph] Donahue, interview 1979.
27. Documents from Sister Sarah Ann Travers, 1979.
28. Mary Eddie [Mary McCourt] Moran, Mrs McKinney, Marion Donahue, Bert and Pat Mulleavey, interviews 1979.
29. March 17th was also the traditional beginning of the maple sugar season, the day the roads were cleared into the sugar bush, to begin tapping the trees. Nelly Brown, interview 1979.
30. Marion Donahue, interview 1979.
31. Information from Normand Legault, Centre de Valorisation du Patrimoine Vivant, Québec, March 1990.
32. Historical material for this section is taken from J.-A. Kirouac, *Histoire de la paroisse de Saint-Malachie*, and Patrick Redmond, *Irish Life in Rural Quebec: A History of Frampton*.
33. "The eastern half then became known as Saint Malachie because its early settlers came from Armagh, where that saint is greatly venerated." Redmond, *Irish Life in Rural Quebec*, p. 10.
34. He founded the parish of Saint Odilon de Cranbourne, which was named in his honour.
35. Elizabeth Courtney Kelly, interview 1979.
36. A dispensation was granted in 1925 to permit the celebration of the feast. See above, p. 81.
37. The Society was founded in 1935 and celebrated its 50th anniversary on Saint Patrick's Day in 1985. Although its numbers are somewhat reduced, it is "looking forward to its 75th anniversary". *Quebec Chronicle-Telegraph*, March 20, 1985, p. 7. See also *La Voix du Sud*, 19 mars 1985.
38. Mrs Thomas [Helen O'Farrell] Quigley, interview 1978.
39. Mrs Thomas Quigley, interview 1978.
40. *Quebec Chronicle-Telegraph*, March 18, 1955, p. 5.
41. His mother was an O'Farrell.
42. *Quebec Chronicle-Telegraph*, March 14, 1956, p. 5.
43. In 1979, square-dancing was reintroduced and taught to children of Irish descent. In the old days, people learned to dance at house parties. There would always be someone who knew the dances and who would teach the young boys, so they would not have to display their ignorance. James Quigley, interview 1979.
44. John O'Farrell, interview 1979. Saint Joseph's Day falls on March 19th.
45. John O'Farrell and James Quigley, interviews 1979.
46. There were 400 people at the dinner. Attendance at the dinner has varied from some 150 in 1986, 200 in 1987 and 1988, to about 350 in 1989. Source, *La Voix du Sud*, passim.

47. *La Voix du Sud*, 19 mars 1985, p. 14; Quebec Chronicle-Telegraph, March 20, 1985, p. 7. Métivier's mother was a Simms.
48. Many people have helped to maintain the Saint Malachie traditions in recent years. Among them have been Joan Quigley Blais, Irene Cassidy, Theresa O'Farrell Gagnon, Alvin Hickey, Rita Hickey, Helen Lafontaine, Stewart Humphrey, Lawrence and Pauline O'Farrell, Francis O'Farrell, Louis O'Farrell, Annie Quigley, Farrell Quigley, Georgette Bernard Quigley, James Quigley, Annie Simms, Joseph Simms, Mary Simms, and Margaret Whealan, as well as the late Eileen O'Farrell Kilganan. The Saint Patrick's Society also received ethnic minorities grants in 1985 and in 1987 from the Québec government to help defray Saint Patrick's Day expenses. While Manigance did not perform at the 1990 feast, they have already been engaged for the 1991 event.

Overleaf:

The 1980 Programme cover was designed by Debbie Babin Healy

St. Joseph's Council C.W.L.

Fifteenth Shannon Irish Show

1980

'His gold has never been found. Maybe it is just a legend, but a legend is like a dream. It could come true ... and it could happen to you!'

CHAPTER VII

The Shannon Irish Show

In the small community of Shannon, located some 30 kilometres to the northwest of Québec City, the Saint Patrick's Day celebration has been gathering momentum for the last twenty-five years. Though the grand Matinées and Soirées have come to an end in Québec City itself, the Shannon people have taken up the challenge and evolved a worthy successor. The Shannon Irish Show has become important over the years as a focal point for the anglophone element in the communities surrounding it, as well as an attraction for the Québec metropolitan area and beyond.[1]

Shannon and the Irish

The municipality of Shannon, like Saint Gabriel de Valcartier, is located on land which originally formed part of the Seigneurie de Saint Gabriel, granted to the Jesuits in 1657. It later became part of the Seigneurie de Fossambault, and was known as *l'établissement Saint Patrick sur la Rivière Jacques-Cartier*, or Saint Patrick's Mission, because of the large number of Irish settlers in the area. In 1824, the whole area was designated as the civil and canonical parish of Sainte Catherine de Fossambault. In 1845 the latter became a municipality, of which Shannon was a part until 1946, when it separated from Sainte Catherine. During this century, the community was reduced to its present size as a result of two federal expropriations, one in 1914 and the other, much more extensive, in 1965, in favour of the expansion of the Valcartier Canadian Forces Base[2] On April 1st, 1981, Shannon became part of the Municipal Regional County of Jacques Cartier, made up of Saint Gabriel de Valcartier, Sainte Catherine, Lac Saint Joseph, Lac Delage, Saint Dunstan du Lac Beauport, Fossambault sur le Lac, Stoneham-Tewkesbury, Sainte Brigitte de Laval and Saint Gabriel Ouest[3]. The Shannon Show rallies people from many of these areas, including C.F.B. Valcartier, as participants or spectators.

Shannon is like much of the Québec area in being a settlement of Irish immigrants who arrived mainly before the great tide of immigration in the 1840s. There is a tendency to belittle the residents' claims to be non-famine Irish, but a look at the early records shows a strong presence of Irish names in the parish registers as early as 1821.[4] There were certainly later arrivals during the famine years and right up to the middle of this century, and ties remain alive between certain families in the community and their relatives in Ireland.

Today, in a Shannon reduced by the successive expropriations, the official population stands at 1250 (in 1990). Of this number, the ratio of anglophones to francophones has dropped from somewhere around nine to one to about one to two. The biggest change has come about in the last ten to fifteen years. The "Irish enclave" has been more and more diluted by the loss of its young people and the influx of city people looking for a quiet place to live. An unofficial estimate puts the linguistic composition of the population at about 30-40% "Irish"[5] to 60-70% French. This is in contrast to ten or fifteen years ago, when the percentage of Irish was much greater, some say as high as 90%.

Kinship and Friendship

When it comes to the Shannon Irish Show, however, these percentages are drastically reversed. Over 90% of the participants in the show and in the audience are "Irish" and anglophones. The francophones who are either in the show itself or in the audience are usually there for reasons of kinship or friendship: they either have a spouse or relative who is Irish or a friend or neighbour who encourages them to come. The rest of the French population either knows nothing of the show or tends to dismiss it as something that does not directly concern them.

There are, of course, those prominent members of the ecclesiastical, political or commercial institutions in the community who are always represented. For example, during the 1990 show, the master of ceremonies welcomed the new mayor of Shannon, Jean-Pierre Soucy, who replaced the Irish mayor, Maureen Maher[6]. The parish priest of Shannon, Father Marceau, as well as the former pastor of Saint Catherine's, Father Painchaud, are always honoured guests at one or both of the performances. Other dignitaries included representatives from Canadian Forces Base Valcartier, and from the Saint Patrick's and Saint Gabriel's Councils of the Catholic Women's League, the president of Voice of English Québec, the president of Shannon Vision, the assistant principal of Alexander Wolff, the Valcartier Base school, city council members, and so forth.

Families, friends and well-wishers gather from far and wide to attend the show. People come from the different parishes in Québec City and from other rural communities. Every year one or two busloads of people from the village of Inverness (Mégantic County) faithfully attend the matinée. Buses are arranged for groups from Québec City, such as VEQ and the Fifty Plus Club. If the Saint Patrick's Parish banquet falls on the same day, people will go to the Mass at Saint Patrick's, rush out to the matinée performance of the Shannon Show, and then back for the evening's festivities in the city. Family members return for the occasion from such places as Ottawa, Toronto, Halifax, and Montréal. Visitors from the United States, as far away as Michigan, arrive for the festivities. For some families, Saint Patrick's Day is a time of reunion similar to Christmas or Easter.

In 1988, a short study was undertaken to discover what ties of kinship or friendship bound together the people most directly involved in the performance of the show itself: the hundred or so persons whose names appeared in the programme, either on the stage or behind the scenes, as performers, stagehands, technicians, and coordinators. It was found that 62% of these more or less "official" participants were members by birth or by marriage (i.e. spouses, children, grandchildren or cousins) of basically only five families. It is no coincidence that these included the names of some of the oldest families in the Shannon area: King, Kiley, Conway, Kelly, Neville, and Maher. Two of these extended families actually furnished a third of all those listed. Approximately nine-tenths of the participants were from Shannon, with one-tenth coming from the surrounding communities or Base Valcartier. Anglophones accounted for 90%, and the francophone participants were all residents of Shannon.[7]

In 1989, another survey among Shannon residents showed that the average anglophone family who has lived for two years or more in Shannon, has participated at least to the extent of having been a member of the audience, if not an actual performer or organizer. Most of the francophones who have participated in the past have also come out of friendship for neighbours or because of family. A francophone member of the audience said she attended because her husband was Irish. Although she could not understand the words to the songs nor the jokes, she enjoyed the singing and dancing.[8] The Shannon Irish

Show thus seems to appeal to anglophones and Irish wherever in the Québec region they may be, and to francophones because of community or family ties.[9]

History of the Show

Early in this century, Saint Patrick's Day festivities in the Sainte-Catherine/Shannon area resembled those elsewhere in the Québec region. People would gather together for "house parties", traditional singing and dancing in private homes. There might be a cake with green icing, someone would play an instrument, and people would sing old songs handed down from their parents. Then in the early 1920s, Mrs Joseph L. Griffin and Miss E. O'Reilly organized concerts which were held in White's Hotel or Sainte Catherine's Church Hall. In 1921, this "Fine Irish Concert" included a musical comedy, "The Limerick Boy", recitations, songs, traditional Irish music and an Irish jig.[10] In 1954, the concerts began to be formally organized by the Saint Joseph's council of the Catholic Women's League, and were held in the Old Shannon Hall. The following year, the C.W.L. offered a supper, as well as the concert.[11] The concerts attracted such large crowds that they had to be discontinued for lack of adequate space. The hall could too easily have become a fire-trap.[12] When the show was started up once more, it was again the C.W.L. who undertook to make it a success. It has continued to be sponsored by the Shannon C.W.L., and is its major activity of the year. During the 25th Show in 1990, the C.W.L., in the person of its president, Elaine Neville, was presented with a plaque in appreciation for the 39 years of work by the League in the community.

The present Shannon Irish Show began its career as an annual event in 1966. In the beginning, it was held at two different times: an afternoon show for the children on the Saturday nearest Saint Patrick's Day, and an evening show on the Sunday or on the 17th, Saint Patrick's Day itself. As the years went by, it gradually developed into a one-day performance in two parts, the Matinée and the Soirée, always held on a Saturday near Saint Patrick's Day. In later years, the Shannon Irish Show has been held on either of two Saturdays, the nearest or the second nearest to Saint Patrick's Day, alternating with the Saint Patrick's Day Hot Roast Beef Supper and Dance put on by the C.W.L. in neighbouring Saint Gabriel de Valcartier. For example, in 1986, 1987, 1988, 1989, and 1991, the Shannon Show was held on March 15, 7, 12, 11, and 9, with the 25th Show in 1990 on the Day itself, Saturday March 17th, while Saint Gabriel's supper and dance took place on March 8, 14, 19, 18, 10, and in 1991 on the 16th. Since many of the same people are involved in the two events, this system of staggering avoids conflict and allows everyone to enjoy both, rather than having to choose between them.[13]

In 1966, the show was held at Dollard des Ormeaux School on Base Valcartier and in 1967 at Sainte Jeanne d'Arc School. From 1968 to 1974, it was held in Sainte Catherine's School Auditorium. The new Shannon Recreation Center was built in 1974, and the shows have been held there ever since March 1975. The Center seats about 450 people and the combined audiences of the two performances have in the past averaged from as high as 1100 people, with standing room only, several years ago, to about 800 in 1989. In 1990, however, almost 900 people attended, about 100 more than the previous year. The organizers use a system of ribbons to keep track of those who have paid their entry fee. These figures take into account, however, the usual number of people who might have neglected to take their token, and of course the official and unofficial participants in the show itself. Thus the true attendance figure is always a little higher than the official one.

Performance and Performers

For the first year or two, the Show relied on a combination of Irish-American and local Shannon traditional songs and local folk dancing traditions, such as Quadrilles and Lancers. As time went by, it settled into its present format, and since the late 1970s it has remained virtually unchanged from year to year, although the exact content will vary according to the person responsible for a particular year's programme. For example, trial and error showed that people were not particularly interested in a show that had an American "Bing Crosby" Irish flavour. Also, the family and community participation mentioned above demanded a format which would allow the exploiting of a variety of skills. If a person cannot dance, it is very likely that he or she can at least sing well enough to be part of one of the singing groups, generally divided according to age. There is also the skit or one-act play, which allows those with some dramatic ability to show their stuff.

At the same time, without being "commercial", the show has come to demand a certain level of competence. Each year, the different parts of the show, even those involving the youngest members, display a quality of performance which can be qualified as semi-professional or even professional. For example, the costumes are new every year for everyone, so there are no "hand-me-downs". At the same time, the professionalism is tempered by the necessity to acquire a spirit of community. If one year, by some happy accident, all the members of the "Pride of Shannon" perform perfectly, the next year, there will surely be one youngster who breaks the perfection of the line, with no one being overly critical. The important thing is for everyone to feel welcome to participate according to their abilities. It is a way of giving the young members of the community a chance to learn confidence and to become competent performers. This does not prevent standards from being kept high, and those who participate in the show year after year may acquire an enviable level of professionalism. This calibre of performance encourages people to keep coming back to the Show year after year.

Another quality, and not a negligible one, is the way people enjoy the show enough to keep putting it on year after year, often in spite of growing difficulties. While it is impossible to examine every performer in the show, a few examples may help to show how much of the show is a family affair, how those who take part in it evolve as performers, and how, for many, it is a long-term commitment.

Allan King, one of the people who sang and played in the very first show, has been in every one since. All six of his children have performed in the show at various times. For example, his daughter, Donna King, began as a youngster in the "Pride of Shannon" in 1968-70, then in the "Lads and Lasses" until 1975. She was in the "Belles and Beaus" and a dancer in the "Pub" in the early 1980s and has been one of the mainstays, singing and playing the guitar in the pub and as accompanist to other groups, ever since. As a student in Montréal, she travelled back and forth every February weekend to practice for the show, and in 1990, even though living in Ottawa, she travelled back to participate once again.[14] Charlotte Kiley, like Donna, has been successively a member of all the different age groups, from the "Pride of Shannon" up to the pub. During the 1986 show, special mention was made of her having "come of age", moving up from the "Belles and Beaus" to the pub.[15] In 1989, while a student in Montréal, she almost decided not to take part, but the idea of missing the show was too much for her, and then, as well as in 1990, she made the necessary trips back and forth to participate in the show.[16]

Photo Edwards, kindness of Maureen Maher

Photo François Vézina

The dancers in the 1967 Show Larry Hamilton, Linda Hood, Carolyn McCarthy, and Pauline McCarthy. Larry was joined in 1990 by five new young dancers, Kevin Hamilton, Matthew Neville, Ryan Kiley, Michael Neville, and Neil Neville.

Photo Stephen Monfette

The 1978 dancers were Donna King, Angela Maher and Wanda Leahy. Accompanying them were accordionist Allan King and Jack Maher on the banjo. "Lannigan's Ball" held no terrors for young dancers Holly Lynn Neville, Mary Ann Neville, Sandy Bélanger, Anna Dick, Krista Nikkel, and Amy Neville in the 1989 Show. Their accompanists were Johnny McClintock on the keyboard, Don Kack, guitar, Eric Corrigan, violin, Allan King, accordion, and Mike Neville, guitar.

Melita Maher, who, with her husband Jack and most of their ten children, was deeply involved in the show until moving to Ottawa after the 1984 show, practised for the "Rovers" in the 25th Show of 1990 "with the help of a tape sent to her Ottawa home".[17] Larry Hamilton, who until 1990 was the only "step dancer" in the show, performed his first Irish jig as a youngster of eleven in the 1966 show. Except for one year, he has danced and sung in every show since then. Typical of some of the younger people, Irish dancers Catherine (Cathy) Kelly and Joanne Conway, who have sung and danced in the show since they were youngsters, emphasize their enjoyment of being in the show. Both maintain that as long as they live in Shannon, they hope to be a part of it.[18] Effie Kiley, Ena Leahy and Mike Neville are also among those who have been in every show in one capacity or another, and often several, since 1966, while Don Kack, Maureen Maher and Jim Kelly have been in almost every one.

In order to coordinate the preparations and ensure a competent level of performance, work on the show has at times begun as early as six months before the date. Rehearsals for the dancers begin in November, and those who are studying Irish traditional dancing know that even though they may participate in competitions and occasionally in other shows, their chief goal is to perform in the Shannon Show. Generally, though, things start to get organized around the beginning of January when the Christmas festivities are over. As the time draws near, songs and dances are finalized and practices may be held as often as twice a week. Costumes must be made, sound equipment rented, sets constructed, publicity arranged, separate and combined rehearsals coordinated, and in all a great deal of work underlies a successful performance. As we saw above, the brunt of the organisation is borne by the members of the C.W.L. and the families of the performers, as well as relatives and friends.

The performers, stagehands and technicians are not the only part of the show, however. There are the other members of the C.W.L. who offer tea and coffee, cake and cookies during the intermission. Other helpers take tickets, run the soft drink concession or bar, direct traffic in the parking lot and generally help out as needed. The people who sew costumes, drive children back and forth to practices and take on other chores are the unsung contributors to the festivities.

All the age groups that are normally found in the community are involved in the performance of the show. The 1988 show was a good example of this. A hundred persons directly involved in the show were mentioned by name in the programme. Of these, half were adults, nineteen years and older ("Rovers", "A Party at the Pub";

technicians, coordinators). Of the other half, a third were adolescents ("Belles and Beaus"; technicians) and two-thirds children, ranging in age from three to twelve ("Pride of Shannon", "Lads and Lassies"). This proportion is not unusual, as some of the young people in their teens tend to drop out for a few years, while often coming back to participate or perform when they are older and can join in the adult part of the show.

The progression of the show is also a sort of progression through life. In the first part of the show, there are singing and dancing performances by everyone from toddlers of three or even only two-and-a-half years of age to grownups. Included in this section, there is often a short humorous play or a performance by a traditional storyteller. During the preparations for the various numbers, the master of ceremonies tells Irish jokes and anecdotes. After an intermission, the second section is exclusively adult, the "Irish Pub": people sitting around drinking and having a good time, while various members of the cast take turns coming forward, alone or in groups of two or three, to sing, dance, or play a tune, following each other the way people might do in a traditional Irish pub. Growing up to take part in the "Pub" is a way of acknowledging that a young person is now considered to be an adult. This second part of the show, the Irish pub scene, can stand alone as a separate performance, such as when it is brought to the elderly at Saint Brigid's Home in Sillery, once Saint Patrick's Day is past, to finish up their celebrations there. It also once served as entertainment for the Saint Patrick's Parish banquet in 1983, but this was exceptional. Generally, except for Saint Brigid's Home, once the show is over, it's over for another year.[19]

The Play

The original 1966 show contained two song medleys by a twelve-member "Chorus", Allan King singing "Let Ye All Be Irish Tonight" and "O'Brien Has No Place To Go", a Quadrille danced by "Shannon Youngsters", interspersed with songs, music, an Irish jig by Larry Hamilton, and a physical education demonstration by Grade five youngsters. The second part of the show was a one-act play: "Merry Molly Malone".

The one-act play, most often one that was bought in Dublin, or occasionally ordered from the United States, has been one of the features of the show from the beginning. Amateur or professional theatricals have always been a feature of Saint Patrick's Day celebrations

Photos Edwards, kindness of Maureen Maher

The play in the 1966 Shannon Show was "Merry Molly Malone" with players Peter Maher, Effie Kiley, Billy Vye, Barbara Knox, Patricia Grouette, Jack Maher (director), Maureen Maher, and Kenneth Smith. The 1967 play was "Mrs Murphy's Chowder", with Maureen Maher, Laura Bouffard, June Lusk, Donny Maher, Raines Walling, Effie Kiley, Linda Déry, and Nancy Gingras.

Photo Stephen Monfette

"The Grand Irish Party", in the Sainte Catherine's Hall in 1971, included step dancer Elmer Thompson, fiddler Mike Murphy, young Robbie Kelly, singer Sylvia Murphy, and Barry Neville on the guitar. The picture of Eddy Conway's grandparents on the wall lends a feeling of the old time house parties to the scene. "The Belle of Boolavogue" was 1988's contribution to the grand tradition of skits and plays. Here are Eugene O'Grady as "Larry the Lad", Clive Kiley as the other "Larry", Theresa King as the "Widow Cassidy", and Germaine Villeneuve as her daughter "Maureen".

FIGURE I

YEAR	TITLE	ACTORS	DIRECTOR(S)
1966	Merry Molly Malone	3 men; 4 women	Jack Maher
1967	Mrs Murphy's Chowder	2 men; 6 women	Jack Maher
1968	The Counter Charm	2 men; 3 women	Jack Maher
1969	Mrs O'Leary's Cow	2 men; 5 women	Maureen Maher, Effie Kiley
1970	The Boston O'Tooles	9 men; 4 women	Maureen Maher, Effie Kiley
1971	Garages & Green Goats	5 men; 2 women	Helena Booth
1971	The Marriage Plan	4 men; 2 women	Maureen Maher
1972	The Spanish Waistcoat	3 men; 2 women	Clive & Shirley Kiley
1973	The New Maid	2 men; 4 women	Helena Booth
1974	A Simple Soap Opera	2 men; 3 women	Helena Booth
1974	The Spinsters	3 men; 2 women	Jack Maher
1975	This is Your Wife	3 men; 3 women	Helena Booth
1976	absent		
1977	The Burthen	2 men; 4 women	Helena Booth
1978	The Face upon the Floor	13 men	Jack Maher
1979	absent		
1980	The Joker Plays Trumps	3 men; 2 women	Jack Maher
1981	absent		
1982	absent		
1983	Casey Taking the Census	1 man; 1 woman	Maureen Maher
1984	absent		
1985	Casey's Description of his Fight	2 men	Rose King, Betty Neville
1986	Casey at Home	3 men; 2 women	Rose King, Betty Neville
1987	The Storyteller	Jimmy King	Betty Neville
1988	The Letter	Jimmy King	Rose King
1989	The Belle of Boolavogue	3 men; 3 women	Maureen Maher
1990	Garages and Green Goats	4 men; 3 women*	Maureen Maher

* Difference in number of women: the lawyer for the defendant in 1990 was played by a woman.

in the Québec region, and Shannon is no exception, as witness "The Limerick Boy" in 1921. In 1954, Mae Derouin and Brother Osmond[20] first directed the play, "Garages and Green Goats". The 1955 play, "Casey Taking the Census", was transcribed from a recording. There was no play as such in 1976, 1979, 1980 and 1982, but the volume of dancers or the semi-dramatic presentation of dancers replaced it. The 1982 "ceili" was a good example, the dancers and singers giving a show within a show. In 1987 and 1988, the dramatic emphasis was furnished by Jimmy King, a traditional storyteller. The play reappeared in 1989, with the "Belle of Boolavogue", directed by the then mayor of Shannon, Maureen Maher. In all, there have been nineteen different plays, with the 1971 and 1974 shows having two. "Casey Taking the Census" was put on for the second time in 1983. For the 25th show [1990], "Garages and Green Goats" was put on for the third time, in memory of its 1971 director, Helena Booth.

The "Storyteller", Jimmy King, is a Shannon folk tradition bearer. His tales were learned from his father and others through oral tradition.

The Dancing

Dancing has always been a very important part of the show. During the first two years, the show relied on dances taken from the traditional dance repertoire of Shannon and Valcartier: quadrilles, square dances, lancers.[21] Melita Maher was responsible for training the "Shannon Youngsters" and "Shannon Dancers" for the show. Then in 1969, Patrick (Paddy) White, an Irish serviceman, began to teach Irish traditional dancing to local youngsters. The first of these, a Three Hand and a Four Hand Reel, were performed in the 1969 show. Paddy's last show was in 1979; he was followed by Nancy Roy who taught the dancers until replaced by Bernadette Short, an Irish dance teacher who has come from Montréal once a fortnight since 1981, to teach local girls. Some of the dancers have been trained by almost all these teachers, such as the senior dancers Joanne Conway, Catherine Kelly, Arleen King, Liane King, Doreen O'Grady, Sherry O'Grady and Tammy O'Grady, as were Donna King, Wanda Leahy and Angela Maher before them. For a while, a few boys took part, but in recent years, only girls have performed, taking the boys' parts when the dance requires it, as in the 1987 "Bonfire Dance". For the 25th show, Tess Leblanc, who has recently begun a Shannon school of step dancing, taught five young boys a step dance, the "Currageen Jig", a first for the show. After 25 years of solo step dancing performances, Larry Hamilton may at last have a successor in one of these boys, repeating the cycle he himself began in the 1966 show.

The favourite dances are reels and jigs, of which there have been over thirty variations. The most popular jig is the Slip Jig, which has been performed on at least ten occasions, as a solo or by two to five dancers. It is followed by the Treble Jig, while "Saint Patrick's Day", the "Humours of Bandon", the "Irish Washerwoman" and "Lannigan's Ball" are other recurrent favourites. Of the Reels, the most popular continue to be the Three, Four, and Eight Hand Reels.

Photo Stephen Monfette

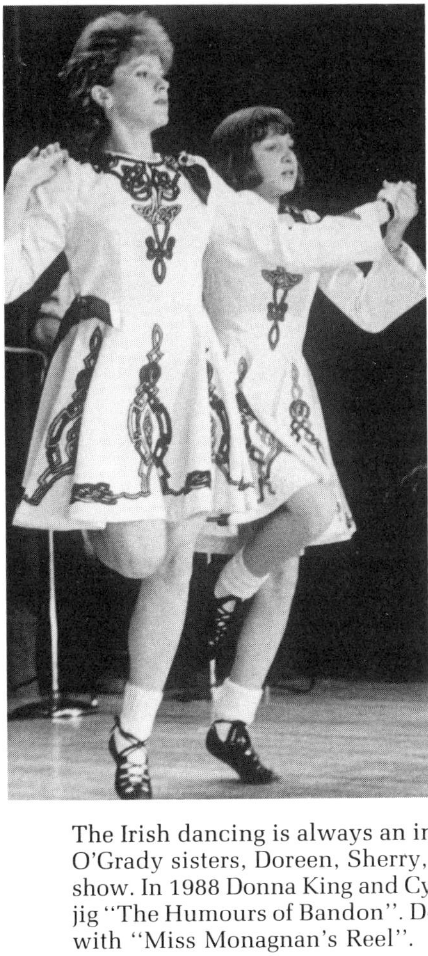

Photo Michèle Young

Photo Ross Corcoran

The Irish dancing is always an important and much enjoyed part of the show. The O'Grady sisters, Doreen, Sherry, and Tammy, dance "The Blackbird" in the 1989 show. In 1988 Donna King and Cynthia Carrier were two of the dancers of the 4-hand jig "The Humours of Bandon". Donna and Arleen King were part of the pub in 1985 with "Miss Monagnan's Reel".

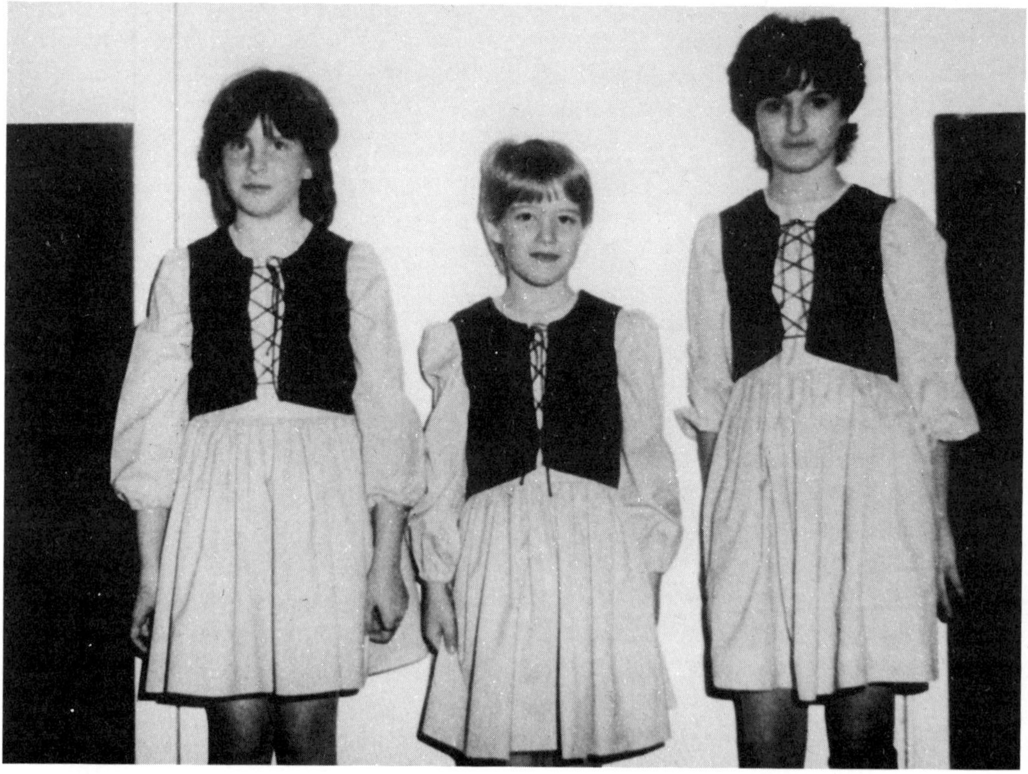

In 1990 the Pride of Shannon make a brave showing. Young Tammy Landry, Lisa Kack, and Mélanie Bélanger take a break from practising "Lannigan's Ball" for the 1985 show.

Jigs and Reels may have names suited to the Show, such as "Donna's Fancy Jig", "Neville's Jig", and "Shannon's Jig"; the "Shannon Reel", "McCarthy's Reel", and the "Tiny Tots Reel". Over the years, well over a hundred different dance numbers have been prepared and performed by Shannon dancers of all ages. For the last few years, the first part of each show has had at least five dance numbers (1980) and as many as eight (1981), with the average being six. While there have been occasional exceptions, such as Donna and Arleen King's performance of "Miss Monaghan's Reel" in the 1985 pub, the only dancing in the "Pub" half of the show has been Larry Hamilton's jigs and reels.

Other favourite dances are the hornpipes, which have several variants. Figure dances have also been popular, particularly those which depict some form of traditional activity, such as the "Donegal Weavers", the "Shannon Weavers", and the "Weavers of Inishmore", where the intertwining movements of the dancers depict the placing of the thread in the weaving of cloth. The "Gates of Derry", the "Loughs and Bridges of the River Shannon", the "Spinning Wheel", and the "Bonfire Dance" evoke various scenes and activities. Other descriptive dance titles are the "Fox Hunter", the "Blackbird", "Miss Brown's Fancy", the "Curragh of Kildare", "High Caul Cap", "Kitty's Rambles", the "Sweets of May", the "Walls of Limerick", and the "Trip to the Cottage".

Instrumental music may also contain reel and hornpipe tunes, such as "Hugh Travers' Jig and Reel", "Boys of Blue Hill" and "Dunphy's and Harvest Home" (hornpipes), "Bonaparte's Retreat", "Humours of Glendart", "Lord Inchoway", the "Millers Reel", and "The Priest's Leap" among others. Eric Corrigan and Tom Conway on the fiddle, Allan King and Rose King on the accordion, Don Kack, Mike Neville, Ralph Haberlin, and Donna King on the guitar, Jack Maher and Danny Stewart on the mandolin and banjo, Shirley Leahy on the spoons, Johnny McClintock on the keyboard, the bodhran drum and other drums, are a few of the musicians who have accompanied the singing and dancing over the years.

The Songs

Songs are an indispensable part of the show, whether sung in chorus by the different age groups, or as solos, duets or trios in the "Pub". Over the years, the songs have not always been enumerated in the programme, but of those programmes where the titles do appear, a compilation shows almost 200 different songs. Over a hundred of these are in the repertoire of the "Pub" singers alone. Of these, more than thirty favourites have been repeated at least two or three times. "Come Back to Erin" was sung as long ago as the 1921 Show, and sung as an opening by Jim Kelly in 1977. Allan King sang "O'Brien Has No Place To Go" in the 1966 Show, and sang it again with daughter Donna in 1984. Ena Leahy is known for her rendition of the "Isle of Innisfree", which she sang again in the 25th Show. A perennial favourite is Jim Kelly's "Women Are Worse (Better) Than Men". While certain favourites do come back from time to time, there is a concerted effort to have as many new songs each year as possible. People find them on records bought in Ireland, in Toronto or the States, and keep an eye out for new sources whenever possible. This results in a tremendous number of different and often unusual songs being added to the Show's repertoire, songs which many people would probably never have the opportunity to hear or learn if there were no Shannon Irish Show. Not included in this survey are the "classic" Irish songs, "When Irish Eyes Are Smiling" and such, which have also appeared regularly as solos or in medleys of Irish songs. There have been local compositions, such as "In the Year of '65", by Pauline McCarthy, sung by the "Belles and Beaus" for the 20th Show in 1965. Protest songs or modern laments such "Four Green Fields" and "Flight of Earls" are common. The songs, humorous or serious, speak of both traditional and modern Ireland, and are an indication of the interest in Ireland which Shannon people keep alive. They are best seen in the context of the different groups which sing them in the Show.

The Pride of Shannon

The performers in the first half of the show are grouped according to their age. As the years go by, youngsters move up from one group to the next, with "graduation" to the adult pub as the ultimate step. They can almost be said to "grow up with the show" and for many this has been the case. The youngest group, known as the "Pride of Shannon", is made up of the littlest citizens, aged 3 to 5, although the occasional 2½-year-old has taken part. In the first shows they were presented simply as a choir or choral group, with some being "Centennial Children" in the 1967 Show, and were in the spotlight for the 1979 "Year of the Child" Show. The name "Pride of Shannon" was first used in 1969 and 1970, and has been

Photo Edwards

Photo Ross Corcoran

Over thirty children participated in the 1967 Show, put on at the Jeanne d'Arc school. In 1984 the Lads & Lassies were still going strong. Here, among others, are Patrick O'Grady, Richard Collin, Darlene Kiley, Kathy O'Hearn, Tammy O'Grady, Rosalie Kack, Cathy Kelly, Doreen O'Grady, Liane King, and Paul O'Grady.

Photo Edwards, kindness of Ena Leahy

Photo François Vézina

Twenty-five years separate the children's chorus of 1966 (with their director Ena Leahy and accompanist Don Kack), and the Lads & Lassies of 1990. The youngsters of yesterday have become the parents of the children in today's shows. The 1966 choir also made a television appearance.

permanently in the programme since 1973. On one or two occasions, they have come second or third, but since 1979 their preferred position is first, mainly to avoid their having to wait too long to come on, especially in the Soirée, which is often after their bedtime. They generally sing one song, one not too difficult, which may or may not have a directly Irish origin, such as "A Daisy a Day", "The Unicorn", "Robin in the Rain", "Inch by Inch", "When Irish Eyes are Smiling". In the 24th Show, they also did a dance, the "Saint Patrick's Day Jig", and in the 25th Show, they sang "The Leprechauns", which had been the opening song in 1974. They have had many different directors over the years, and the result is always satisfying. The little ones are always warmly applauded and seem to get a taste for show business which brings them back from year to year.

Lads and Lassies

The next age group, which has always been under the direction of Ena Leahy, is made up of the elementary school children, the 6-12 year-olds. They were the last to receive a distinctive group name; their first official mention as "Shannon's Lads & Lasses" appears in the 1974 programme. Four years later, their name was modified to "Lads and Lassies", and remains the same today. While they have appeared in many places in the show, by 1983 they had been stabilized in a "chronological" position, following the "Pride of Shannon". In 1989 and 1990, they were grouped together with the few adolescents remaining from the "Belles and Beaus". They usually sing one or two songs, sometimes with soloists. Occasionally, as in 1980 and 1984, they may integrate a dance number. In 1982, they built their presentation around a well-known Irish theme: "Young Emigrants". Lorena King was a soloist for the song "The Emigrant's Letter", while John Kelly had the solo in "The Hat My Father Wore". The following year, Tracy Feeney, Cathy Kelly and Liane King were the soloists for "One Road" and "Sweet-Forget-Me-Not"; this last song, one of their favourites, they repeated in both the 1988 and 1990 shows. In 1986 they had only one song, "Tipperary's my Dream", but it had five soloists: Lorena King for the first verse, Jason Kack and Cynthia Carrier for the second, with Cathy O'Hearn, Richard Collin and Monique St-Pierre for the third. Their songs always have an Irish flavour, such as "An Irish Girl For Me" and "I'll Tell Me Ma". This is one of the largest groups, with anywhere from 20 to 30 youngsters taking part, often in spite of the usual distractions. Richard Collin, an 11 year-old soloist in the 1985 show, thought it might be his last, because of other activities such as Scouts and hockey.[22] Yet he managed to stay with the "Lads & Lassies" in 1986 and 1987. The performance by these young people shows the results of such dedication and hard work, and their growing assurance is always pleasant to watch.

Belles and Beaus

The adolescents, who acquired the title "Belles & Beaus" in 1973, have usually been one of the smaller groups. It is more difficult to get the teen group together, because of their varied interests and outside commitments. This age group also furnishes musicians, stagehands and technicians, as well as singers and dancers. At times during their high school years, some have been participants in the show put on by Saint Patrick's High School in the city, such as Barry and Peter Maher, Louanne McGrory, and Geraldine O'Shea in the 1970s. Because the teenagers have so much to give, the organizers have always been grateful for their participation in the show. Their status of sometime child, sometime adult seems to be reflected in their place in the show: they usually come after the "Lads & Lassies", but have also on occasion followed the "Rovers". Their selections for the programme are something of a rehearsal for the adult section of the pub, to which they could in principle graduate when they reach "drinking age", and have, in the past, shown the most versatility both in choice and types of presentation. They have used younger children dressed up as little animals or leprechauns to illustrate songs. In 1983 they tried their hand successfully at singing "Fanny Power" in Gaelic. That same year they had everyone sing along "My Wild Irish Rose", and during the song, they came down and distributed roses to members of the audience. They have integrated dance numbers, and poems expressing Irishness[23]. They have used comic effects, as in such songs as "Kitty McGee", "The Old Woman from Wexford", "Mary Mack" or "Uncle Nobby's Steamboat". They may choose love songs such as "Come to the Bower" or the "Gypsy Rover", or patriotic songs about the troubles in Ireland, like "Belfast Mill". They have also mingled popular songs of the day with the more Irish oriented selections.

In 1985, in tribute to the 20 years of sponsorship of the Show by the Catholic Women's League, their director, Pauline McCarthy, composed a special, song: "In the Year of 65".[24]

Photo Patricia O'Donnell

Photo Monik Simard

In 1979 and 1988, the Belles and Beaus brought the fervour and commitment of the young people to the Show.

Photo Francois Vézina

Photo Ross Corcoran

The Shannon Rovers of 1990 brought together scattered friends of many years and young people growing up in the show: Marcelle Neville, Louise Carrier, Maureen McCarthy, Diane Hincks, Jennifer Patterson, Melita Maher, Joanne Conway, Sherry O'Grady, Betty Babin, Angèle Daigle, Carolyn Kiley Therrien, Betty Neville, Sherril King, Rosita Kelly, and Rose King. The Rovers of 1986 were Marcelle Neville, Louise Carrier, Betty Neville, Karen Neville, Marguerite Genest, Joanne Myre, Betty Babin, Catherine Young, Rosita Kelly, Sherril King, and Rose King.

[Charlotte Kiley]
In the year of sixty-five
A great love we felt inside
'T was a dream of long ago
To recapture ever more
Our great love for Erin's shore
So—Hand in Hand—
We did plan
Our Irish Show.

[Belles & Beaus]
Oh How grand it feels
Dancing jigs and Irish reels
Hornpipes and some
Tapping Too
Singing songs—or put on plays
We express in different ways
Love for the land that
Our ancestors knew.

[Maureen McCarthy]
Though the years will slip away
We'll not forget our younger days
And all the good times spent with you.
Thanks to the Catholic Women's League
For sponsoring this event indeed
Good luck to you—and to future shows
From the Belles and Beaus.

In 1986, Charlotte Kiley and Maureen McCarthy took over the direction of the "Belles & Beaus", and Maureen continued in 1987 and 1988. Hard work and lively talent have always made the "Belles & Beaus" a much appreciated part of the show. But in 1989, and again in 1990, because of their diminishing numbers, what remained of the Belles (no Beaus made the transition), about seven girls, joined with the "Lads and Lassies" in the programme, and the "Belles & Beaus" have, at least for the moment, withdrawn from the spotlight.

The Shannon Rovers

The "Shannon Rovers" first came on the scene as a group in the 1971 Show, directed by Melita Maher. This first group included both men and women, many who had sung the year before in a number called "The Spinning Wheel". By 1974, they had evolved into an all-women group. The 1975, tenth anniversary "Rovers" were Louise Carrier, Pierrette Carrier, Barbara Côté, Dale Feeney, Rose King, Mary Lewin, Mary Lou King, Diane Maher (now Hincks), Pauline McCarthy, who also directed them, Karen McKeaney, Betty Neville, Marcelle Neville, and Karen Walsh. It is interesting to note that some of these same people were still in the 25th anniversary show: the 1990 "Shannon Rovers" were Betty Babin, Louise Carrier, Joanne Conway, Angèle Daigle, Diane Hincks, Rosita Kelly, Carolyn Kiley Therrien, Rose King, Sherill King, Melita Maher, Maureen McCarthy, Betty Neville, Marcelle Neville, their director, Sherry O'Grady, and Jennifer Patterson. Passage into the "Rovers" now marks a coming of age as an adult woman, and often includes members of the C.W.L. Their position in the programme varies, but is generally, as befits their adult status, one of the last numbers in the first half of the show. On three occasions they have been the opening number in the show, while still performing another number later on. Their personal song repertoire includes, among others, "My Green Valleys", "Patsy Fagan", "The Silver Sea", "Out on the Myra","Marie's Wedding", "Galway City", "Free-Born Man", "Dublin in My Tears", "After All These Years" and "The Mermaid".

Shannon's Irish Pub

Shannon's "Irish Pub" is an entity in itself, a type of variety show, which uses the framework of a "pub gathering" to display songs, dances and instrumental numbers in a relaxed, but well-paced atmosphere. The idea grew out of the traditional "house parties"[25], where those with various talents could be called upon to perform, in the days when television did not exist and people, especially in rural communities, had to make their own entertainment. The 1968 Shannon Irish Show featured "An Irish House Party to Celebrate the Homecoming of 'Paddy' who is returning from America". It was directed by Ena Leahy and Gary Bowles. Effie Kiley played the mother, Katie O'Brien, Jack Maher, the father, Tim O'Brien, and Danny Maher, the son, Paddy O'Brien himself. The guests were Sheila Corrigan, Larry Hamilton, Harold Kack, Don Kack, Jimmy Kelly, Rosita Kelly, Allan King, Rose King, Richard Leahy, Ena Leahy, Shirley Leahy, Roy Maher, Carolyn McCarthy, Mike Neville, Elmer Thompson and James O'Shea. That year the Quadrille formed part of the "house party" entertainment.

Someone then came up with the idea of a gathering in a traditional Irish pub setting, where, as the evening progresses, people grow merrier and almost everyone is called upon to perform in some fashion: singing, playing an instrument, dancing jigs and reels. It was called "Saint Patrick's Day at the Pub", and for the first time came at the end of the programme. In 1970 and 1973, it was called "Paddy's Pub", but in 1971 it was a "Grand Irish Party", and in 1972 "An Irish Get Together". Ena Leahy has been its director for the whole 23 years, while ever since 1972, Terry Neville has been the master of ceremonies. In 1973 it began to be presented as a separate section after an intermission. Its name in 1974, "A Gathering at the Crossroads" evokes a traditional Irish practice: when the pubs were closed on

Photo François Vézina

Photo Monik Simard

The "Irish Pub" remains the favourite get-together of Shannon's adult performers. In the 1990 show were Charlotte Kiley Provencher, Arleen King, Ena Leahy, Richard Leahy, Eric Corrigan, Allan King, Larry Hamilton, Shirley Leahy, Jim Kelly, Don Kack, Jimmy Maher, and Donna King. M.C. Terry Neville, hidden behind Larry Hamilton, is slightly more visible in the 1988 photo, just behind Richard Leahy. Others include Danny Stewart on the banjo and Mike Neville on the guitar.

Photo Ross Corcoran

In the 1990 "Pub", Eric Corrigan plays a medley of traditional fiddle tunes, accompanied by Mike Neville and Don Kack on the guitar, and Shirley Leahy on the spoons. Marty Conway and Jimmy King enjoy "Casey's Description of His Fight", the 1985 skit.

Sunday, people would meet at the crossroads (or "the cross") to have a good time. The 1975 version was called "An Irish Stage Party", but from 1976 on, the various names have had some connotation with a pub: "Irish Pub Party" (1976), "A Party At The Pub" (1983, 1988), "Saint Patrick's Day at the Pub" (1984, as in 1969), "Shannon (or Shannon's) Irish Pub" from 1977 on with the variant "Outside Shannon's Irish Pub" in 1980, while in 1989 and 1990 it was called simply "The Pub".

Over the years, many people have performed in the "Pub" according to their availability, while some participants have been in it for all of the 23 years. Among those who were in and out of it for periods varying from two to fifteen years are: Tom Conway, Gerry Deveau, Ralph Haberlin, Robbie Kelly, Rosita Kelly, Vincy Kelly, Carolyn Kiley, Jimmy King, Kerry Ann King, Rose King, Henry Lacasse, Todd Leahy, Wanda Leahy, Earl Leblanc, Jack Maher, Martha Maher, Roy Maher, Terry Maher, Gordon McAlpine, Carolyn McCarthy, Esther McCarthy, Barbara McGrory, Claire Murphy, Sylvia Murphy, Barry Neville, Jackie Neville, Danny Stewart, and Elmer Thompson.

In the 25th Show (1990) Eric Corrigan played the violin, Larry Hamilton did his step dancing, Don Kack, Donna King and Mike Neville[26] played the guitar and sang, Allan King had his accordion, Johnny McClintock was on the electronic keyboard, while Shirley Leahy added the harmony and played the spoons. Ena Leahy, whose specialty is traditional Irish ballads, sang one of her favourites, "Isle of Innisfree". The previous year, she had sung "Four Green Fields", a powerful ballad with strong Irish political overtones. Donna King sang "Flight of Earls", a modern emigrants' lament over the necessity to leave Ireland to find work, reminiscent of the departure in 1607 of the Celtic Earls and the end of Celtic Ireland. The song ends on a note of hope of return, however, since "airplanes fly both ways". Donna has sung similar songs in the past, such as the "The Island" (1985), which spoke of those who left home (Ireland) but who will always be part of the community. Another tribute to Ireland was sung by Charlotte Kiley Provencher, "Erin's Lovely Home", a song handed down in her family, learned from her father, who had it from his mother, and her mother in turn. Arleen King sang "My Dear Old Galway Bay", and Jimmy Maher another favourite, "The Nightingale".

Jim Kelly, Larry Hamilton, and Richard Leahy added a comic note to the proceedings with "Rielly's Daughter", the opening song and one of the "Pub's" favourites. Then came "Wooden Wedding", a sort of "Irish rap", in which a breathless pace must be maintained. "Twenty-One Years", sung by Richard Leahy, is a sort of "Irish Blues" about a man serving a term in Dartmoor prison, and missing his loved ones. A favourite with the audience is Jim Kelly's "Women Are Worse Than The Men", the story of a man who lets his wife be carried off by the devil. She causes so much trouble in Hell, that the man sees the devil "bringing her back". Then "This shows that the women are" he pauses and the audience shouts "worse" or "better"—"than the men, they can go down to Hell and come back again."[27] "Women's Lib" in a traditional ballad! Don Kack's "Brannigan's Pup" would make a pit bull turn tail and run, while Allan and Donna King sang a duet about his "Navy ('Navvy') Boots."

At the end of the "Pub", Terry Neville bid everyone goodbye with his usual "Irish" wish: "If you're driving, don't drink. You might go over a bump and spill some." The closing song, "Who is the Man?—who does not love the land where he was born..." again evoked the theme of liberty for Ireland. It was also used as the finale in the 1989 show. Other "patriotic" closing songs in the past have been the "Holy Ground" (1981) and "Home to Mayo" (1983), while a frequent finale has been a Medley of Classic Irish Songs.

The Opening

An important person in the Show is the Master of Ceremonies. He not only introduces the different numbers, but must amuse the audience with a running commentary, which includes typical Irish jokes[28], while the scenes are changed behind the curtain. He must thus be alert to the signals transmitted from the technicians and at the same time relaxed and amusing. The very first Master of Ceremonies was James (Jimmy) O'Shea and he emceed the Show for fourteen of the twenty-five. Other M.C.'s have been King Kiley (five shows between 1978 and 1990), Danny Maher (1977), Jim Kelly (1983), Terry Neville (1985-1986) and Clive Kelly (1987-1988).

Every year the opening number sets the mood for the Show to come. While there is an element of stability in the other parts of the Show, every effort is made to vary the opening, so that no one can necessarily predict it. This certain amount of suspense prevents a feeling of "sameness" from creeping in. There have been recitations, such as Danny Maher's "A Toast To The Irish" in the very first Show, which Lorena King took up again in 1987. Then in 1967 Kerry Ann King and Suzan Déry chatted "Over the Back Fence", while 1968 featured songs by the Chorus. "We're Off To Dublin Town" set the mood in 1971. In 1973 and 1974 "Leprechauns" brought a touch of Irish whimsy to the Show. The "Pride of Shannon" were the openers in 1969 and 1970, "Shannon's Kiddies Band" in 1972, and in 1979, the Year of the Child, "The Shannon Children" were featured.

The tenth anniversary Show, 1975, found Kenny King and Barry Maher introducing the Show as "Pat and Mike". A similar skit by Wayne Conway, Glenn Feeney and Gregg Kiley opened the 1983 Show. The whole cast appeared in a Grand March-On in 1976. The curtain opened in 1977 on Jim Kelly and the "Shannon Rovers", singing "Come Back to Erin". "The Shannon Rovers" did the honours again in 1978, 1984, and were joined by Larry Hamilton in 1986 for "We'll take you back to Ireland". The 1985 Show's Invitation to "Come by the Hills" featured Allan Copeman and George Fraser on the bagpipes, as well as an adult chorus. The 1982 opening combined a poem by Danny Maher, while the voice of Ena Leahy singing "Kerry Dancers" served as music for the dancers. Irish and traditional dance numbers opened five Shows from 1980 to 1990, among them a "Slip Jig" and "Lancers" (1980), "The Sweets of May" (1988), "Three Tunes" and "Lannigan's Ball" (1989), while the 1981 and the 1990 Shows brought on an "Irish Stew" of dancers.

Behind the Scenes

The organisation of the Show puts a heavy burden on the shoulders of the coordinator or coordinators, who must see that all the elements come together as a coherent whole on the final day. Coordinators over the years have included Gary Bowles, Marty Conway, Barbara Côté, Jackie Griffin, Clive Kiley, Effie Kiley, King Kiley, Jack Maher, Maureen Maher, Melita Maher, and Terry Neville. The team of Effie Kiley and Gene O'Grady has successfully coordinated the shows for the last ten years, including the 25th Anniversary Show.

There are also the stagehands and technicians, who are rarely visible, except for a quick curtain call at the end of the first half of the Show. Yet their collaboration is crucial. Danny Neville has been stage manager for all but a few of the shows; Jack Maher and Lou Babin were the others. Though it is impossible to list them all, Eddy Conway, Wayne Conway, Earl Corrigan, Kathleen Corrigan, Keith Cotnoir, Christine Dick, Roy Dick, Glenn Feeney, Johnny Feeney, Pat Feeney, Gloria Hamilton, Diane Hincks, Doreen Kack, Clive Kiley,

Gregg Kiley, King Kiley, Pat Kiley, Patricia Kiley, Jimmy Kitching, Wayne Lannin, Darren Maher, Jimmy Maher, Dave Neville, Elaine Neville, Jimmy Neville, and Karen Nikkel were just a few of those who filled the jobs of stagehands, sound and light technicians, dressmakers, or took care of the programme and the publicity.

For the first few years, the organizers of the Show solicited funds from sponsors who advertised in the programmes, although in 1968, since there were no sponsors to pay for printing, the women typed all the programmes themselves. By 1974, fund raising had replaced the sponsors and the programmes have since been free of ads. As the years go by, the programmes have become more elaborate. Besides giving the names of all the performers and organizers, they contain the titles of all the songs and dances, and even, in the last few years, a short description and a bit of the story behind many of the dances.

The show has had its share of unexpected trials and tribulations. In 1973, when everyone arrived at the Sainte Catherine's Hall for the evening show, the electricity was out: no lights, no mikes, the $100 sound system rented for the occasion couldn't be used. The show went on by candlelight, with Easter candles furnished by the parish priests as footlights on the front of the stage. The dancers went on first, because they could manage without amplified music, then the musicians with their acoustic instruments, and finally the singers. There was no curtain, since it was run by electricity. This gave the organizers the idea of doing a show without a curtain the following year.[29] Then in 1985, the water suddenly went off in the Shannon Recreation Center. Volunteer firemen worked throughout the afternoon to replenish the water supply so the evening Show could continue as scheduled.[30]

Will The Show Go On

The Shannon Irish Show attracts people from all over the Québec City area, and is an important focus for Irishness during the Saint Patrick's Day celebrations. Having grown out of a local folk tradition of festivity which resisted Americanisation, it has developed a quality all its own, a blending of the best of Old World and North American Irish traditions. One could almost say that it is the local substitute for the Saint Patrick's Day parade, particularly since the latter's disappearance in Québec City. It is a community affair, bringing people together in a common undertaking, and it serves to

Photos François Vézina Prints Pierre Cayer

Typical of the many workers behind the scenes over the years are Darren Maher, Jimmy Kitching, Wayne Conway, Keith Cotnoir, Danny Neville, Eugene (Gene) O'Grady and Effie Kiley, coordinators, Elaine Neville, C.W.L. president, Roy Dick, Dave Neville, and Glenn Feeney in the 1990 Show. And the Hall is always well filled with the most important people — the appreciative audience.

Though a span of more than thirty-five years separates the 1954 concert in the Sainte Catherine's Hall and the 1990 Show in the Shannon Center, the enthusiam remains undiminished. Alan King shared the stage with Philip and Johnny Murphy in that early show.

emphasize family connections and cooperation. As an added attraction, it also maintains a high standard of professionalism in performance.

However, it is obvious that the Shannon Irish Show is a major undertaking, which mobilizes the time and energies of a great many people during a good part of the winter months. At the same time, the largest part of the organisational burden falls on the shoulders of a relatively small number of the same people year after year. Every year it becomes a bit more of a struggle to bring people together for the show: young people are leaving the village and even the city, for schooling and work, while those who remain find they have ever more demands on their time. The composition of the Shannon community is changing, with more French newcomers than Irish, leaving a shrinking pool of resources upon which the organizers can draw. Every year the question arises: Will there be a Show next year? Yet many remain optimistic. Thus far, when Show time rolls around, people get busy at it once again.

Notes

1. In 1980, the community was the focus of a feature page article in the Montréal *Gazette*, with half a page of illustrations by Aislin: "Buried in Quebec, an Irish enclave", by Tim Burke, *The Gazette*, Saturday, March 15, 1980, p. 45.
2. See Lise Deveau et al., *Where Green is Worn: Shannon*, p. 62-75, for details of these expropriations.
3. For further details on the history of the community of Shannon, see *Where Green is Worn*, p. 18-19.
4. *Where Green is Worn*, p. 103 ff.
5. For Shannonites, both English and French, the term "Irish" refers to anglophones regardless of their actual ethnic origin.
6. Maureen Conway Maher was mayor from 1979 to 1989.
7. Nancy Schmitz and Monik Simard, "Research Note", p. 80-83.
8. Author's notes.
9. A roll call of family names appearing in the programmes since 1966 shows a good mixture of Irish and French, though the numbers of participants of each are in the proportions mentioned in the text: Amarandos, Babin, Bélanger, Beliveau, Bergeron, Bisson, Booth, Boudreau, Bouffard, Bowles, Brousseau, Carrier, Chabot, Collin, Comeau, Conway, Corrigan, Côté, Cotnoir, D'Entremont, Daigle, Denis, Déry, Deveau, Dick, Donaldson, Egan, Essiambre, Feeney, Gauthier, Genest, Gingras, Griffin, Haberlin, Haché, Hamilton, Henry, Hincks, Kack, Kelly, Kiley, King, Kirkwood, Knox, Lacasse, Lachance, Landry, Lannin, Leahy, Leblanc, Lefebvre, Maher, McAlpine, McCarthy, McGrory, McLaughlin, McNulty, Mercereau, Montgomery, Murphy, Myre, Neville, Nikkel, O'Grady, O'Hearn, O'Neill, O'Shea, Patterson, Pouliot, Rioux, Roberge, Stewart, Surette, Thériault, Therrien, Twardawa, Veilleux, Verrault, Vienneau, Whitehead.
10. *Where Green is Worn*, p. 78.
11. *Where Green is Worn*, p. 77-79.
12. Effie Kiley, interview 1990, and *Quebec Chronicle-Telegraph*, March 14, 1984, p. 8.
13. This form of cooperation is typical of the members of the extended community formed by M.R.C. Jacques Cartier.
14. *Quebec Chronicle-Telegraph*, March 6, 1985, p. 9, and March 21, 1990, p. 2.
15. Author's notes.
16. *Quebec Chronicle-Telegraph*, March 8, 1989, p. 1, and March 21, 1990, p. 2.
17. *Quebec Chronicle-Telegraph*, March 21, 1990, p. 2.
18. Interviewed by Monik Simard, March 12, 1988.
19. A notable exception occurred on the 9th of September 1985. The Québec government invited the entertainers from the Shannon Irish Show to give a performance in the Shannon Hall for a group of Irish Parliamentarians, on a visit to Ottawa and Québec. There were nineteen guests at the concert, which was made up of some of the dancers from the first part of the show, along with the Shannon Rovers, and the Pub.
20. Religious name of James Mangan.
21. Tess Leblanc, performer and step dancing teacher, is preparing a study of traditional dancing in the Shannon area during the present century.
22. *Quebec Chronicle-Telegraph*, March 13, 1985, p. 20.

23. In 1984, they performed an original poem: "Oh to be Irish! If only for today". See below, p. 252.
24. *Quebec Chronicle-Telegraph*, March 20, 1985, p. 8.
25. Akin to the French-Canadian "veillées".
26. At 75, Mike Neville was the oldest person in the show and was accorded a special mention as well for his participation in all twenty-five shows.
27. This is a variant of the traditional Child ballad 278, "The Farmer's Curst Wife"; a similar theme is found in a traditional folktale, Aarne-Thompson tale type 1164, "The Evil Woman Thrown into the Pit".
28. The following brief example is taken from the 1990 Show: "Husband: I wouldn't have married you if I'd known how stupid you are. Wife: You should have known it the minute I asked you." There are also Pat and Mike and Catholic/Jewish jokes, as well as the occasional political satire.
29. *Quebec Chronicle-Telegraph*, March 21, 1973, p. 2; Melita Maher, interview 1978; Betty Neville, *Quebec Chronicle-Telegraph*, March 6, 1985, p. 17.
30. *Quebec Chronicle-Telegraph*, March 13, 1985, p. 20.

Overleaf:

Irish for a day by consent and descent: Sister Eleanor Keller proudly wears the shamrock; a young Chinese colleen pins a feast-day decoration on Tim O'Connor's lapel.

Happy St. Patrick's Day!

Photo Ross Corcoran

Photo Jacques Boissinot

CHAPTER VIII

A Look to the Future

Studies of ethnic festivals have become commonplace in the last quarter of the 20th century, as the notion of multiculturalism, or polyethnicity, replaces the melting pot mentality of earlier decades. Global preoccupations have, paradoxically, been accompanied by the emergence of neo-nationalist efforts on the part of ethnic entities of various sizes to emphasize their survival as a unit. At the same time as such forms of economic decentralisation as free trade and the European Economic Community are on the rise, a new non-material awareness of self-identity continues to grow on the regional and local level. "National" groups within present nation-states (Québécois, Bretons, Basques, and Lapps) continue their demands for political autonomy, while renewed national boundaries are being defended (Poland, Lithuania), and old ones reformed (Germany).

In a recent article on ethnic identity, J.A. Williams remarks that

> Certain scholars embody a static view of ethnicity, defining it almost entirely in terms of biological descent and of social behaviour—segregation, conflict, and mobility—reflected in aggregate data. Scholars who give more weight to cultural studies offer alternative definitions. In *Beyond Ethnicity*, for example, Werner Sollors contrasts the ethnicity of descent with that of consent, ethnicity sustained by voluntary efforts as well as by external pressures and boundaries. ... The ethnicity of consent constitutes a *via media* between the extremes of cultural isolation based on the ethnicity of descent, on the one hand, and the submergence of everyone in a standardized national culture, on the other.[1]

Québec Irish Identity

Festivity often serves as a way of focusing ethnic identity. The analysis of Saint Patrick's Day in Québec as an event central to the affirmation of Irish identity, reveals that while the notion of conflict is not entirely absent, the concept of the "ethnicity of consent" is particularly relevant to the situation of Québec City's Irish community during the festive period. It is virtually less important to *be* Irish, than to celebrate Saint Patrick's Day. As one informant put it: "Saint Patrick's Day is for the Irish and those who want to be Irish."[2]

The first cultural distinction, or marker, separating the Québec Irish from the majority population is the use of the English language. Contrary to the usual situation in Canada and the United States, English, in Québec, is a minority language. Its use, however, as the working language of a long-dominant minority, has resulted in the abnormal situation of the functional unilingualism of a significant number of English speakers. While this occurs mainly in Montréal, isolated examples can still be found in Québec City today. Although the Irish, due to their "middleman" position, are generally bilingual, they are categorized by themselves and by others as English speakers.[3] This distinction has precluded the need for them to define themselves through the preservation of the Gaelic language. It is usually taken for granted that the language of the Saint Patrick's Day celebrations is English. At the Shannon Show, French people who attend are often unable to understand the anecdotes and patter of the Master of Ceremonies, but realize that this is an essential part of an "Irish" event. In spite of a French presence at many levels of festive activity, the most important positions are held by the Irish. While the head table at the Saint Patrick's Day banquet often includes local French personalities, the guest speaker, when there is one, has always been an "Irish speaker".[4]

Looking back over the more than two hundred years of St Patrick's Day celebrations in Québec, it is easy to see why the Irish are often called a "persistent people". This talent for survival has earned for them the grudging admiration of their French Canadian neighbours, who are themselves known for their attachment to and success at *survivance*. Nevertheless, while the continuity of the Irish presence in Québec has been unbroken since before the end of the French Régime, the numbers of those, especially among Catholics, who can claim exclusive Irish descent are proportionately few.

> The range of physical types acceptable as members of a people can be truly enormous without compromising the sense of a common identity or altering the recognition of the group as a separate entity by outsiders.[5]

Although marriage with members of other English speaking descent groups is common, particularly among the Irish Protestants, the religious factor has favoured intermarriage of Irish Catholics with the French Catholic element, leading in many cases to assimilation by the majority population. In Québec, a person named O'Neill, Ryan, or Ross may be French speaking, while the name Leblanc, Métivier, or Vallières may belong to an English speaking "Irish" man or woman. French speakers with Irish names, or those with an Irish relative or two, may choose to celebrate, even in the face of opposition, as was sometimes encountered on Saint Patrick's Day in the Chien d'Or.[6] Many Irish who in their daily life simply identify themselves as anglophones, make an exception for Saint Patrick's Day.

> On Saint Patrick's Day, I'll come out with my ribbons and everything. I'm not shy to let anybody know I'm Irish.[7]

Even members of the same immediate family may choose contrasting identities. Several French speaking or bilingual informants whose ancestry included both French and Irish, mentioned that while some members of their family had opted to celebrate Saint Patrick's Day in a big way, not all felt that the feast was relevant for them because of their French heritage. In the Québec context, this ideology of mono-ethnic descent barely conceals a polyethnic reality for both French and Irish.

> The variety of peoples who thought of themselves as Irish marked the British North American colonies as much as it did Ireland itself.[8]

The original Irish population of Québec included not only Catholic Irish of Gaelic and Norman descent, but also Protestant Anglo-Irish and Scots-Irish, those descendants of the settlers of the "plantations" in the North of Ireland. Thus, the belief in some form, no matter how remote, of Irish biological descent is an essential element for the ethnic definition of the Québec Irish. This often leads to distinctions of "levels" of ethnicity, depending on how "pure" the Irish component may be.

> They say Québecers are more Irish than people in Ireland. — The Irish from Boston didn't know half the songs we knew.[9]

The ethnicity of consent nevertheless supposes a commitment to one or another ethnic option, French, English or Irish, no matter what genes the person's biological inheritance may contain.

On the other hand, the celebration of Saint Patrick's Day is not limited to those whose ethnic identity either by consent or descent is Irish. The idea of being "Irish for the day" extends to members of other "ethnic" groups, including non-Europeans. The performers in the Saint Patrick's high school show offer a good example.[10] In 1990, a look at the programme showed that about 50% of the cast was comprised of students whose family names were French, while oriental and other non-Irish names made up around 6%. Throughout the history of the parades, Matinées and Soirées, there have always been a significant number of French participants.

> The French citizens appear to consider Saint Patrick's Day as one of their own holidays for they turned out in great numbers and were extremely enthusiastic.[11]

And though their participation has never gone so far as to include a francophone guest speaker at the Saint Patrick's Day dinners or banquets, it would be difficult for most Saint Patrick's Day activities to take place without some form of French moral or physical support.

"Another popular notion ... that attaches to many persistent peoples is the possession of a homeland."[12] This is particularly true of the Irish, whose ties to the mother country, while nostalgic, are often only too real, as witness the material support of modern IRA freedom-fighting activities by certain North American groups.[13] Saint Patrick's Day was often an occasion to bring the troubles in Ireland to the attention not only of the Irish community but of the general public as well. The editorials on March 17th took Irish politics as their theme in both the French and the English newspapers. Throughout the 19th century and up until the proclamation of the Free State in the 1920s, the Irish situation had a direct influence on Québec celebrations. The parade and banquet were frequently cancelled during the darkest days of the Famine and the periods of the troubles. The psychological influence of the Famine itself on the Québec community was out of proportion to the reality, due largely to the proximity of the immigrants on Grosse Ile. The actual Québec Irish population was composed principally of pre-Famine Irish immigrants.[14]

Ireland as a country furnishes the bulk of the thematic content of the festive activities. Songs contain stereotyped descriptions of Irish culture, such as the countryside: "Galway Bay", "Isle of Innisfree"; the promise of an eventual return to the mother country: "I'll take you home again, Kathleen", "Danny Boy"; humour: "Rielly's Daughter", "Wooden Wedding"; rebel songs, encouraging resistance to English occupation of the North: "Four Green Fields"; the economic plight of today's Ireland: "Flight of Earls". Irish dancing, particularly the "Irish Jig", has always been part of the theatrical entertainment, in the shows and at the banquets, and at the present time, Irish competition dancing is taught by a professional to the dancers in the Shannon Show. Irish and Irish-American plays were obligatory choices for the dramatic offerings at the matinées and soirées, whether their themes were familiar ones or not.

Semaine de Solidarité Irlandaise

du 10 au 17 mars

Mercredi 10 Soirée multiculturelle Hotel Hilton à 20 h Contribution Volontaire : $3,00	**Dimanche 14** Films: au Café de la Résistance 815 Côte d'Abraham. 14 h Pourquoi les Irlandais mentent? 15 h 30 Entrevu avec Síle Darragh – ex prisonnière. 19 h 30 L'enjeu des Partisans
Mardi 16 Qu'est-ce qui se passe en Irlande du Nord? – Débat public au Café de la Résistance 815 Côte d'Abraham. à 20 h – Personnes ressource.	**Mercredi 17** Fête de la Saint Patrick au Centre Récréatif St-Jean Baptiste 80 Rue St-Jean (85 Richelieu) à 20 h. Musique irlandaise avec Les P'tits bûcheux.

1982

> They had Lady Gregory and Synge, and Irish American plays because they were easier to come by; and lots of the really Irish plays, we didn't know what they were all about, to tell you the honest truth.[15]

> [The audience] took [the melodrama] so seriously that sometimes they wouldn't speak next day to the guy who played the villain. There was a case when the hero was asleep at the critical moment, and somebody jumps up and says, "Cripes, wake him up!" He thought it was real.[16]

The speeches at the banquets, like the sermons at the festive Mass, have repeatedly stressed the theme of the history of Ireland and her saints and heroes, as a model for living in the adopted country, and as a force for education in Irish heritage: "We learned our history as a people at the Mass and the Banquet".[17] Many a dinner or reception speaker also used the occasion to give his audience an illustrated tour of Ireland, especially before travel to Europe, with the possibility of a visit "home", became popular in the 1970s.[18]

With the expansion of travelling opportunities during the 1980s, the Québec Saint Patrick's Day celebrations have benefited from a certain measure of "cultural revival". Young and old have visited Ireland in search of relatives or ancestors, and to familiarize themselves at first hand with conditions in the divided Island. In March of 1982 young French activists held a "week of Irish solidarity" in Québec, including films, lectures and an interview with an ex-detainee from the North. Many young people also began to listen to contemporary Irish folk and rock music, and protest songs found their way into the repertoires of the high school and the Shannon Show performers. Yet this "search for green roots" remains on a sentimental level. There is no feeling of belonging ultimately to another country; the young people consider themselves first and foremost citizens of the New World, not the Old.

Besides a common homeland, the Irish pride themselves on the timeless aspect of certain more spiritual features of their cultural heritage. A poem composed by Pauline McCarthy to be recited in the Shannon Irish Show of 1984, brings out the elements of this heritage which are most valued by the community:

> Oh to be Irish if only for today
> We are proud of our Irish heritage
> Our culture has survived
> We are grateful to our ancestors
> For keeping it alive
> We acknowledge with pride
> Our saints, scholars and people of the arts
> For through them we can all express
> The joy that is in our hearts

Yes sing Irishmen sing today
Celebrate with us this glorious day
We the Belles and Beaus
Have a favor to ask of you
Just turn slightly, smile,
Shake the hand of the person next to you
And may God bless and take a liking to you
We sure do in every way
Oh tis great to be Irish
If only for a day.[19]

The picture painted here is of a people of saints and scholars, who prize religious, intellectual, and artistic achievement above all, despite the occupational reality of the community, composed not only of priests, nuns, and teachers, but of merchants, labourers and civil servants as well. It also projects a more cheerful image of the Irish, as against the reality of the suffering their ancestors underwent both in the mother country and upon arrival in the New World.

Saint Patrick's Day also permits the proliferation of visible symbols of ethnic appurtenance. Since the Irish share elements of overall North American culture with English and French Québecers, the content of the everyday material culture, such as dress, housing, or foodways of the various groups is largely interchangeable and outwardly homogeneous. Life style distinctions are more subtle and are usually expressed by choices in social relations and alternative educational and recreational practices. Since the Irish share the Catholic religion with the majority population, one of their most significant "contrastive strategies"[20] has been the building of their own "ethnic" church and the founding of their parish. Saint Patrick's parish gives the Québec Irish a "continual organisational existence"[21] which helps to define the community as a separate unit, in spite of its actual polyethnic composition.

The Irish founded and maintained English schools within the French Catholic school system, while the Irish Protestants and the rest of the English speaking population frequented the Protestant school system.[22]

> The Good Shepherd Nuns taught us English in their school. Everybody repeated Grade Four rather than go on to French school.[23]

The Irish excelled in sports, such as hockey, particularly during the early decades of the 20th century, and this aspect is among those highlighted on Saint Patrick's Day when Irish accomplishments are evoked.[24] Their perennial reputation for extravagant drinking and fighting remains part of their image in Québec City, and the frequenting of taverns for the informal "dipping of the shamrock" on Saint Patrick's Day tends to reinforce such an impression. Throughout the history of the feast-day, however, the tendency has always been to emphasize the orderly conduct of the participants during both public and private activities in an attempt to counteract this particular stereotype.[25]

During the festive period, the shamrock, the reminder of Saint Patrick's sermon on the Trinity, and the colour green, predominate in dress and decoration.

> Today we saw more than a few [French] Canadians who, out of affection for their true Irish friends, or because of family ties, sported the shamrock or the green ribbon, just as did the Irish themselves.[26]
>
> My brothers and I, on Saint Patrick's Day, would put on the biggest shamrock we could find.[27]

These symbols have become a universal marker of Irish ethnicity wherever the Irish have settled in the world. The explosion of green dress, decorations, balloons and flags during the parade of 1921 was a good example of the symbolic use of the colour green to express the support of the Québec Irish for political autonomy in Ireland. For the Irish, green is considered the colour of defiance, and for this reason green dress was once banned in Ireland, giving rise to the famous Boucicault ballad, "The Wearing of the Green".[28] Although it is proudly worn outside Ireland as the symbol of Irish ethnicity, many homeland Irish refuse to wear it, believing it to be an unlucky colour.[29]

In 1954, a local Québec Irishman published a poem on the front page of the *Chronicle-Telegraph* which spoke so directly to the Québec experience that readers frequently requested that it be reprinted.

Saint Patrick's Day In Quebec

Saint Patrick's Day will ever live
In old Quebec, I'll tell you why:
If all the Irish were to leave,
The French would never let it die.

Their stores betray a knowledge deep
Of things that please an Irish heart;
Green ribbons, harps and fair colleens,
A blackthorn stick and donkey cart.

And Irish husbands who don't seem
To wish to mark the Day are taught
A lesson when their eyes behold
The shamrocks their French wives have bought.

So each St Patrick's Day we'll toast
The gallant French for standing by;
Long live the Seventeenth of March!
The French will never let it die.

Slievenamon[30]

In addition to emphasizing the privileged relationship between the Irish and the French, this poem includes a number of visual symbols used on cards and in decorations, by which popular culture defines Irishness, not only for the poet, but for most emigrant North American Irish as well: green ribbons, harps, fair colleens, blackthorn sticks, donkey carts, and shamrocks. To this list we may add repetitious material taken from cards and other objects sold in card and curio shops: leprechauns, thatched cottages, clay pipes, green or black hats with buckled band, and even, during the height of Smurfmania, a Smurfleprechaun, which was available in Librairie Garneau, a Québec stationers and bookstore, during the week before Saint Patrick's Day in 1986.

Dynamics of Saint Patrick's Day

From earliest colonial times in Québec, the celebration of Saint Patrick's Day has been the occasion for reconciling the political, religious and linguistic differences inherent in the Québec situation: the longtime economic and social dominance of English speaking Protestants from 1760 until the middle of the 20th century, the religious and political autonomy of the French Catholic majority, and the intermediate position of the Irish Catholics, who must resolve the paradox of being both accepted and rejected at the same time by each of the other linguistic and religious extremes.

Every celebration managed to bring together a certain share of the three elements, while underscoring other divisions, this time inherent in the Irish community itself. The separations along the lines of parish, village, social status, or interest group, although much diminished in recent times, reflect in part the clannish nature of the Celt. The often tragic history of the Celtic population in Ireland, Scotland and Wales reminds us that their loss of political autonomy was attributable in part to their own inability to ignore clan or tribal differences at critical moments in their confrontations with their common English enemy.[31] On the other hand, the presence of these elements in temporary harmony during the Saint Patrick's Day festivities is a tribute to the capacity, possessed to some extent by most

1954

1958

1955

1956

1920

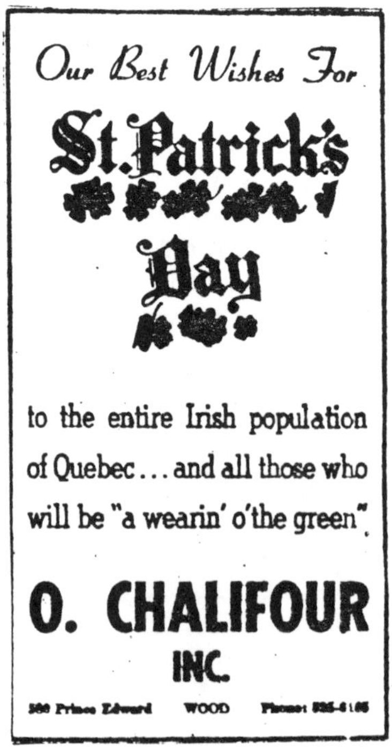

1961

The Quebec Chronicle and Quebec Chronicle-Telegraph

New World Irish and honed by their mediatory status in Québec society, to resolve differences and present a united front.

Preparations for the festival draw together the Irish, their relatives, friends and sympathizers,[32] as well as different interest groups within the wider anglophone community, according to parish, village, or religious affiliation. The actual event, Mass, banquet, or show combines elements from all these groups in varying proportions. For example, representatives of the Protestant clergy are present at the feast-day Mass and the Château Frontenac banquet; the mayor and various provincial and municipal officials attend the Shannon show; and the school performances include children from the urban and rural populations and different ethnic groups.

Elsewhere in North America, the parade has remained the Saint Patrick's Day observance par excellence,[33] because of its affirmation of Irish identity and continuity of presence. In New York, for example, it also went from being a Protestant manifestation to a Catholic one, developing a strict religious orientation, as it needed to be a public demonstration of religious values in a sometimes anti-Catholic "pluralistic" society.[34] The line of march of the Philadelphia parade recalls the history of the Irish population of the city.[35] These parades also emphasize the participation of the Irish in the civil, political, and religious life of their new country. The parade in Québec City embodied these characteristics, but with a slight shift of emphasis. It served to reaffirm the respect of the Irish for the religious and civil authorities of the city and the province. The route of the parade included reviews at the archiepiscopal palace and city hall, where letters and addresses were tendered as expressions of loyalty by the Irish, as responsible citizens and as faithful children of the Church. The procession also passed before the headquarters of the various Irish and other national associations and institutions: the Sarsfield Club, the Tara Hall, the home of the presidents of the different Societies, and the presbytery of Saint Patrick's parish.

Both French and English newspapers were always sympathetic to the parade, and published pertinent announcements and coverage.[36] In the Québec context, overt anti-religious prejudice was inappropriate. The gradual disappearance of other anglophone elements from the parade was more likely due to political differences concerning Irish independence, while Canadian Orangemen displayed anti-French rather than anti-Irish Catholic sentiments. Newspaper accounts tended to accentuate the decorum with which the parade was conducted. The lack of the rowdiness expected of the Irish on festive occasions emphasized the docility toward religious and civil authority which the Québec Irish leaders wished to demonstrate. Like the Republican Irish parades, many American ones developed a militaristic aspect, in order to display their unity and power in the face of discrimination. This aspect was not particularly essential to the Québec parade, since no one doubted the loyalty of the Québec Irish to the British Empire.[37] The Irish participation in the Boer War and the Québec Irish rejection of the American "Fenian invasion" show how the evolution of the Irish on either side of the border diverged in certain important ways according to their different historical and cultural situations in the New World.

The Québec parades tended rather to favour sporting, temperance and occupational associations, such as the Sarsfield Amateur Athletic Association, the Total Abstinence and Beneficial Society, and the Catholic Order of Foresters. The absence of a need to aggressively display their access to power may explain why the Québec parade was eventually discontinued, while the Montréal one is still going strong. The Irish in Québec City, in spite of the normal stresses and conflicts inherent in a bilingual society, were in a less defensive position than their confrères in other parts of Canada and the United States. As their numbers diminished, they preferred to finance dinners and shows, while evoking climatic conditions as a justification for abandoning the parade.[38] Other important parades in Québec have suffered similar fates. The French Saint Jean Baptiste parade has disappeared in favour of a patriotic show, although it was revived in Montréal in June 1990. The only remaining parade is that of the Winter Carnival, which survives because of its commercial and touristic character. While people "simply do love a parade"[39], Québecers seem to prefer a spectacular show.

Another important aspect of the Saint Patrick's Day celebrations is the role of the various national and religious associations. The first of these, the Saint Patrick's Society, and its temporary rival, the Friendly Sons of Saint Patrick, had as their original purpose the organisation of a dinner to celebrate Saint Patrick's Day. The Hibernian Benevolent Society, the Irish Protestant Benevolent Society[40], and later the Ancient Order of Hibernians, also held festive dinners. The Saint Patrick's Literary Institute and, for a while, the Catholic and Literary Institute, sponsored Matinées and Soirées. The history of Saint Patrick's Day is also the history of the rise and fall of these "national" societies, whose role was to safeguard the traditional forms of festivity, while creating new forms to capture the interest of a fairly sophisticated public.[41]

Photo Nancy Schmitz

Photos Frank Scardina

Emblem of the Saint Patrick's Literary Institute, the association that sponsored the Matinées and Soirées for over a hundred years. Emblem of the Ancient Order of Hibernians, Division No. 1, Québec, who sponsored the feast-day dinners and teas for many years. These silk ribbon ornaments are black on the reverse side, to be so worn at funerals of members. The emblems have been handed down in Gerry O'Connor's family for almost a hundred years.

Traditional decorations: the tricolour of the Republic; a replica of the Tara brooch; a shamrock of Connemara marble; the Shannon Show's 25th anniversary ribbon. Popular buttons worn on Saint Patrick's Day. Some are offered by brewers of Irish beer, while others are products of the greeting card industry.

Saint Patrick's Literary Institute on Sainte Anne street as it appeared in 1924.

1856 — ERIN GO BRAGH — 1924

St. Patrick's Literary Institute

68th Grand Annual Soirée

UNDER THE AUSPICES OF

ST. PATRICK'S LITERARY INSTITUTE

AUDITORIUM
QUEBEC

MONDAY EVENING
March 17th, 1924

LARRY-O

A two Act Musical Comedy

Written, directed and staged by Mr. and Mrs. H. Quart

Overture—Irish Airs .... *Orchestra.*

Introductory Remarks:

MR. J. T. QUINN, *President St. Patrick's Literary Institute*

The associations came into being and went out of existence according to the specific needs of the times. During the final struggle for Irish independence in the 1920s, there were in Québec as many as three branches of the Self Determination for Ireland Association. Many of these societies were local branches of international associations, such as the Ancient Order of Hibernians, which is still going strong in other parts of North America. The Ancient Order of Hibernians took over the dinners and shows from the Saint Patrick's Society and the Saint Patrick's Literary Institute around the middle of the 20th century, while its Ladies Auxiliary encouraged an awareness of Irish heritage among the young. As the Québec Irish move toward the 21st century, few of these associations remain. While the Saint Patrick's Society is still active in Saint Malachie, in other areas, including Québec City, the celebrations have become the responsibility of the various councils of the Catholic Women's League, and the Saint Patrick's Parish Social Committee.

Other associations, whose objectives are not specifically directed toward the Irish community, have taken advantage of Saint Patrick's Day to show their appreciation for the achievements of the Irish among them by an appropriate celebration. Among these are the service clubs: Kiwanis, Optimist, and Rotary Clubs held their usual luncheons or dinners around an Irish theme. The Athletic Club held a dinner, while the Curling Clubs, as a prelude to their dinners, held a thematic series of matches, such as Ireland versus the World, and later the Ladies Shamrock Bonspiel. Certain clubs for senior citizens, such as the Fifty Plus Club and the Veterans Club, have always included Saint Patrick's Day in their calendar of social events.

An important characteristic of Saint Patrick's Day festive activity in Québec has been its flexibility. No function is so immutable that it cannot, in the long term, adapt to changing political, economic or social conditions. The Mass has been the one unchanging observance over the last two hundred years, while other events have had more chequered careers. The Saint Patrick's Day banquets have a varied and colourful history. The parades have come and gone. The Matinées and Soirées had their heyday, but have been replaced by alternative performances. Temporary overlapping or conflict of activities has always been resolved in the long run to the benefit of the community as a whole. For example, in the late 1960s, as many as five or six similar dinners took place on the feast-day evening itself. Since the beginning of the 1980s, a greater effort has been made to adjust the various activities over an extended time period, in order to allow maximum participation at each event. Saint Patrick's Day celebrations remain an important exercise for concentrating the energies of the reduced community.

Whither Saint Patrick's Day

As the 20th century draws to a close, how should we expect Saint Patrick's Day in Québec to evolve?

Looking back over the history of the feast, it is striking to note to what degree it has waxed and waned over the years without ever actually disappearing. Like Saint Patrick's church, it has evolved from humble beginnings into grandiose circumstances, only to finally adjust itself to a more modest existence. Its strength lies in its polyethnic character. Protestants and Catholics, francophones and anglophones have all, in different ways and at different periods, helped it to survive. Thus in 1990, though in reduced circumstances, it is alive and well, both on a formal and an informal level. Every year, the organizers of the Shannon Show wonder if there will be a show the following year, and so far there always has been. The Mass and the banquet organized by Saint Patrick's parish are still going strong. The green beer drinking habitués of the various pubs continue to make merry far into the night.

If the festival is to survive, however, it will do so because a certain element in the French population will have adopted and modified it to respond to the expectations of young people. While the English Catholic schools continue to favour Saint Patrick's Day celebrations, there is no corresponding interest in the Protestant schools. The average age of the participants in the basic English parish activities is relatively advanced. As Irish and English speaking young people leave the city for study and employment in Montréal and elsewhere, it becomes more difficult for the senior members of the community to keep up the momentum.

French Québecers are well known for their ability to assimilate elements from various ethnic groups into their mainstream culture, either by direct contact with the bearers of the different traditions, as is the case with Saint Patrick's Day celebrations in Québec, or indirectly through the media. This would not be the first time that Québecers have adopted festive behaviour in response to the commercial development of a holiday. Halloween is a good example. Trick-or-treating was virtually unknown in the early 1960s, while today schools and families celebrate with decorations, costumes and door-to-door collection of treats and pennies for UNICEF. Easter eggs were traditionally made of chocolate; kits for the decoration of ordinary eggs have become common only since the 1970s. This can be seen as a result of exposure to the general North American content of these celebrations by way of television, magazines, and chain-store marketing campaigns. The Québec Winter Carnival is another example of the commercialisation of festivity.

It is possible then that part of the final answer may lie in the increasingly commercial aspect of the feast. Saint Patrick's Day greeting cards were few and far between in the 1960s and could only be found in English. They have gradually increased in number and variety, with cards in French making their appearance in the 1970s and 1980s. In March of 1990, Librairie Garneau stocked fourteen different models of Saint Patrick's Day cards, nine in English and five in French. The brewers of Harp and Guinness beer supply shamrock decorations and hats for the staff and buttons for the patrons in pubs where their brew is available. Certain disco bars have adopted the policy of offering green beer at half price to patrons dressed in green on the feast-day evening.[42] It is likely that Saint Patrick's Day will serve as an occasion for festivity and a target for the commercialisation of seasonal materials as long as the greeting card and brewing industries find it profitable. In this respect, the proximity of the Irish minority in the rest of Canada and the United States can be considered an asset.

Under no circumstances, however, should the vitality of the Québec Irish be underestimated. In the final analysis, Saint Patrick's Day will certainly continue to be celebrated by the Irish community and those closely connected with it for some time to come. For, after all, everyone is Irish on Saint Patrick's Day.

Notes

1. John Alexander Williams, "Italian-American Identity, Old and New," p. 7.
2. Melita O'Neill Maher, interview 1978. A widely known variant of this is: "There are two types of people, those who are Irish and those who want to be." Or as the young people put it: "If you're not Irish, fake it." Unnamed informant, 1990.
3. In areas with a traditionally important Irish element, the term "Irish speaking" refers to an English speaking person.
4. Leo McCullen, interview 1978.
5. Castile and Kushner, *Persistent Peoples*, p. xvi.
6. See above, p. 110.
7. Unnamed informant, 1979.
8. Marianna O'Gallagher, "The Irish in Québec", p. 255. As Kildare Dobbs notes: "The Irish [in Ireland] are not a single, homogeneous ethnic group. — Catholics, of Gaelic or Norman origin, form the majority in Ireland as a whole; Protestants of English, Scotch or other origin are a majority in Northern Ireland," *in* "Ireland and the Irish Canadians", p. 6.
9. Doris Coveney, interview 1978.
10. This is brought home rather delightfully by the sight of a young Chinese colleen in a long Kelly-green skirt, with a shamrock on her blouse, earnestly singing: "If you're Irish, come into the parlour..."
11. *The Quebec Telegraph*, March 17, 1921, p. 1, as well as in *L'Evénement*, 18 mars 1921, p. 7: "Many thanks to the [French] Canadians who helped make the [feast-day] the grandest possible." Author's free translation.
12. Castile and Kushner, *Persistent Peoples*, p. xvii.
13. In 1983, some representatives from Dublin supposedly boycotted New York's Saint Patrick's Day parade because of Grand Marshal Michael Flannery's affiliation with the IRA. See Kelton, "New York City St. Patrick's Day Parade", p. 99-102.
14. "In the post-Famine era the volume of emigration from Ireland to Canada dropped dramatically. The U.S.A. became the prime destination." Houston and Smyth, "Irish Emigrants to Canada: Whence They Came", p. 34.
15. Unnamed informant, 1978.
16. Unnamed informant, 1978.
17. Unnamed informant, 1978.
18. Many Québec Irish took advantage of these trips to seek out possible relatives; the notion of "home" existed even when the speakers were the fourth or fifth generation born in Québec. See Sollors, *Beyond Ethnicity*, chapter seven: "The Cultural Construction of Descent" for a discussion of the notion of "second" and "third" generation.
19. *Quebec Chronicle-Telegraph*, March 21, 1984, p. 1.
20. Term used by Sollors in discussing Barth's concept of boundary construction, *Beyond Ethnicity*, p. 28.
21. Sollors, *Beyond Ethnicity*, p. 28.
22. This distinction is maintained on the level of school participation in Saint Patrick's Day festivities. The Protestant schools organize no school-wide or community celebrations. One Protestant informant in 1979 remarked that he

had never seen the Matinées as a child, although he did wear a green ribbon to school on Saint Patrick's Day.

23. Unnamed informant, 1978. This was before the building of the Girls' School.
24. The Québec Hockey Club won the Stanley Cup in 1911 and 1912. It seems that when Lord Stanley donated the cup in 1893, it was on Saint Patrick's Day: *in* "Souvenir [Programme of] St Patrick's Day, 1913," p. 11.
25. See above, chapter II, passim.
26. *Le Soleil*, 17 mars 1899, p. 1. Author's free translation.
27. Mildred Wallace, interview 1978.
28. This song had such strong symbolic significance that it was reprinted in English with complete text and full piano accompaniment in *Le Soleil* on Saint Patrick's Day, 1900, during the pro-Irish delirium of that year, and again in 1903. See chapter III, note 5.
29. This is not solely because of its link to the "troubles", since green is sometimes considered an unlucky colour in other parts of the world.
30. *Quebec Chronicle-Telegraph*, March 17, 1954, p. 1. Slievenamon was a pen name of Desmond Lonergan. The poem was reprinted on the editorial page in 1956, 1969 and 1973.
31. Roger Chauviré noted that "Gaelic society, which was so closely and so firmly woven together in the smaller groups, was unsuccessful in its attempt to organize itself on the higher levels": *A Short History of Ireland*, p. 63. Kelton qualifies the New York Irish as "A community of people displaced from a country famous for intercounty chauvinism and rivalry", *in* "New York City St. Patrick's Day Parade," p. 98.
32. "All my French relatives came to the show to see us." Unnamed informant, 1978.
33. Kelton notes that "There are now 175 St. Patrick's Day Parades held each year in the United States," p. 93.
34. Kelton, p. 98
35. Clark, *The Irish Relations*, p. 200.
36. As an example of other journalistic reactions to Saint Patrick's Day, Kelton, p.100, observes that the *New York Times* continually disapproved of the New York parade. In Québec for the last few years, the only newspaper which regularly covers the Saint Patrick's Day events is the English language *Quebec Chronicle-Telegraph*. Coverage in *Le Soleil* up until 1988 was generally assured by journalist Monique Duval. Since her retirement, Alain Castonguay seems to have taken up the cause with his coverage of events in 1990. No reference to the 1989 celebrations in Québec appeared in *Le Soleil*, though the paper did run syndicated articles on the 1989 Montréal parade on March 11th and 13th. The Saint Malachie celebrations are regularly and enthusiastically covered by their regional paper *La Voix du Suc*.
37. The closest the parade came to having a quasi-militaristic character was after the Second World War, when it was temporarily revived by the high school cadets.
38. This was a poor excuse, since at the end of the 19th century and the beginning of the 20th, people often marched ankle-deep in slush and through windy drifts without being in the least discouraged.
39. Clark, p. 203.
40. While the Saint Patrick's Society included both Catholics and Protestants, Article II of the Constitution of the Irish Protestant Benevolent Society [founded

in 1959] limited membership to "Irish Protestants only and their descendants, being Protestants". Membership in the Society had dwindled to a mere handful by the time it was dissolved in 1981.

41. The Saint George's, Saint Andrew's, and the Irish Protestant Societies held dinners mainly to finance their charitable purposes. When they were no longer in a position to do this successfully, they pooled their resources and disbanded. See chapter IV, note 14. On the other hand, the Saint Patrick's Society of Saint Malachie has actually increased its activities in recent years, to the extent of receiving grants from the Ministère des Affaires culturelles, in 1985, and the Ministère des loisirs, de la chasse et de la pêche, in 1987, under the programme of aid to ethnic minorities. Cultural heritage programmes are another possible resource for the encouragment of traditional festive activity.
42. This recalls an advertisement in the *Quebec Chronicle-Telegraph* on March 17, 1955, which promised that "Anything GREEN brought in to Richelieu Cleaners on Saint Patrick's Day will be done at HALF PRICE!"

SELECT BIBLIOGRAPHY

Annales de l'Asile Sainte Brigitte, 1877-1944.

Archives de l'Archevêché de Québec, Saint Patrick's I, 55, 1853.

Arensberg, Conrad. *The Irish Countryman*. New York: Macmillan, 1937.

Bulletin des Recherches Historiques, vol. XLV, n°. 8, Aug. 1939.

Barth, Fredrik. *Ethnic Groups and Boundaries: The Social Organization of Culture Difference*. Boston: Little, Brown, c.1969.

Bieler, Ludwig. *The Works of St. Patrick*. Translated and annotated by Ludwig Bieler. London: Longmans, Green and Co., 1953; Ancient Christian Writers, n° 17.

Bilodeau, Julien ed. *St-Sylvestre se raconte: 1828-1978*. Le comité des recherches historiques sous la direction de Julien Bilodeau, historien. Ste-Marie (Beauce): Imprimerie Le Guide, 1978.

Bowen, Desmond. "Ultramontanism in Quebec and the Irish Connection", in O'Driscoll and Reynolds, *The Untold Story: The Irish in Canada*, vol. 1, p. 295-305.

Burke, Tim. "Buried in Quebec, an Irish enclave", *The Gazette*, Montréal, March 15, 1980, p. 45. Illustrations by Aislin.

Byrne, Donald E. Jr. "The Race of the Saints: An Italian Religious Festival in Jessup, Pennsylvania", in *Journal of Popular Culture*, vol. 19, n° 3 Winter 1985, p. 119-130.

Castile, George Pierre and Gilbert Kushner eds. *Persistent Peoples: Cultural Enclaves in Perspective*. Tucson: University of Arizona Press, 1981.

Castonguay, Alain. "Les Irlandais ont célébré leur fête", *Le Soleil*, 18 mars 1990, p. a-2.

Chauviré, Roger. *A Short History of Ireland*. Toronto: New American Library, 1965.

Clark, Dennis. *The Irish Relations: Trials of an Immigrant Tradition*. Toronto: Associated University Presses, 1982.

Danaher, Kevin. "Calendar Customs and Festival Practices in Ireland", in Feder & Schrank, *Literature and Folk Culture: Ireland and Newfoundland*, 1977, pp. 111-128.

Danaher, Kevin. *The Year in Ireland*. Cork: Mercier, 1972.

Deveau, Lise and Charlotte Kiley, Angela Maher, Esther McCarthy, Timmy Murphy. *Where Green is Worn [Shannon]*. Shannon, Québec: Municipality of Shannon, 1983.

Dobbs, Kildare. "Ireland and the Irish Canadians", in O'Driscoll and Reynolds, *The Untold Story: The Irish in Canada*, vol. 1, p. 3-14.

Doughty, A.G. and N.E. Dionne. *Quebec Under Two Flags*: A Brief History of the City from its foundation until the present time. Québec: The Quebec News Company, 1903.

Duckett, Eleanor. *The Wandering Saints*. London: Collins, 1959. "Saint Patrick: Ireland in the Fifth Century", p. 30-46.

Dufour, Lynn. "La St-Patrice à Québec", in *Culture & Tradition*, vol. V, 1980, p. 55-66.

Duval, Monique. "La fierté et le ralliement des Irlandais", *Le Soleil*, 17 mars 1979.

Duval, Monique, "Là où il y a des Irlandais, c'est aujourd'hui la fête", *Le Soleil*, 17 mars 1988, p. A-18.

Evans, E. Estyn. *Irish Folk Ways*. London: Routledge and Kegan Paul, 1957.

Feder, Alison and Bernice Schrank. *Literature and Folk Culture: Ireland and Newfoundland*. St John's: Memorial University of Newfoundland, 1977.

Gale, George. *Historic Tales of Old Quebec*. Québec: The Telegraph Printing Company, 1920.

Gale, George. *Quebec 'Twixt Old and New*. Québec: The Telegraph Printing Company, 1915.

Greenough, William Parkes. *Canadian Folk-Life and Folk-Lore*. Toronto: Coles Canadiana, [1897]/1971

Guérin, Mgr Paul. *Les Petits Bolandistes: Vies des Saints*. Paris: Bloud et Barral, 1872. "Saint Patrice, Apôtre d'Irlande", tome 3, 17 mars, p. 467-478.

Guerin, Thomas. *The Gael in New France*. Montréal: privately printed, 1946.

Halpert, Herbert. "Ireland, Sheila and Newfoundland", in Feder and Schrank, *Literature and Folk Culture: Ireland and Newfoundland*, p. 147-172.

Houston, Cecil J. and William J. Smyth. "Irish Emigrants to Canada: Whence They Came", in O'Driscoll and Reynolds, *The Untold Story: The Irish in Canada*, vol. 1, p. 27-35.

Kelton, Jane Gladden. "New York City St. Patrick's Day Parade: Invention of Contention and Consensus", in *The Drama Review*, vol. 29, n° 3, Fall 1985, p. 93-105.

Kirouac, Jules-Adrien. *Histoire de la paroisse de Saint-Malachie*. Québec: Laflamme & Proulx, 1909.

LeBlanc, Barbara. "To Dance or not to Dance: The Case of Church and Group Social Control in Cheticamp, Cape Breton Island, Nova Scotia", Québec: Université Laval, 1986, unpublished M.A. thesis.

Literary and Historical Society of Quebec. *Historical Documents, Series 8*, vol XI, Québec: The Daily Telegraph Job Printing House, 1906.

Luireach Phádruig. St Patrick's Breastplate. London: Catholic Truth Society, n.d.

Mannion, John J. *Irish Settlements in Eastern Canada: A Study of Cultural Transfer and Adaptation*. Toronto: University of Toronto Press, 1974.

Marie Ursule, Sister. *Civilisation traditionnelle des Lavalois*. Québec: Presses de l'Université Laval, 1951 (Archives de folklore 5-6).

McQuillan, D. Aidan. "Beaurivage: The Development of an Irish Ethnic Identity in Rural Quebec, 1820-1860", in O'Driscoll and Reynolds, *The Untold Story: The Irish in Canada*, vol. 1, p. 263-270.

Mulchrone, Kathleen. *The Tripartite Life of Patrick*. Dublin: Hodges Figgis & Co., 1939.

Nadeau, André. *Histoire de la paroisse de Saint-Patrice de Beaurivage: 1871-1946*. Québec: Ernest Tremblay, 1946.

O'Driscoll, Robert and Lorna Reynolds eds. *The Untold Story: The Irish in Canada*. Toronto: Celtic Arts of Canada, 1988, 2 vols.

O'Farrell, John. "Irish Families in Ancient Québec", in O'Driscoll and Reynolds, *The Untold Story: The Irish in Canada*, vol. 1, p. 281-294.

O'Gallagher, Marianna. *Grosse Ile: Gateway to Canada 1832-1937*. Quebec: Carraig Books, 1984.

O'Gallagher, Marianna. "The Irish in Québec", in O'Driscoll and Reynolds, *The Untold Story: The Irish in Canada*, vol. 1, p. 253-261.

O'Gallagher, Marianna. *Saint Brigid's, Quebec*. Québec: Carraig Books, 1981.

O'Gallagher, Marianna. *Saint Patrick's Québec. The Building of a Church and a Parish, 1827 to 1833*. Québec: Carraig Books, 1981.

O'Leary, James M. *History of the Irish Catholics of Quebec: St. Patrick's Church to the death of Reverend P. McMahon*. Québec: Daily Telegraph Print, 1895.

Patrick, Saint [See Bieler]

Quebec Chronicle-Telegraph ed. *100th Anniversary: St Patrick's Parish, St Brigid's Home, Quebec*. Québec: Quebec Newspapers Limited, 1956.

Redmond, Patrick M. *Irish Life in Rural Québec: A History of Frampton*. n.l.: privately printed, [1977].

Rivet, Monique. "Les Irlandais à Québec 1870-1968", Québec: Université Laval, 1969, unpublished M.A. thesis.

Roberts, Kenneth. *March to Quebec, Journals of the Members of Arnold's Expedition*. New York: Doubleday, 1947, p. 492.

Robinson, Johanne and Marie Gauvin, Sally Lavallée, Helen Hamilton, Lorna McBain. "St-Gabriel-de-Valcartier: Histoire et développement", Projet Eté Canada au Travail, 1983, unpublished report.

Roy, J.-Edmond. *Souvenirs d'une Classe au Séminaire de Québec*. Lévis: Imprimerie de l'Auteur, 1905.

Schmitz, Nancy. "La Saint-Patrice: fête d'identité et de cohésion ethnique", in *Que la fête commence*, sous la direction de Diane Pinard, Montréal: Société des Festivals Populaires du Québec, 1982, p. 78-83.

Schmitz, Nancy. "Research Note: Significance of Core Family Participation in the St Patrick's Day Show (Shannon, Québec)". With Monik Simard. *Canadian Folklore canadien*, vol. 11, 1-2, 1989, p. 77-83.

Short, W.T.P. ed. *Journal of the Principal Occurences (sic) during the Siege of Quebec by the American Revolutionists under Generals Montgomery and Arnold in 1775-76*: London, Simpkin and Co. Stationer's Court, 1824. Reprinted in Literary and Historical Society, *Historical Documents, Series 8*, vol XI, 1906, p. 87.

Sollors, Werner ed. *The Invention of Ethnicity*. New York/Oxford: Oxford University Press, 1989, "Introduction: The Invention of Ethnicity", p. ix-xx.

Sollors, Werner. *Beyond Ethnicity: Consent and Descent in American Culture*. New York/Oxford: Oxford University Press, 1986.

Stevenson, John. *Moore's Irish Melodies*. Boston: Oliver Ditson, [1852].

Walling, Richard and Catherine O'Connor, Lynn McCauley, Alain Castonguay. *Our Heritage: A tribute to the Irish community of Québec*. Québec: Council of Irish Heritage, 1979.

Williams, John Alexander. "Italian-American Identity, Old and New: Stereotypes, Fashion, and Ethnic Revival", in *Folklife Center News*, volume XI, 1989, number 4, p. 4-7.

Newspapers

Action Catholique
Le Canadien
The Daily Telegraph
L'Événement
L'Événement Journal
Le Journal de Québec
The Morning Chronicle
The Quebec Chronicle
The Quebec Chronicle and Quebec Gazette
Quebec Chronicle-Telegraph
The Quebec Gazette
The Quebec Mercury
The Quebec Telegraph
Le Soleil

Souvenir Programmes of Saint Patrick's Day

1912
1913
1919
1924
1964
1965

INDEX

INDEX OF FAMILY NAMES

INDEX OF DATES

Printed by the workers of
Les Éditions Marquis, Montmagny, Québec
for Carraig Books
February 1991